Here Now the News

An Inside Scoop into New York's Best-Loved Anchors

Jerry Barmash

ISBN 979-8-218-39681-7 (paperback)
ISBN 979-8-218-41329-3 (Ebook)
ISBN 979-8-218-39682-4 (audiobook)

"Jerry Barmash reveals in his excellent and informative *Here Now the News*, some of the most insecure and crazy personalities to ever appear on broadcast news. Fistfights, backstabbing, racism, sexual dalliances, and a considerable amount of alcohol abuse are just a few of the tidbits Barmash, who has covered the NY market for many years, chronicles with revealing interviews and spot-on observations."
Don Dahler, critically acclaimed author of *Fearless* and *A Tight Lie*

***

"It was great to learn the television news business from the bottom to the top. And we had so much fun doing it!"
Pia Lindström, former WNBC anchor

***

"*Here Now the News* by Jerry Barmash is an inside look into the New York newsrooms of the past. It's a little bit of history, a dash of gossip, and a cup full of memories of the golden age of local TV news."
Ernabel Demillo, Chair, Communication & Media Culture, St. Peter's University

***

"*Here Now the News* is a fascinating and insightful look back at the rich history of TV anchors in New York. I've known Jerry Barmash for a long time and have to say, I can't imagine a more knowledgeable and insightful person to report and relay this important history."
David Paterson, former governor of New York

Contents

Acknowledgments

I'm indebted to the broadcasters and other professionals who were willing to be interviewed, providing insight through their colorful anecdotes and memories.

As a self-published author, I'm even more grateful to Adam O'Brien, whose work with the manuscript helped mold it into a book. As someone who hadn't written a book before, I relied heavily on his expertise, which made it easier to address the queries. We were on the same page from the start.

I also want to thank Adam Hay for sharing my vision to bring the cover to life with his incredible design.

Introduction

1

B roadcasting books are not a new phenomenon. Even television shows and movies have taken audiences behind the scenes, though they are sometimes based more in fiction than reality. They have been a popular part of culture, from *WKRP in Cincinnati* to *Anchorman*.

The book that you are reading is all based on real events, not the Will Ferrell version. You could call it a period piece, although that usually makes me think of Victorian-era royalty. This period is primarily about the 1970s. Depending upon who is reading this, it may be considered either recent history or ancient history for the short-attentioned, social-media enhanced millennial.

It's about the world of the anchor when only "man" belonged in that title and group. It was before news managers concerned themselves with being politically correct. This was a time when a white man delivered the news nightly without any company or any resistance. That was the earliest of early news "men."

But the tide slowly started to ebb in the late 1960s. This book looks at the changes that brought a new look to TV news in New York City and that would set the standard nationwide.

While some of the key players are no longer with us, I conducted dozens of interviews, painting the picture of news reporting, gathering, and of course, anchoring in the explosive decade of the 1970s and beyond.

Timing is everything, and I was fortunate to connect to several important figures before their passing, among them Al Primo, who created the *Eyewitness News* format; Chauncey Howell, a longtime WNBC reporter; former *Today* host Jim Hartz; and legendary meteorologist Frank Field.

You'll get firsthand accounts of the individuals at the heart of this book, with personal anecdotes throughout.

The seed for this book was first planted several years before Donald Trump ran for the presidency in 2016. The news media would later be branded "fake news," a spot that would prove hard to remove, but in the era highlighted in the pages ahead, we were yet to be infiltrated by outlets blurring the lines between news and opinion. This is about pure journalism.

Male anchors today, across all local markets, share facetime with female counterparts. Today's norm also allows any minority representation the ability to anchor. But as we see, that was not the case a half-century ago. While these stories center in New York City, they may as well have been be Anywhere, USA. Executives were under the impression that only men counted for ratings.

Now, in the post #MeToo movement, the pendulum has swung the other way, with dual women anchors in some locales, most prominently on Fox's *Good Day New York*. Women, once not even an afterthought as parts of the audience, have been recognized for the importance their demo brings.

As someone who's been in broadcasting for more than three decades, I've always had an interest in how an anchor delivers the news.

Growing up in New York in the late 1970s, it was a pleasure to watch *Eyewitness News* at its zenith. Specific memories fade, but I knew this was original must-see TV, even as an adolescent. My family was a WNBC home, meaning some sort of loyalty each night. Even with soap operas (or as my grandmother called it, her "stories"), it was always about the NBC programming. It spilled over to network news. In an era without the Internet or, dare I say, smartphones, ABC, CBS, and NBC were the only option.

Having said that, I was an avid ABC prime-time watcher, led by the slew of comedies (e.g., *Three's Company, Happy Days, Laverne & Shirley,* and *Too Close for Comfort*).

Another reason why you stuck with a station: The remote control was not the ubiquitous piece of TV equipment of today. Changing channels would mean lifting yourself from the sofa and manually turning the dial. I know this might be hard for anyone under 40 to visualize. Picture the difference between choosing a different book to read from your bookshelf versus browsing to a new website.

Once remote-control technology was prevalent, though, you'd easily switch newscasts based on favorite anchor.

Option two was WCBS, usually vying for second place throughout the decade. By the time the 1980s rolled around, WCBS was gaining a presence in our living room—and I was finding myself more aware of the names Jensen, Smith, Martin, and Marash.

As for the newscasts at ABC's flagship: Even without watching *Eyewitness News (EWN)* regularly, I knew they were popular. It was a matter of style, preferring one station over another. But clearly, *EWN* found the secret sauce for bringing local news to viewers. Whether you tuned in nightly or occasionally, it can't be denied what WABC was accomplishing, and still is.

This book's title *Here Now the News* is an homage to Roger Grimsby, who helped put *Eyewitness News* on the map. His four-word introduction (after giving his name) became another familiar part of each evening's newscast.

To commemorate *EWN*'s the 50th anniversary, the New York Emmy Awards gave its highest honor at the 2019 gala—the Governor's Award—as the program reads, "WABC Proud to Celebrate 50 Years of *Eyewitness News*." It recognizes extraordinary and unique contributions to the television industry.

The amazing feat for television news was not without some controversy, as the Emmys chose to focus on the current on-air personalities and not honor its past (save for a video montage). Aside from creator Al Primo, none of the familiar faces from decades earlier was feted that night. As Pedro Guzman, the veteran city reporter told me during a personal health crisis that kept him off the air for an extended period, "Out of sight, out of mind."

The milestone also led to a montage on the newscast as anchor Bill Ritter, who quite capably followed in the footsteps of legends Roger Grimsby and Bill

Beutel, broke format for his weekly public affairs show *Up Close*, inviting John Johnson and Doug Johnson to reminisce about the old days.

Local news was still in its infancy in the 1960s, with crude production values. However, a confluence of events in the 1970s made this *the* decade for the local news anchor.

As you'll see, those (mostly male) anchors had different styles. Some could come as close to crossing the line with their repartee. As for appearance, some must have been a Hollywood casting director's dream; others would make Columbo proud with their rumpled look.

Even as a young viewer with no reference point to the past, I knew these were special moments in the annals of broadcasting.

In the end, this became much more than simply a book about broadcasting. It's about egos, power, sexism, and racism. The names you'll see in the pages that follow are stars of local news in New York City. However, their story plays on a large scale, and not just because of the exposure many of them got at the network level.

The talent worked in other markets, usually as a pit stop before landing in the Big Apple. Most anchors came to New York and never left, though one person comes to mind who climbed Mt. NYC only to find an avalanche, causing an abrupt exit.

For the last several years, I've interviewed dozens of people from various stations: Anchors, reporters, managers, producers, and writers with unique perspectives on an explosive time in the TV news business. While Grimsby, Beutel, Jensen, and Snyder are no longer with us, they are remembered by many who worked with them.

This book began to take shape shortly before the era of "fake news" would be ushered in by former president Trump. His use of Twitter to assail journalists has caused damage on many levels. Those who believe in Trump, and take his words as gospel, think the left-wing, liberal media have an implicit bias against the right. Trump cemented a feeling in ways we never expected to hear from a sitting president. Those who make a living covering the news, at most outlets, feel the attacks are unwarranted and potentially dangerous.

This "drain the swamp" mentality toward the media is not new, of course. The most famous (or infamous) offender was Richard Nixon, who had an enemies list featuring many TV reporters. It's amid the backdrop of his administration that this book opens. As Nixon returns to Washington, the television news landscape is beginning a whirlwind of change. We'll see the how coverage of local news in New York evolves from the doldrums of the 1960s to big ratings and even bigger personalities. But these anchors were trusted, if not always true to themselves. They had a look and style that made you keep tuning in. But they could be brash and opinionated.

These were anchormen and yes, the start of anchorwomen. As a group, they were a talented bunch, well-read and experienced. They were up for the challenge that could only come from New York. Some of these anchors were trailblazers. These were the local anchors that made a difference in the market and the country.

Unfortunately, several of those anchors are long gone. But many others helped color the pages with their stories and anecdotes. On-air talent, news directors, writers, and producers provided insight into the anchors and their broadcasts.

The world of fake news didn't exist when the anchors in this book arrived in New York, and they still resonate with viewers, decades after they formed a long-lasting bond. There was nothing fake about their experience, knowledge, or delivery, though sometimes these anchors were almost too real.

Thanks to their decades of airtime, a first name is all that's needed to identify many anchors: Chuck, Rolland, Sue, Ernie, Roger, Bill. Throw in a "Jensen," too. These chapters should help give a good understanding of their greatness, along with their weaknesses.

If Mount Rushmore was a symbol of New York's all-time anchors, it would be difficult to choose only four faces!

The anchor wasn't a new concept, but it became a household word in the 1970s, thanks in no small part to the personalities and skills of the people who sat in the chair during the decade. This group became part of the family and, in turn, the first superstars of local news in New York.

"So many of the stories were somewhat similar, so it was really the personality of the anchor that defined each of the stations," said Ron Simon, Curator for the Paley Center for Media since the 1980s. "Every station was using the new videotape technology, so the anchors were the constant presence that could give humanity as the station was developing."

No Internet, no cable networks, no mobile devices. Over the air newscasts were the only game in town, but for one channel it was quickly becoming appointment television.

Ushering the new decade meant a chance to turn the page on the worst upheaval in American history since the Civil War. The 1960s featured a rising death count in Vietnam, civil rights marches, and the assassinations of Martin Luther King Jr. and the Kennedy brothers.

But on the horizon in the 1970s was a new kind of ugliness in the form of the Watergate scandal. The decade was synonymous with the seedy Times Square and rampant crime, leading to art imitating life in such movies as *Death Wish* and *The Taking of Pelham One Two Three*. Of course, an infamous *New York Daily News* front page forever fossilized (and immortalized) New York of that era: "FORD TO CITY: DROP DEAD."

Local news coverage had moved past the nascent days of the 1960s, if only barely. (Videotape, if you could find it, was in its early days. Long before the high definition or digital quality, it was recorded on clunky 2-inch quad reels.)

Anchormen were the "overriding compelling reason" for viewer loyalty, former WABC GM and VP Kenneth MacQueen told *The New York Times* in 1975.

A random *TV Guide* listing from 1971 shows just that. Take a look at the 6 pm time period and you'd find Jensen anchoring on WCBS and Jim Hartz on WNBC. The anchor team was still an anomaly except for trailblazing WABC and its fledgling *Eyewitness News*. The new format had just started in 1968, but the legendary pairing of Roger Grimsby and Bill Beutel would have to wait two more years. Watching the immediate success at WABC made dueling anchors the norm.

Also in the minority was having minorities as anchors. Norma Quarles was the earliest Black female to fit the bill when WNBC put her on the evening newscast. In the early 1970s, Melba Tolliver, a former nursing student turned receptionist, was another important figure in the history of racial inclusion in the broadcasting ranks. However, her ascension was more about happenstance than hard work. Carol Martin was a popular hire by WCBS in the mid-70s, while another Black woman, Carol Jenkins, was finding her niche at WNBC. Before that, she was on the street for WOR.

All of them were gifted individuals, and each laid the groundwork for Sue Simmons to become one of the most beloved anchors in New York history.

In the 1950s and 1960s, a typical nightly newscast would run for about 15 minutes, if at all. When *The Tonight Show Starring Johnny Carson* debuted in 1962, it was allotted an hour and 45 minutes. However, NBC gave affiliates two openings, one at 11:15, complete with Carson's monologue, and at 11:30, with the guests and sketches.

However, more stations expanded their newscast to 30 minutes, thus causing viewers to miss Carson's comedic look at the day's events. To fix this problem, from February 1965 to December 1966, NBC gave their opening "segment" to Ed McMahon and musical director Skitch Henderson.

By January 1967, Carson demanded the network drop the 15-minute segment, and thus the show did not begin until he walked through the rainbow-colored curtain.

During that time, networks produced local broadcasts. It's not until the late 1960s when local stations took control of their own newscasts.

Before knowing the anchors of the period, you need to understand New York of the 1970s. "Most of the reporters were only interested in becoming anchors," veteran New York City reporter Chauncey Howell would recall.

This was a time when the Big Apple was a big mess. Crime was at historic proportions. Hollywood disparaged New York with movies like *Death Wish*. Times Square was a cesspool of porn and prostitutes. The economy was also in the toilet.

Prior to this era, anchors were almost exclusively men who delivered the news each night alone. Minus the cutting-edge technology of today, the anchor team would gain notice in the coming years.

Helping the anchors gain popularity, the early evening newscasts on the three main affiliates ran a full hour from 6–7 pm. By the 80s, the news department, seizing on the revenue, expanded to the commonplace two hours. The stations eventually cut the length on the back end, airing network news at 6:30, and plugging a full hour block of syndicated shows in the highly lucrative prime-time access period—the 7 pm slot where *Jeopardy!* and *Wheel of Fortune* have lived side by side since 1984.

2

Stars of WCBS

Rolland

The decade was barely underway when one new face would emerge in New York. For viewers, Rolland Smith was not just bringing a different way to connect using the written word. Until Smith's arrival, facial hair was an odd commodity for the anchorman. In short order, the dark mustache was more of a calling card than the tie-clip (lavalier) microphone.

It's 1970, and Smith is starting his long association with WCBS/Channel 2. Like many who landed in New York, Smith was brought in as a weekend anchor and correspondent. Soon, though, his talent would take him to the high-profile weeknight slot.

If not for happenstance, Smith's resume might have looked quite different.

His first trip to New York predated his WCBS gig and included a meeting with WABC/Channel 7 and Al Primo, credited with establishing *Eyewitness News*, first in Philadelphia, then in New York. Smith would also reconnect with his former boss from his days at WISH-TV in Indianapolis. As fate would have it, Bob Hoyt was now the assistant news director at WABC.

They wanted—and got—their man, or so it seemed.

However, a week after meeting with WABC management, Smith accepted a position as White House and national correspondent with Metromedia Television. "I wanted that job," he recalls.

Upon alerting ABC of the dramatic developments, he says Primo was very upset. Instead of signing on the dotted line, Smith and Primo parted ways less than amicably.

When asked if he felt put out by the failed negotiations 45 years earlier, Primo could only muster a "Yeah."

A year after filing Washington-based reports for Metromedia stations, including New York's WNEW/Channel 5, Smith was dropped as national correspondent.

Smith was not quite 30 years old, and his career was already in jeopardy. There wasn't much need for fretting, though. He received a call from Metromedia management about joining the station as co-anchor with Bill Jorgensen and George Sherman on the upstart *Ten O'Clock News*.

He was part of the team, getting valuable experience in his one year at the desk. While in New York, Smith also took on the role of United Nations correspondent for the Metromedia group.

It all came crashing down for Smith on one decision he made.

In an effort to attend his son's elementary school performance, Smith taped his assignment from the U.N. and put it "in the can." News director Ted Kavanau was livid when he found out that Smith had pretaped the report. Both men carried a temper at times, helping ignite the situation. Smith was fired.

"Ted was very impetuous," former anchor John Roland said. "But he loved us like his family."

Within 40 minutes, Smith returned home and got a serendipitous call from Marty Haig, the assistant news director at Channel 2/CBS.

"Is what we hear true?" Haig asked. Smith answered affirmatively. He met with the station brass 24 hours later and started at the "Deuce" two weeks later.

It was Roland who paved the way for Smith's entry at WCBS, placing the call to Haig, and singing the praises of his talented pal. Smith wouldn't forget that gesture. At the New York Emmy Awards in 2017, Smith and Roland appeared as part of the 75th anniversary of WCBS (honored with the prestigious President's Award) and the Emmy's 60th anniversary.

"You changed my life with that phone call," Smith told Roland.

Kavanau tried using Roland, good friends with Smith, as a liaison to clear the air of his embarrassing outburst. "Do me a favor, call Rolland. Tell him I'm sorry, all is forgiven," Kavanau told Roland.

Even with Roland's help, it was happening so fast for Smith, whose stock was clearly rising. An apologetic plea from Kavanau to take a day off and start fresh the next day fell on deaf ears.

"No thanks, I accepted something else." Smith told him.

However, a half-century later, Kavanau has no regrets about his decision terminating the future, legendary broadcaster at WNEW (now known as WNYW).

"I don't know what he could have *done*. All I know [is] what he did was intolerable," Kavanau admits. "To turn down a major assignment, he didn't leave me any choice. It was not a mistake. It had to be done."

Still, John Roland thought Smith's move "took guts," as he had a family and needed a job to support them with no guarantees that a job offer would follow so quickly.

Years later, their paths would cross when Smith was being sought for a job by the WWOR news director. Kavanau, as VP of news, had to sign off on the personnel decision.

"I could have kiboshed that, if I didn't want Rolland," Kavanau says.

But in late 1970 after Smith's initial interaction with Kavanau his career trajectory would never be the same!

***

The Odd Couple

As the disco decade began, Jim Jensen was already an established presence on WCBS. He solo anchored the 6 pm newscast, while Bob Young led viewers through the nightly stories at 11.

It wasn't until 1973 that WCBS/Channel 2 made its own news with a dual anchoring format, promoting Smith and hiring Dave Marash. The tandem would only last a handful of years (in its first incarnation) but they would become one of most successful anchor teams in New York history.

A typical grooming move, Smith was named the weekend anchor and, on the streets, reporting the other three days. As for literal grooming, Smith added the famous mustache to look older and more established. It was also the era of the mustachioed swimmer Mark Spitz, winner of a then-record 7 gold medals in the 1972 Munich Summer Olympics.

Smith even recalls meeting the Olympian. "Oh, you're the guy I'm supposed to look like?" Spitz told his doppelganger.

But Marash broke in with WINS Radio in New York City where he honed his sports and news skills for a year. He looked up to morning anchor Jim Gordon, who also was known as play-by-play voice of the New York Giants, Knicks, and Rangers. Marash recalls asking Gordon what the secret was to thread the needle between on-air sports and news.

"'It's really simple,' Gordon told his protégé. 'Just know what you're talking about.'"

After news station 1010 WINS, he worked at Metromedia's WNEW Radio when staffers grabbed the picket lines led by Marash as the strike chairman. Once the deal was agreed upon for AM and FM talent in 1968, "I got fired two days later," he recalls.

Marash, following a successful turn at WCBS Newsradio 880, was hired in late 1972 as the station's late evening sports anchor. Primarily a sports reporter on the radio side, Marash gained a serious news feather in his cap covering the Olympic Games in Munich.

Within five months, Marash was given the high-profile promotion of 11 pm co-anchor with Smith.

"It was such an unheard-of switch at that time," Marash says. "I was the new sports guy. I was enjoying myself doing that and was prepared to do it for as long as we were all happy with it."

But management made the move because Marash proved so popular with viewers. Ratings soared in the second half of the newscast that featured his sports report.

That was just fine with Marash's new partner. The sports and radio background posed no animosity. "I did sports a couple of times. It depends on your interest," Smith says. "When you're starting in your career and working your way up to the big leagues, you do everything."

As Marash puts it: He was "credentialed" for the gig, having done news in New York City since 1967. But Marash was a transplanted New Yorker from the south—Atlanta to be specific—where his father was a civil servant. The Marashes, and young Dave, bounced around from city to city, like the voice of one those train conductors in the 1940s movies—Atlanta, Miami, Richmond. When he was 15, the family settled in White Plains, New York, where his father would become human rights commissioner.

To delineate past from present, WCBS created a new look for the Smith/Marash tandem, originating directly from the newsroom.

As part of the promotion, a newspaper ad showed them sitting in the newsroom with Smith glancing at Marash's script. "What you'll see on the Channel 2 Newsroom is a news team reporting in a refreshingly comfortable style," the ad read.

However, as the late news director Ed Joyce wrote in his 1989 autobiography, they had to do "more than move the broadcast into our newsroom or we'd be hanging our hats onto a gimmick. The key in my mind was our sportscaster, Dave Marash."

"The set on a news studio in the 1970s looked kind of abstract, sort of halfway between a newsroom and a game show set," Marash remembers.

The newsroom production wasn't only there to tell the audience–"This is something different!" There was a tangible factor at play as well. Having the news wires just steps away from the anchors gave Smith and Marash a chance to have breaking news before the competitors. Marash recalls one of those moments when they "scooped" the competition.

"When Spiro Agnew resigned as vice-president [in October 1973], he timed his resignation so that the wires carried it at something like 11:26 pm," Marash says. "They were confident that this would bury it, because who was going to be able to watch the wire machine, get the bulletin, and get it up to the news studio?

"In fact, we're sitting at our anchor desk and hear the wire machine bells ringing. We were actually the one television station in America—east of the Mountain Time zone—that got it on our late news."

That led to a print campaign in the summer of 1973 titled, "No News Team is Closer to the News than Rolland Smith and Dave Marash," as we see them chatting at their newsroom desks.

Another advertisement was popular in 1973, stating that they were inches away from the teletypes and telephones. "If a story breaks while they're broadcasting, you'll get it as soon as they do." The ad said it's "where they're most comfortable."

Marash and Smith had different on-air styles and presentations. Led by the newsroom as their broadcast home, the bearded Marash came up with the idea to work in his shirt sleeves. Smith, a mustachioed '70s anchor, had the full "uniform." (A variation could be found in 2018 as all WNBC anchors on Saturday newscasts took a casual, no tie approach.)

"I didn't look like most anchors. [Then] there was Rolland, the handsomest guy since Clark Gable, and a man who looks fabulous in a suit," Marash recalls. "I think it was a very synergistic combination."

At the height of the duo's acclaim, WCBS seized the moment with a new 1975 ad campaign. "Smith/Marash have a chemistry and a style that's been absent from the New York scene for many years."

The theme was "More and More Viewers are Watching the Smith/Marash Anchorteam." (They did spell anchorteam as one word. Worse, though, it went into print with movie critic Joel Siegel's name spelled as "Seigel.")

Veteran broadcaster Frank Cipolla, who grew up watching the Smith/ Marash team, agrees it was a winning formula.

"[Rolland] was the more staid, traditional, well-dressed, focused news guy. Rolland, you could tell over the air, had a certain elegance to him and a certain wonderment to him," Cipolla says. "Dave Marash was his rumpled little brother." (Actually, Marash is only five months younger.)

However, not everyone fell in love with their chemistry.

Al Primo, a pioneering local news producer, tried luring many competitors to WABC. But not Marash.

"I never got the Dave Marash thing, to tell you the truth," Primo admitted. "He violates every basic rule for success in our industry. He's overweight, got a big beard, tall, not particularly witty. It's like, 'Why is he there?'"

Primo, at the time of this interview, was long since retired from the daily grind at ABC's Channel 7, but kept the competitive juices flowing about yesteryear.

"That's probably harsher than I have a right to be."

Ed Joyce certainly "got" Marash. As the former news director at WCBS wrote in his autobiography, the bearded Marash was "the poet," who "seemed to fill that kind of role for us."

He pointed out that former chairman/founder William Paley was a Marash fan. "[I'm] gratified that Mr. P. felt that way," Marash says. "[But] puzzled to find out so indirectly."

Loyal WCBS viewers also understood this was no experiment.

"Dave and I were the first anchor team to do it shirt sleeves from the newsroom with coffee cups in front of you," Smith recalls. "I was always dressed in a suit, because that's my nature. Dave's nature is he'd rather be in shirt sleeves and smoking a cigar. That was new; that never happened before. That's one of the reasons why we were successful, because we were down and direct."

Another print ad campaign at the height of their popularity focused on their differing styles as an asset for viewers. In October 1975, WCBS paid for a full page in *New York* magazine. The perfectly coiffed Smith and the bushier Marash were separated by text reading, "The only thing they have in common is their personal, yet professional approach to reporting the news."

"Switch to Channel 2 and see the difference."

The anchor duo complemented each other in all facets of the broadcast, but the contrasting appearance sealed the deal with viewers. Marash claims the 11 pm newscast was at or near the top for most of their time. It was a relatively short stint in the annals of New York TV news—less than five years—but Smith and Marash remain fan favorites.

Smith believes those rolled-up sleeves and bushy beard gave Marash the ability to connect with so many people.

"He could be construed as a vocal intellectual as well as a common man," Smith says of his former partner. "He was Copland's 'Fanfare for the Common Man.'"

Thanks to time doing sports, Marash says he was more adept at being off-the-cuff than his partner.

"In general, Rolland's style was more traditional and buttoned down," Marash says. "My writing was more colorful."

Smith adds: "Dave knew a lot of things about a lot of things, and he was able to express it, not only as a good writer, but also in conversation. I knew with Dave, and Dave knew with me that each of us did our homework. When we started doing the 11 o'clock together, I knew that Dave was well read in, and he knew that I was well read in. If anything happened, we could maneuver around it with a degree of professionalism that I think at that time, and all times, CBS/Channel 2 was looking for."

While there was a great chemistry between Marash and Smith when the red light shone, they weren't best friends, but did have an enormous respect for one another.

"Dave to me is one of the finest intellectuals and one of the smartest people I ever had the pleasure of working with," Smith says.

Marash adds: "When I was off camera I would be out, either going to sports events or going to hear jazz or other forms of music. Rolland was much more a 'stay home with family and kids' guy, and wasn't a particular sports fan, and wasn't a particular jazz or music fan. But did we get along? Absolutely. I love the guy. He is one of the nicest, one of the kindest, one of the most loyal people you'll ever meet."

It's those attributes, Marash says, that created the perfect recipe for a winning anchor team.

"He rooted and grounded the show for viewers who were looking for a familiar kind of news. And he did such good job of that they [the viewers] were willing to cut me some slack to be more colloquial, more slangy, more snarky, more individual in my writing style and in my presentation style," Marash recalls.

"He was a very good ad-libber," Smith remembers. "He could talk about anything, so it was nice to have that. I was the yin; he was the yang."

Although it wasn't a regular ritual, Smith and his guitar did visit Marash a couple of times for an impromptu jam session that included the late Joel Siegel, who was the movie critic at WCBS before moving to WABC and *Good Morning America*.

"We'd have a great time," Smith remembers. "It was fun."

That unorthodox newscast began to supplant the mighty *Eyewitness News* with the vaunted Roger Grimsby and Bill Beutel. As their tenure began, WCBS premiered a portable camera for live coverage. It was the first such device in New York and only second in the country. The network debuted the shoulder-mounted camera at the presidential conventions in 1972. As *The New York Times* wrote, "The camera is capable of direct, instantaneous transmission of images and sounds to the news studio and to the viewer's screen, by way of a series of microwave dishes on top of the Empire State and Chrysler buildings."

"By the second or third year we were together that it was a very even fight," Marash contends. "We would win as many as they would win, and NBC was well up the track.

"We were like Diane [Sawyer] and Brian [Williams] today, and [WNBC] was like CBS has been since Dan's [Rather] numbers started to collapse, not really in the hunt."

By 1970, *Eyewitness News* was already starting to gel with viewers, causing a rare three-way race among the newscasts. It also caused them to reevaluate. For example, Bob Young was removed from the late broadcast on WCBS, giving Jim Jensen the solo anchor slot at 6 and 11.

"Jensen is better able to handle the new set and format," Michael Keating, WCBS news director at the time, told the *Times*.

They were using a new horseshoe-shaped desk set, at which several WCBS personalities can sit and perform. "It will all be very loose," Keating said.

WNBC had more struggles until finding its footing with *NewsCenter 4*. To compete with *Eyewitness News* in those early days, Channel 4 started by panning the camera, showing talent chatting on the set. It was a copy of WABC's end to their newscasts where the team would congregate and make some wisecracks as the credits rolled and the announcer spoke.

Even though it was still three and a half years until WNBC's new design and format caught everyone's eyes, they were experimenting with a wide-open, free-swinging approach by early 1971. WNBC claimed they wouldn't do their nightly casts like their rivals uptown at WABC.

News director Steve Cohen missed out on the Marash/Smith magic the first time around. But he brought the popular team together in 1981 after Marash was on ABC's *20/20*. It was the familiar 11 pm time slot, but this time no special treatment—they broadcast like everyone else in the studio. Marash wore a suit and yes, he still had the signature facial hair, which Smith poked fun at in a welcome-back promo.

"Dave Marash, the Newsbreaker who doesn't know the meaning of a close shave."

By this time, the Smith/Marash pairing was going up against WNBC's Chuck Scarborough and Sue Simmons, who began their legendary on-camera marriage in 1980. WABC featured another popular option, Ernie Anastos and Brooklynite Rose Ann Scamardella.

"[Channel 2 was] not really on my radar," Simmons remembers. "They must have been doing better than we were when I first got here. But I would always look to *Eyewitness* as the competition.

Another popular WCBS promo aired in 1978 with the theme "Nobody Does It Better." A pulsating news theme is combined with reporters (John Tesh, Chris Borgen, and John Stossel) as they assemble stories for the evening. Then the anchors come into focus. We see Carol Martin typing, Rolland Smith walking to the studio with his copy, and Jim Jensen briefly on the phone. As the time flashes 5:58 pm, Smith is on set. The next shot has the anchor reading on air. Switch back to Jensen as the digital display flashes 5:59, and he is seen tightening his tie before beginning the broadcast.

Unfortunately, lightning didn't strike twice at Channel 2, and by 1983 Marash exited for WNBC, where he was an investigative reporter. Still, Smith holds a special place for the time they shared whether the cameras were on or off.

"[He's] the quintessential journalist. One of the most brilliant men, anchors, and friends that I've ever had the pleasure of working with."

***

Michele Marsh

Smith had nearly 20 years at CBS in New York, meaning the majority of his time at the anchor desk was actually with another partner. Once Marash left (the first time), just drop an "a" from his name and you'll find Michele Marsh. The brunette was a longtime pairing with Smith on the late newscast into the 1980s.

Marash also worked many broadcasts alongside Marsh. "She was a very attractive anchor who projected a nice friendliness on the air," Marash admits. "I don't think she had any interest in news per se. I think she was a performer and not a news person."

Marsh passed in October 2017 at age 63, after battling breast cancer.

"I always liked Michele, just a nice lady," Len Berman says. "We always had a nice relationship."

Marsh was part of the growing trend ushering in the fairer sex. The stock of WCBS colleague Carol Martin, WNBC's Jane Hanson, Sue Simmons, and Carol Jenkins was rising. WABC's Rose Ann Scamardella was also on that short list.

Smith also co-anchored numerous newscasts with the late Vic Miles, who plugged up a hole for a year until Marsh was on board. She worked at Channel 2 well into the 1990s before the infamous "Black Friday" when the station, with news director Bill Carey at the helm, fired many anchors and correspondents.

She joined John Johnson, who made the jump to WCBS, as midday anchor at WNBC, and was subsequently fired on that day in 1996.

"She was a true professional and an outstanding woman journalist in a field dominated by men," Johnson said upon hearing of her death.

Marsh would also team with Scarborough on the 6 pm until 2003 when her contract wasn't renewed.

"It was all business," Berman asserts. "It really wasn't a reflection on her abilities."

Berman, who worked with Marsh at WCBS and then at WNBC, recalls her best attribute, "The audience liked her and that's not easy, and it's certainly not easy in New York. That's really important and underrated in our business."

"He Was Larger Than Life"

T hen there's Jim Jensen, who completed the longest 6 pm tandem with Rolland Smith at Channel 2.

Jensen could have been hired from central casting as a local anchor. He was old-school.

"He was larger than life," sportscaster Warner Wolf says. "He was the consummate professional."

John Corporon, who helped launch the *Ten O'Clock News* at Metromedia and later brought the *Independent News Network* to fruition, also praises Jensen as a classic anchorman. "He was very credible," Corporon said. "He was never totally satisfied on the ratings, but he was competitive, highly competent, and totally professional."

Jensen made his bones during the 1967 Newark riots, leaning into the camera, which would become his trademark move, and presenting a calm demeanor.

"I had watched Jim for years and always thought he was the epitome of what an anchorman should look like and how a news script should be read," remembered Frank Field. "When I met Jim, my first thought was that he should be playing Gary Cooper roles in Hollywood. He was a heroic figure, and his delivery was impeccable."

So, it's probably not a shocker to learn that the Jim Dial character in *Murphy Brown* (played by Charles Kimbrough) was reportedly based on Jensen.

Jensen was from the era of solo anchors, but WCBS, already seeing the future with Grimsby and Beutel attaining mammoth success at WABC, and their own Smith and Marash duo, decided it was time for Jensen to share face time at 6 pm.

Steve Bosh, later known for his work at WPIX alongside Pat Harper, got the first shot with Jensen.

Eric Ober, who had a 30-year career at Channel 2, remembers that Bosh was asked to change his first name from Jim, "so it wasn't the 'Jim and Jim' show." There was no middle name option for Bosh.

"They gave me three names: Michael, Steven, and one other," Bosh remembers.

He selected Steve, and it became his professional moniker for the rest of his career. However, another name controversy followed. How would his first name be spelled on the air? Management chose "Stephen."

"It's show business," a WCBS reporter told *New York* magazine at the time. "The next day Bosh came into the newsroom and everyone called him Stephen. It's as if Jim Bosh never existed."

"The only persons who called me Jim are some members of my immediate family," Bosh recalls.

But the surname was unique.

"When I got to New York, I was the only B-O-S-H in the damn phone book," he says. "Eight million people and I was the only Bosh, which is kind of incredible."

Although Ober says Bosh was a "perfectly decent anchor," the short-term pairing was, ultimately scrapped, but not the idea. Smith was later broached by management.

"It did not work out, and to this day I really don't know why, to be honest with you," Bosh admits. "I'm confused by the whole thing. I don't mull it over in my mind. It's just the way the business is."

Upon further reflection, Bosh provides one possible factor for his premature exit at WCBS.

"When you have an agent who has several clients, oftentimes there are two or three competing for the same job, you lose a job that way, too. So, you never know what it is."

But he claims a lack of rapport was not the cause for the Jensen/Bosh breakup.

"Our chemistry was perfect. It was almost, I want to say father and son, but it was along those lines," Bosh says about the professional relationship with Jensen.

Jensen logged more than 10 years at Channel 2 when Bosh came on board from KDKA in Pittsburgh. He was younger, but Bosh wasn't nervous sitting alongside the veteran.

"As far as performance, no," Bosh says. "Was there a difference in experience? Yeah! I learned a lot from him and from others in the newsroom as well: Vic Miles, Ralph Penza, and Linda Ellerbee."

Penza, in fact, was given the 11 pm anchor duties with Jensen in January 1972 to halt sagging ratings. He joined WCBS in 1963 as a producer and became a versatile reporter. But to younger readers, Penza is best remembered for his time at WNBC as a senior correspondent and weekend anchor.

Before 1975 was over, Steve Bosh was off the anchor desk, and Rolland Smith was in at 6 pm. Smith was already at the Deuce for more than five years. The experiment would only last a few months, despite the 34-year-old Bosh "being groomed for bigger things: perhaps co-anchor on the WCBS 6 pm news."[1]

"That's how they used me," Bosh jokes, "to open up that co-anchor [position]."

Don't feel bad about Bosh—after a stint at WPIX, his TV career has taken him to Dallas and as a staple in San Diego on KUSI since 1991.

---

1. "The Name's the Game at WCBS." *New York Magazine*, September 22, 1975.

Despite the trailblazing quality of his efforts at Channel 2, there was no animosity from the stalwart Jensen about encroaching on his solo anchor territory.

"Actually, he and I became good friends," Bosh says.

Jensen may not have indicated any ill will, but there was a sea change that astute viewers may have picked up on.

"When I first got there, I could only read one story per segment (or block)," Bosh recalls. "Then gradually that kind of increased."

However, one change that didn't happen on the newscast—top stories were always Jensen's domain.

"If there was a reporter on the set or in the field, they'd never toss back to me. It was always tossed back to him," Bosh says. "Which is fine with me. I didn't care about that."

However, filling in on the late newscast gave Bosh a more natural cadence without Jensen.

"I'd anchor with either Marash or Smith and it would bounce back and forth."

They began to understand the concept that ratings success meant success in all demographics. As coveted as men 25–54 have always been, no longer could the newscast only focus on them. While Bosh was approximately 15 years Jensen's junior, their pairing didn't capture new viewers.

"Jim was one of the older anchors," Ober says. "I think he was always a good, solid anchor. Co-anchoring him with Carol Martin probably was based on feeling that they would have more appeal to younger women."

Bosh says it was also the right time to promote females from within.

"They were doing reporting jobs and they were doing a good job, and there was no reason for them not to anchor," Bosh says. "That's just the way the trend was going. It has to start somewhere."

Despite Bosh's numbered days at WCBS, it meant a lot to him professionally and even personally. He was introduced to his future wife, Cindy, by Carol Martin. Cindy was a 20-year-old English major at Hunter College, taking a class taught by a retired VP from CBS. She got the school's annual internship, spending plenty of time at the copy machine, located next to Bosh and Martin's desks.

"One day, Carol came over to me and said, 'He really likes you. Can he ask you out?'" Cindy Bosh recalls.

A simple answer in the affirmative led to the timid Bosh courting the student (15 years his junior) with a note asking her to a Broadway show. The rest is history. But it could have taken a more public track. After the internship, she says Ober offered her an on-air position.

"[He] wouldn't remember this for anything in the world," she says.

However, Bosh felt it could harm their budding relationship. So, she went to law school, while he wore the broadcasting pants in the family.

After showing off her matchmaker skills, Martin was eventually picked to join Jensen at the anchor desk. However, before that pairing would materialize, Rolland Smith was asked to take the seat next to Jensen.

"Can you work with Jim?"

"Of course, I can work with Jim," Smith says. "I love Jim."

But wanting further confirmation that he wouldn't be stepping on Jensen's toes, Smith spoke directly to his mentor, 15 years his senior.

"I can't be subservient to you, Jim. I have to be a co-equal with you on the air."

"I have no problem with that," Jensen responded. "You're like my little brother."

Jensen was clearly the star anchor at the CBS flagship, but Smith was never in the shadow.

While Jensen was easy to get along with in the newsroom and the studio, Ober acknowledges that Jensen "would have preferred staying a single anchor." (As head of the *CBS Evening News*, Ober added Connie Chung to Dan Rather's venerable broadcast.)

Jensen did understand the business of ratings and was frustrated by not being part of the market's top news program, which more times than not he wasn't.

"It's a very competitive environment, and I don't see anything wrong with that," Ober says.

With Smith's matinee idol looks on display, WCBS used the dual team to its advantage this time, securing female watchers.

"He and Jim were a fine anchor team and made it all look easy," Frank Field said. "I never saw Rolland raise his voice under fire."

Steve Cohen said in his book, *The Newslife: from Arkansas to Aruba*, "Jensen had a classic style of what was called the 'A' anchor."

Together, they would bring viewers the dinner broadcast until Smith's exit in 1987.

Richard Reingold, former WCBS assistant news director, says there was mutual admiration.

"One never confided to me about the other that he was unhappy about the other... What you saw is what you got."

Smith says he never felt competitive with Jensen, who treated him with courtesy and was professional. "As a man [Jensen] I respected. He was a good broadcaster," Smith recounts.

But as good as Jensen was for New Yorkers, he never made the transition to the national scene. "I think he wondered why he wasn't called upon to do the network news," Former WCBS sportscaster Warner Wolf says. "I think that was always in the back of his mind. He would have been great."

Alas, the network gig eluded him.

"Sometimes I've thought about it. But I don't waste a hell of a lot of time thinking about it," Jensen said. "If it happens, it happens. If it doesn't, I'll keep doing what I'm doing until something better comes along."[2]

Given the symbiotic nature and close proximity of studios in New York, it wasn't always automatic for talent to get promoted.

---

2. Magelof, Peter M., Lustig, Warren I., and David M. Levine, directors. *Anchors Away*. NYC TV, 1975.

"Sometimes they're very much attuned more to local stories, or they don't have that one story that can catapult them to the national scene," Simon explains.

Jensen did get a chance to shine for an audience on a larger level. It was 1966, and CBS had the annual presentation of the Masters Golf Tournament. Limited commercials would greet viewers, a staple of the coverage to this day. The opening announcement would be given by someone on camera before each broadcast, showing the event's popularity for fans and a priority for CBS hierarchy.

The unique intro was the request of Tournament Chairman Clifford Roberts, who wanted to hear gravitas in the welcoming message. Someone outside of sports was sought to take the plumb, albeit brief, assignment.[3]

Walter Cronkite and even former president Dwight Eisenhower were discussed, but not available. Ed Sullivan was also mentioned as a possibility. But Roberts balked at having a show-business personality.

In the end, neophyte anchor Jensen was chosen. Roberts had seen his reporting. He would bring the air of dignity and confidence that Roberts needed to start the telecast.

But that wasn't the end of the story. In the final taped version, Jensen identified himself incorrectly as a news correspondent, causing a crisis among the Masters honchos. While the average person watching would not know the difference, Jensen technically was not a correspondent or a reporter, and not for the network.

There was talk of editing the word correspondent, but time was running out before the broadcast, so that was a non-starter. Of course, no sooner did Jensen tell golf enthusiasts his title than the phone in the control room rang. Bill McPhail, VP of sports, was the one who answered. Jack Schneider, number

---

3. Jenkins, D. (1967, April). "An Eye on the Masters." *Sports Illustrated.*

three at CBS behind William Paley and Dr. Frank Stanton, was on the other end. [4]

Producer/director Frank Chirkinian was standing nearby when the fateful call came in.

"Bill, just tell Schneider that Cliff Roberts promoted Jensen," Chirkinian said.[5] He was undeterred by the Jensen mess, much more focused on-camera angles and overall production values for his live coverage.

Smith, who would create a larger presence at the network than Jensen, was happy to log 17 years at WCBS, with his various anchor teammates. "In many ways I still wish I was [there] today," Smith admits.

Jensen would remain at WCBS for three decades and was usually known for his easygoing style with colleagues.

"He was a hard man with tender heart," Smith says.

Jensen's crusty exterior wasn't usually a problem for Reingold either, who said he was "wonderful to work with."

But Reingold didn't take long to recall a moment of classic Jensen. One day, while anchoring the 6 pm broadcast, he called Reingold in the control room, balking at a "People in the News" story. Jensen refused to tell viewers about the latest celebrity divorce, deeming it too salacious for the evening news.

"I told him, 'This is not the time to be bringing it up.'" Reingold says. "'If you've got a problem, I'm happy to hear it. But 30 seconds before coming out to you is not the time to be telling me. So we're coming out to you, and you better read it!'"

Reingold, in the 20s at the time, set the line in the sand. Jensen acquiesced, reading the gossipy story, and their relationship persevered.

But Jensen wasn't about to give in with reporters. They had to think quickly, as the anchor could ask them a follow-up question in their live shot. If correspondents were ill-prepared, Jensen would pounce on them for everyone to see.

---

4. Jenkins, D. (1967, April). "An Eye on the Masters." *Sports Illustrated*.

5. Jenkins, D. (1967, April). "An Eye on the Masters," *Sports Illustrated*.

"They were insightful questions, but you might not have an answer," Smith says.

Jensen would also look forward to showing off his sports acumen.

"You really had to be prepared. You didn't know what he was going to ask you," Wolf remembers.

While Jensen was extremely knowledgeable about baseball, Wolf says boxing wasn't in his sweet spot—such as one time not understanding how a fighter could have a 74-inch reach.

That humorous moment notwithstanding, Wolf says those interactions got him charged each night.

Early in his Channel 2 career, Smith was stumped by Jensen. "I remember one time he asked me something and I said, 'Jim, I have no idea what you're talking about.'"

That aside, instant chemistry emerged.

"He was just a fun guy to hang out with," Smith recalls. "Not on a social level . . . I'm talking professionally."

One time, that fun translated into uncontrollable laughter during the newscast. Jensen butchered the name of Bhagwan Shree Rajneesh, the Indian guru, leading Smith to snicker off-mic next to his partner.

Still laughing, Smith has to gain composure for the next story, while Jensen begins to guffaw.

"Finally, we lost it. But fortunately, the next story was a lead to commercial, and we were able in that two-minute timeframe to get ourselves together."

No laughs, but when Frank Field arrived at WCBS in 1984, he and Jensen made several deadpan promos. For example, one shows the local news legends side by side with Jensen singing his new weatherman's praises. "His professionalism and experience have earned him the trust of millions. To me, Frank Field is not only one of the finest newsmen I've ever met, he's one of the finest people I've ever met."

Field replied with his own compliment: "Now let me say something about this man. Jim Jensen is a terrific judge of character."

Steve Bosh was the first permanent co-anchor with Jensen. "I always looked up to him." Bosh says. "All of the younger people, everyone wanted to be him."

Smith says viewers didn't know that the oft-crusty Jensen had a great sense of humor and was personable off-air.

When Frank Field bolted to WCBS after more than two decades at WNBC, Jensen was stunned to learn that it wasn't a joke, telling Field, "This is just great. At least I won't have to deal with weather clowns."

Eric Ober, a former VP of news, recalls that personality shining before one particular broadcast of the *CBS Evening News with Walter Cronkite.*

"I'll never forget this because Jim was just a funny guy: He teased Walter, who anchored that night from China, then kind of twinkled at the camera and said, 'And I'll be eating at a Chinese restaurant in Newark.'"

Ober says it was a loose newsroom and Jensen, despite being the star, was a fun guy to be around. That's where Jensen, the team's softball pitcher, could also be found practicing.

"It was a great place to work in those days," Ober recalls.

Smith doesn't recall ever clashing with Jensen on (or off) the air. "I'm an easygoing guy. I always tried to not let ego get into the mix."

Steve Cohen, a former WCBS news director during the late 1970s and early 1980s, enjoyed working with Jensen.

Cohen recalls, "[He was] a wonderful, great, classic anchorman."

Over at rival WNBC, Sue Simmons says, "Jensen was quite accomplished. I put him in the same category as Chuck [Scarborough]."

Len Berman, who had a legendary run at WNBC of more than a quarter-century, first got noticed by sports fans at WCBS in 1979. He was the weekend sports anchor, often filling in on the "A-team" where he sat near Jensen.

"One day between the Six and the 11 o'clock news, [Jensen] was reading a book about Israel," Berman recalls. "I was stunned."

That image burned in Berman's mind, having never seen an anchor read a book, let alone a non-Jew learning about the "homeland."

"That impressed the hell out of me," Berman says.

It's not such a far-fetched thought, as Jensen had a knack for jumping off paper and teleprompter when warranted.

"He was as good an ad-libber—he's right up there with the best of them, local or network." Ober says. "He just could handle any situation."

Jensen had another skill that viewers didn't see, but was evident most nights in the control room. "He had great ear-mouth coordination," Ober recalls. "You could tell him something and he was superb at smoothly ad-libbing. He was a pleasure to work with."

Occasionally, technical glitches would hit the air, and Jensen made the viewers aware of the problem. He paid attention to all elements of his newscast: If a tape didn't play, Jensen didn't miss a beat in summarizing the report.

Those are some reasons Al Primo had a fondness for Jensen. Primo said he tried many times to get the Channel 2 stalwart in a "Circle 7" blazer.

"He was just too smart of a guy to throw it all away for this sub-start thing," Primo remembered.

As the "dean of New York anchors," Jensen took the role seriously. Berman, early in his three-year tenure at Channel 2, was backup for lead sportscaster Warner Wolf. Berman quickly learned the power of Jensen.

Trying to make a name for himself in the market, and especially at WCBS, Berman showed a large breasted woman as part of the hockey highlights and added the line, "The Rangers go up by a pair."

Following the broadcast, Jensen approached the new sports personality. "Son, we don't do things like that here at CBS."

Still, Berman says, the venerable anchor wasn't difficult to work with.

Jensen was such a natural, equipped at all aspects of news anchoring. It was his writing and off-script abilities that set him apart from his contemporaries.

"I always assumed at some point we would lose Jim to the network," former station manager Ober says. "But CBS in those days was a separate place."

Bill O'Reilly, who dabbled at WCBS, had designs to replace Jensen at the anchor desk, before beginning his trajectory to the national level. As *The Man Who Would Not Shut Up: The Rise of Bill O'Reilly* uncovered, the future Fox star would get his shot at the anchor desk occasionally on weekends, but that only angered O'Reilly more.

When reporters such as political correspondent Tony Guida refused to ask Governor Hugh Carey about a negative poll, O'Reilly was quick to confront. With the cameras rolling, O'Reilly faced the wrath of the governor and rushed back to the studio to air the encounter unedited during Jensen's newscast. O'Reilly expected to become the WCBS conquering hero for taking on Carey, but a call to William Paley nearly got O'Reilly ousted.

A stern warning followed from CBS VP of News, Ed Joyce, who told him that he was rude to the governor. "We can't have that here at Channel 2."[6]

Instead, Michele Marsh quickly became the darling of the Deuce.

While she wouldn't be confused with Walter Cronkite for her news acumen, "at least you have to concede that she is prettier than Rolland Smith," one viewer said.

Needless to say, Jensen's one-time news director Ed Joyce was a member of the Jensen Fan Club. In his 1989 autobiography, *Prime Times, Bad Times*, Joyce called Jensen "the most natural anchor talent I've ever seen."

And while many looked no further than Smith when it came to looks at the station, Joyce says Jensen could hold his own in that department. "Blessed by luck and Danish parents, Jensen is one of those tall, strikingly handsome people who can create a wave of turning heads whenever he enters a room," Joyce wrote. "I've seen that happen in cities where no one is aware that's he's an anchorman on New York television."

As for the timetable, it was before Bill Beutel was in place, so Primo was ready to have Jensen and Grimsby together on the desk.

"I think maybe they could have worked together," Primo admitted. "We didn't get him, because he knew he had the deal of the century."

---

6. Kitman, Marvin. *The Man Who Would Not Shut Up: The Rise of Bill O'Reilly*. New York, NY: St. Martin's Press, 2007.

Smith, a great anchorman in his own right, was more concerned with being professional, making sure facts were checked—twice—and getting as many sides to a story as possible.

"I think that my colleagues recognized that in me, as I recognized it in them."

Plus, as Len Berman says, "He was a bit looser. He wasn't the stentorian anchor that Jim Jensen was."

And that mustache didn't hurt, "He looked like a soap opera star. I know the female audience loved him," Warner Wolf says. "He had a good presence and was very believable."

The 1970s are legendary for the anchors' carousing. Some stories have the talent drinking in between the 6 and 11 pm casts. Smith wouldn't comment on that but does say he and Jensen were smokers. Smith stopped in recent years.

"When both of us had cigarettes lit, you could see waves of smoke coming up between the two of us on the 6 o'clock set," Smith recalls.

Smith kept in touch with Jensen until his death in 1999. The longtime colleague marked the sadness surrounding Jensen's passing with another tragic circumstance: His son Lee was dying of brain cancer.

Smith recalls, "Jim would call me once every couple of weeks, when I was no longer working there, and asking how my son was doing.

"I'd be at the hospital. My cell phone would ring and I would be talking to Jim."

Jensen and Smith's son died weeks apart.

At Jensen's funeral he said, "I come here with a heavy heart because my son had just passed."

Smith says, "For me, Jim was always a good friend, anyway you looked at it."

Jensen had his own family tragedy and demons to bear. A second marriage dissolved and in 1979 his son Randall was killed in a hang-gliding accident. The famous anchor, feeling the burden of guilt, couldn't cope. He turned to drugs.

He opened up about his personal struggles with *People* magazine in 1989.

"I never handle emotional things well," Jensen said. "I was back at work a week after my son was killed. Everyone was telling me how brave I was. I didn't think I was brave. I thought there was something wrong, but I didn't know what."

Jensen recalled his daughter telling him the unthinkable news, causing his knees to buckle and wanting to throw the phone into the wall.

Battling with himself, Jensen's focus would switch at the snap of a finger from current activities to thoughts of his dead son.

"After that, it was a slow descent that manifested itself by my becoming more and more reclusive, feeling kind of gray," Jensen said.

For Jensen, cocaine was the drug of choice, starting at a party in the early 1980s.

"An intelligent person such as me, doing something so hideously stupid. Next thing you know, I had a problem." Jensen said his drug use was primarily alone on late nights, a couple of times a week, with occasional weekend binges as well.

Cohen says, "It was one of the great tragedies in his life, which sent him on a spiral into oblivion."

Jensen said he was never stoned on the air but admitted to being a "little erratic" in the newsroom. "My temper would be short, and I wouldn't be too consistent in the way I treated people. Sometimes I would be abrupt or I'd be silent. I started missing work. I'd miss family functions. You start to look a little seedy around the edges."

The station picked up on the odd behavior, and in the summer of 1989 suggested a urine test.

Ultimately, he was treated at a facility, getting all drugs out of his system, including Valium, which he took for four and a half years because of a sleep disorder from anxiety. However, Jensen recognized that Valium posed a bigger problem than the cocaine.

"I thought it was like an aspirin tablet; when I wanted to stop using it I would just quit. Trying to come off Valium can be brutal, but I became determined."

He stayed in the hospital for six or seven weeks, but severe leg and back pain would ensue beginning the Valium withdrawal. Jensen would sleep seven hours for the week and eat minimally. He'd be forced to take constant hot baths to find any relief from the pain. There were swings between feeling ice cold and sweating.

"It was absolute, sheer hell," he recalled.

One of his daughters, at the time seven years sober from alcohol, helped her father through the most difficult point in his life.

"Daddies are supposed to be the source of help; kids are supposed to come to daddy. But I had to go to my kids and ask for help. That was a humbling experience."

Once the Valium and its side effects were out of his body, depression set in.

"You feel as though there's no future left, you might as well die." Jensen recalled in the *People* interview.

He started taking antidepressants daily, attending Alcoholics Anonymous meetings each day, and seeing a psychiatrist every week.

Losing his anchor chair to a senior correspondent position ruffled his feathers initially, but he understood that WCBS had a job to do.

"I mean, I wasn't very dependable."

The lead anchor for nearly three decades was demoted to the Sunday morning (taped during the week) public affairs show. Forced to retired in 1995, Jensen died of a heart attack four years later.

"He was like the local Walter Cronkite," Howard Stern sidekick Robin Quivers said in a broadcast after Jensen's death.

"I remember as a little kid just growing up, watching him all the time," Stern reflected.

When Jensen made his private ordeal public, he received something stronger than meds.

"I've got seven boxes of mail in my office. People on the street, they pat me on the back. It's wonderful. They're all pulling for me. I can't let them down," Jensen said.

"Over a period of time I learned about the early tragedies which affected him," Frank Field said. "It pained me to see him reproached by a news director who could have been his son. The last time I met Jim he was walking down

Madison Avenue. He was no longer at WCBS and appeared gaunt. I am glad I hugged him."

"It was stunning to me to see his personal business come out over the years," Simmons says. "I just pictured him as a straight arrow. Apparently, he was not a straight arrow."

Still, Cohen says, "It never affected him on the air."

Most of Cohen's face time with Jensen away from the studio was spent talking about the weighty matters of life. "He always felt that he had a shot at being the next Cronkite, or the next Rather," Cohen remembers.

Because of New York's position as the top market, the talent pool is already network quality, although the transition for the anchor is not as easy.

"So many of the local anchors are first perceived as variations of a network anchor personality," Ron Simon, curator at the Paley Center, says. "Jensen, obviously, had some Cronkite in him, in a way."

Jensen also wouldn't miss an opportunity to chat about baseball—one of his other passions. One Opening Day, Jensen and Cohen took the subway to Yankee Stadium, where the car was filled with passengers showering praise for the popular anchor, "Hey Jim! I love you, Jim!"

"He was New York. He was everything about it and believed it wholeheartedly," Cohen says. "The side of him that was a journalist really believed that he would make a difference, and did make a difference in his life. And when his life went crazy, he had to try and manage that. But at his core he was a gentleman who wanted to do the right thing."

By the time the adept Jensen debuted at Channel 2, he was a broadcasting veteran, having made stops in his hometown of Kenosha, Wisconsin; Peoria, Illinois; and Boston.

Serendipity brought Jensen to New York.

He was the pool reporter assigned to cover the Kennedy compound in Hyannisport following President Kennedy's assassination. That work caught the attention of the execs at WCBS, hiring him in 1964. Jensen's first taste of WCBS would be in a typical "grooming" role: weekend anchor and backup weekday anchor for Robert Trout, the veteran CBS News man. Trout, beginning in

1952, pulled down double duty as network correspondent and WCBS evening anchor. Jensen succeeded him on June 18, 1965.

The year before, WCBS started branding "Channel 2 News," a title that would last into the 1990s.

Rolland Smith was seen as the right counterpoint to whoever was sitting next to him, especially Jensen.

"[He] was a very thoughtful, very connected literary figure with a great soul that ran through him," Steve Cohen says. Those balancing acts were by design to bring the largest possible audience to the nightly newscasts. "That era, knowing that everything was at stake everything we said really mattered, and at least one-third of New Yorkers were going to watch us on any given night, was just so heady."

Of course, this wasn't unique to WCBS/Channel 2. WABC had Roger Grimsby and Bill Beutel, while the Chuck and Sue era started at WNBC.

"You got this enormous sense that everything mattered, but at the time nobody took each other seriously," Cohen says.

This was prior to the cable news proliferation, and well before any use of the Internet, mobile devices, or social media for news gathering.

"What you did in local news in the 70s and early 80s did matter, and we used to get 30 shares," Cohen says. "It's not like today where if they get a 10 or a 12, they're happy campers."

While today social media apps are used as tools to promote a newscast or story, in the "good ol' days" it was a simpler time. The product was only for the audience via one platform—television.

Despite the serious battle for ratings, WCBS anchors poked fun at each other and the union to make the newsroom more fun for everyone.

"There was a white phone that had a red bulb on it. When it rang, it was somebody at Black Rock. So whenever it would ring, everybody would scatter," Cohen says. "And Jensen would casually walk with a cigarette hanging out of his mouth and say, 'Are you going to answer that fucking thing or do I have to answer it?'"

4

"A Real Newsman"

As for the competition, Rolland Smith watched them frequently when not working, and met his contemporaries many times at functions. Smith knew all the counterparts well, from Roger and Bill to Chuck and Tom.

"I always enjoyed their company," Smith says. "I never felt challenged by them or that I was in competition to them. We were all trying to do a job. We were storytellers, and each of us told it in the way that was right for us and our management."

"[WNBC] had Tom Snyder, who never made it in New York," Marash says. "A tribute to New York's taste."

Marash's thoughts aside, Snyder did rise to national prominence on NBC's *Tomorrow* show, using the Johnny Carson lead-in to his advantage. Once that fizzled, Snyder returned to the anchor desk at WABC in the early 1980s.

"He was a real newsman," former WABC colleague Mara Wolynski remembers.

Snyder's return to New York was also the tail end for Grimsby at WABC and in the industry.

Wolynski says, "They both sucked the air out of the room. It was kind of like two bull elephants at the watering hole."

Al Primo, executive producer of *Eyewitness News*, had Snyder under contract in Philadelphia, but their paths never crossed in New York. While he mentions Snyder in his autobiography, in a 2017 email Primo said he would be pleased to chat about Snyder, who he called one of the "giants in our lives."

Back to the 1970s, with ABC out of the picture (for now), NBC made the next bid for the star's services.

In 1976, Snyder was still a premiere face at the National Broadcasting Company. Not only did he host the 1 am show, he was newsreader of the live 8:57 pm weeknight *NBC News Update*. Because of the prime-time spot, a 1976 *People* magazine article said this gave Snyder the largest audience of anyone in the business. Months earlier, though, he was dropped as NBC Sunday night anchor.

But in the late 1970s, Snyder was actually considered the heir apparent to replace John Chancellor on *NBC Nightly News*, a position that ultimately went to Tom Brokaw in 1982.

"People felt comfortable and safe with him," Snyder's daughter Ann Marie Snyder says. "When you feel comfortable and safe with someone, you're more likely to open up and talk about things than you are when you feel fearful and guarded."

Snyder, who won an Emmy Award in 1974 for Special Classification of Outstanding Program and Individual Achievement, was able to thread the needle from news to entertainment, but always considered himself a journalist and broadcaster.

"He felt like [*Tomorrow*] was a deeper dive into people than you'd ever get on news," says Ann Marie Snyder.

You'll notice that more in early seasons of *Tomorrow*, before NBC turned it into more of a ratings grab.

But Snyder wasn't universally loved. Just look at a 1977 *New York* magazine article, describing him as an "unorthodox anchorman," who was "abrasive, salacious."[1] Those traits would set him apart with viewers, but would cause constant consternation with his bosses.

John Huddy Sr. was told by many, and directly by Snyder years later, that NBC brass offered the high-profile seat—Snyder's life-long dream. The announcement was expected to be made official in the coming days. The exuberant Snyder went out drinking and rushed to tell colleagues prematurely.

As the story goes, high-ranking members of NBC News showed up at his door the next morning—as early as 5 am. They rescinded the offer. Snyder was shell-shocked by the reversal of fortune.

The rug was pulled from beneath Snyder after the news division apparently rebelled against the promotion. Bill Small took over as NBC News president in 1979.

"The network news organization said, 'We'll walk,' and they took back the offer," Huddy says.

Huddy learned about it from Snyder during another drink-fest, relaying how he went to the NBC offices in anger and spray-painted insults on every door, including some of the female staffers.

"[It shows] insight into the kind of guy he was," Huddy says.

However, Huddy was not aware of any drinking that was noticeable on the air. Snyder saved his belts and shots for after the broadcast. Huddy recalls Snyder stashing a bottle of booze in his office drawer, which "always concerned me."

Snyder would show off the bottle with black lines on the side.

"The janitor comes in here to clean and he's been drinking my booze, so I put a line where it was when I last drank the whiskey," he told Huddy. "I don't want him drinking my booze."

With Fred Silverman in charge of the network in the spring of 1979, Snyder got another network assignment: anchor for a revamped *Weekend* news magazine show. He replaced Lloyd Dobyns and Linda Ellerbee. By this point, Snyder was pulling down $600,000 a year for his weeknight interview show. It

---

1. Van Horne, Harriet. "New Business Like Show Business." *New York Magazine*, March 21, 1977.

was important to cement their star at NBC—not only had his name been long rumored to replace John Chancellor at *Nightly*, reports had resurfaced that he could jump ship to ABC News.

As Snyder told the *Washington Post*:

> Certainly I have been approached by other people and certainly I have had conversations, but throughout this whole negotiating period with NBC, it was my desire, if it was at all possible, to stay there for a very simple reason: I've been there for almost ten years and I know the people there who are involved. Not so much the new executive echelon, but the people that I have to deal with—the producers, the crews, the technicians, the secretaries, the production people—and so it makes my life a lot easier to stay here.[2]

Snyder shuttled from LA to NY throughout the life of *Tomorrow*, but his daughter Ann Marie claims bringing the outspoken personality to the Big Apple wasn't just to resuscitate WNBC's news viewers. There was another incentive.

"They made a deal with him: 'If you go out there and you help us, we'll give you *Nightly News*.'" she says. "That was the deal that was made, and we all know that didn't happen. He was dangled that carrot."

Nightly News was no longer the must-see TV of Huntley-Brinkley, who had their final broadcast at the start of the decade.

There is no question about the talent of Snyder, but at times it appeared management had trouble getting the best out of him while keeping him happy. There was a "square peg, round hole" situation with Snyder.

There was also concern that Snyder's main skills, especially that sharp tongue and wit, would cause more problems than a straight news reader. They worried

---

2. Shales, Tom. "The Prime Time of Tom Snyder." *The Washington Post*, April 14, 1979.

he could bring too much opinion to the newscast and make them look bad. Of course, it would not be the first-time bosses would act on those feelings. Consider Howard Stern at WNBC-AM, or David Letterman on his first late-night show. (Ironically, Letterman and Snyder would cross paths a couple of times in the years that would follow.)

When NBC and Snyder had grown tired of each other, it was Letterman who moved seamlessly into the historic show, after Letterman's previous tenure at a short-lived morning show.

When he moved to CBS, Letterman didn't forget Snyder's talents in creating a show from his production company, Worldwide Pants, while putting Snyder back in his familiar time slot.

"Every single rating point," a 39-year-old Snyder said, "is worth a million dollars to the network."

Trying to straddle the line between newsman and entertainer, even within a broadcast, Snyder admitted, "Which Johnny am I? Chancellor or Carson? Ask NBC."

Primo said, "He was so talented, he could have been either."

However, by 1995, Snyder was not as ambitious, opting for a more reflective outlook.

"I'm the luckiest person in the world," he said. "I mean, jeez, I really don't have any great talent. I don't sing, I don't do any of that stuff. I mean, I get in one lifetime to follow, to work behind, both those guys on the wall behind you."[3]

Snyder was looking at framed photos of Johnny Carson and David Letterman.

At the height of Snyder's popularity, he gained a new legion of fans, thanks to Dan Ackroyd's send-up on *Saturday Night Live,* in which he exaggerated Snyder's chain-smoking, machine-gun firing laughter, and his signature response to guests: "Alright, sir."

---

3. Shales, Tom. "Tom Snyder: The Last Word." *The Washington Post,* January 22, 1995.

"I don't do that," he told Bob Costas on his NBC talk show *Later* in 1989. "It was flattering when he did it." However, Snyder did admit that he pulled back a bit after seeing the impression.

In 1991, Snyder made a brief return to Rockefeller Plaza and the overnight, filling in for Costas on *Later*. What followed was a contentious 30-minute interview with another NBC alum, Howard Stern, which ended with Snyder walking off the set as the credits roll, allowing Stern to hawk his video.

But, moments before the less than amicable split, Stern and Snyder found some common ground.

"I thought the Dan Ackroyd thing was a scream," Stern says.

Snyder acknowledged, "Fabulous. Unbelievable."

"And that's what turned me on to you," Stern admits. "But you think it ruined your career."

"No, it didn't ruin my career at all. It made me." Snyder responded. "Imitation is the sincerest form."

His former *Tomorrow* producer, John Huddy Sr., concurs. The impression instantly lifted Snyder to a larger following. "It made him more famous because there were a lot of people who never heard of him—didn't stay up until 12:30 and 1 o'clock in the morning. It took him into another whole dimension, in terms of celebrity, and I don't think he had any problem with that at all."

As a teenager, Ann Marie Snyder recalls the Ackroyd impression being an important moment for her father as the 1970s zeitgeist.

"It identified him as a real force in culture," she says. "If you're getting parodied on *Saturday Night Live*, you're somebody."

During the April 1976 episode, Ackroyd's Snyder tells President Ford's press secretary Ron Nessen, "As well as working on this popular late-night program, I also do a minute of prime-time news every night on the network. Everybody knows this, of course. They work me hard here. I sometimes do local news. I'm a workhorse here."

While Snyder was pleased with Ackroyd's impersonation, it was the characterization from another SNL's alumnus that got under his skin. Joe Piscopo portrayed him as a failed broadcaster living in a skid row hotel, who interviewed the doorman.

"That to me was hurtful. I did better than that," Snyder said.[4]

While there is no denying that Tom Snyder's career was long and widespread, it didn't always last as long as it might have at various stops.

"As a human being, I didn't like him," Huddy Sr. said. "He made a lot of enemies. He could be absolutely despicable and then completely different."

Huddy's hatred for Snyder as a person would, at times, boil over into fisticuffs. Although not an overly impressive specimen, standing 5′ 11″ and 180 pounds, Huddy had fighting instincts, in part from his father who was a professional welterweight boxer.

"I tend to throw punches from time to time," Huddy recalls. "I stood over [Snyder's] desk. I was a big guy, but not a fighter, kind of a pear-shaped guy."

As the *Tomorrow* show hung in the balance, Huddy felt the pressure. Making matters worse, in February 1981, a *Playboy* magazine interview sent ripples when its cover stated Snyder "bites the hand that feeds him."

"I have no reason not to hit you right in the fucking mouth and throw you out that window!" Huddy screamed. He didn't, but it was yet another example of the frayed relationship between them. "He had no discretion," Huddy recalled. He pointed to the incredible view from Snyder's office and his large salary as reasons he should have been happy in his network role, not a sad figure who disrespected colleagues.

Later that year, Snyder and company had taken the show on the road for a special interview. Huddy orchestrated an interview with Egyptian president Anwar Sadat, as the African nation was facing extreme tumult.

However, after they arrived, Huddy received an urgent call from someone high up in the Egyptian government. The interview was off. Huddy threatened to hold a press conference once they got back to New York.

---

4. Meisler, Andy. "Tom Snyder Reconsidered: Everyman At 57." *New York Times*, May 8, 1994.

"Your own bureau chief told us not to do it, that Tom Snyder was an evil man and that Tom Snyder interviewed prostitutes and dominatrices," the government official told a stunned Huddy.

He responded that the news division was given a black eye by Snyder's coup within the network. Eventually they agreed to have dinner with Snyder to get the interview back on track. During the meal, a nervous Snyder noticed guards with machine guns.

Snyder was willing to skip the historical perspective of the big "get" and head to the tarmac instead.

"Johnny, this is dangerous. We gotta get the hell out of Dodge, right now!" Snyder told Huddy.

As Huddy kept pushing for the interview with Sadat, Snyder decided it was time to leave, as the former producer recalled.

"He pulled the rug right out from under me. He really fucked me," Huddy said.

The producer had to call to explain the situation to Roger Ailes and the president of NBC, who said it was "vintage Tom Snyder."

They would stay for the behind-the-scenes tour of the Pyramids before moving on to another important interview in Paris.

"Two weeks later, when we would have had this thing cut, edited, and on the air, Sadat was assassinated," Huddy said. "That was another time I wanted to fucking wring his neck."

Summing up his association with Snyder: "It was incredibly mixed. I don't think I ever met anyone in show business that I had so many different professional feelings about, journalistic feelings about, and emotional, personal, psychiatric feelings about. He covered all bases."

Ann Marie Snyder, a youngster as her dad's star soared, uncovered more about the man for her documentary. But she wants to ensure the world knows about his greatness.

"He asked the question. He worked for the people. He didn't work for the network," she says. "That's what set him apart. He wasn't a lap dog for ratings."

When Snyder died in 2007, *Saturday Night Live* creator/producer Lorne Michaels spoke to *The New York Times*, recounting the early days of the show when Dan Ackroyd would portray Snyder: "The character took on another life. And he loved us doing it."

By the 1980s, Snyder needed fine tuning, if not a complete overhaul. After the NBC years deteriorated, Snyder's future was uncertain. The man, who was now larger than any local news anchor position would provide, was given a reboot when WABC offered him a chance to anchor.

His days at 30 Rock (or the West Coast version in Burbank) were marked by declining numbers as the new decade started and the highly publicized feud with Rona Barrett (another link to Roger Grimsby). Snyder felt unwanted at the network after David Brinkley was given a newsmagazine show. That was reason number one for Snyder to feel "thrown out" of NBC News.

WNBC would add Jack Cafferty in 1977 as a replacement for Snyder on the 6 pm broadcast. The station would call it the *Scarborough-Cafferty Report* as part of the two-hour *NewsCenter 4* block.

But in the decade that followed, Cafferty would be more famous an hour earlier when he would anchor with Sue Simmons for the uber-popular *Live at Five*.

While Snyder was still a hit on *Tomorrow*, he eventually ran out of "tomorrows" in the next few years among attempts to change the audience and even the format.

It took Snyder's agent, Ed Hookstratten, to resurrect the floundering career, creating and fielding the best situations for his (still high-priced) client.

When the smoke cleared on the negotiations, Snyder was back in local news, back as an anchorman, and back in New York. Working at the vaunted *Eyewitness News*, though, had failed to reconnect Primo and Snyder in New York. The deal included hosting of a magazine show on ABC-owned stations. As reported by *The New York Times*, Snyder was getting an estimated $700,000 a year for the three-year contract. Another piece of the pact would give Snyder a network news presence, if he performed well.

But, of course, the 11 pm newscast was already doing just fine, thank you, with Ernie Anastos and Rose Ann Scamardella. John Severino, then-president of ABC, said Snyder was hired to expand WABC's ratings lead.

To make the WABC deal come alive, although it was arguably D.O.A., Hookstratten urged the former *Tomorrow* host to stay under the radar for six months, potentially creating some buzz for his talents.

Before it was official, the agent had several offers on the table. Snyder was wanted for a local/national combo at CBS, but the $1 million per year price tag proved too rich for their blood, and the boys at Black Rock balked.

CNN, barely out of the honeymoon phase as a broadcaster, was also courting Snyder as evening anchor. However, he had no interest in a move to Atlanta.

ABC remained on the short list, along with a group of Metromedia stations for his services.

Hookstratten wanted the ABC package to include a late-night news and interview show, but Phil Donahue was already signed as a contributor. Plus, Roone Arledge, ABC News president, wanted Snyder to restore his journalism skills on the local level before grabbing a network presence.

At Metromedia, Snyder was close to anchoring a 10 pm newscast for their group of stations.

Robert Bennett, senior VP, told the *Times* at the time, "At first I was not aware ABC was a factor."

Ultimately, Bennett made an offer, which Snyder's agent turned into a negotiating ploy. He delivered that information to ABC, which was slow to respond. The next day, though, Snyder was signed and sealed to work for the Alphabet Network.

Pia Lindström, who spent time at the anchor desk with Snyder and Chuck Scarborough in those nascent days at WNBC, says she didn't emulate either man. However, she found that she did admire Scarborough because of that now-legendary consistency.

"[Snyder] was more temperamental, and many performers are," Lindström says.

That temperament was a fan favorite of viewers and interviewees, but could be a thorn in NBC's side.

"He wasn't afraid to speak his mind," Ann Marie Snyder says. "What he didn't want to do was report or say something that wasn't true."

Snyder didn't let his views appear on the broadcast, despite being considered controversial. If someone would dodge Snyder's questions, he'd push back for his viewers.

In producing a documentary about her father, Ann Marie looked through the prism of being an adult to better understand his skills and popularity. She says he had to take his lumps from management "because you couldn't put him in a box. So, a lot of time with special people, they have to tear you down because that's the only way they can qualify their own mediocrity."

By comparison, seasoned pros in the New York market towered over Scarborough. Jensen earned $180,000. Beutel brought home $250,000 a year, while his counterpart, Grimsby, according to the report, made $200,000. However, topping them all at $450,000 was Snyder, splitting time between local anchor duties on WNBC and the network's late night *Tomorrow* show.

"Many of the anchors like Chuck Scarborough got network exposure but were very much tied to the community." The Paley Center's Ron Simon says. "Especially in the 70s and 80s, I guess, stations really used their news anchors as a way to promote the identity of the station."

Frank Cipolla recalls a story about Snyder, who was considered a talk show personality, but wanted to show WNBC bosses that he had news chops. So, Snyder put together a whole newscast.

"The writing was superb, and it was perfectly timed," Cipolla says.

What was not timed perfectly was Snyder and Primo in New York. While the acerbic anchor and host ascended just fine with NBC, he did not get to join *Eyewitness News*, as his star was still rising in the 1970s.

He was the "ultimate communicator," said Primo, KYW news director.[5]

---

5. "Talk Show Host Tom Snyder Dies at 71." TODAY.com, July 30, 2007.

Snyder would become such a popular anchor and host that in 2008 he was inducted into the Broadcast Pioneers of Philadelphia's Hall of Fame.

Meteorologist Frank Field, who died in July 2023 at age 100, said Snyder was one of the best anchors he ever worked alongside (NBC's Frank McGee was the other).

"Tom was absolutely made for news in television. He just did what he had to do, and unfortunately sometimes it wasn't what [management] wanted him to do," Field remembered.

As an interviewer, Snyder "always used to tell me, I listen to what they're saying and I ask the questions that the average guy would want to ask, not a formulated question," Primo said.

Snyder's former boss also praised him in his memoir, *Eyewitness Newsman,* saying he was a "pioneer when it came to different styles of reporting." Primo writes that he was one of the "key people in developing the *Eyewitness News* reporting style that has become the standard in today's journalism."

Furthermore, Field and Snyder had a strong chemistry off camera as well. "Tom became one of my dearest friends. Tom learned I was going to celebrate my 35th wedding anniversary for immediate family only. Tom didn't care," Field recalled. "He flew in from Los Angeles with a case of Dom Perignon and surprised us at home. He kept us in stitches for several hours and left in his limo that same evening after kissing all the Fields. Tom was on the red eye back to L.A."

For Lou Young, a reporter at the Big Three New York stations, worked with Snyder at WABC in the early 1980s.

"I remember in the lobby when the elevator door opened, I just said hello to him like he was a long-lost friend. I'd never met the man," Young recalls. "I was reacting to him just as any fan might, and he got a kick out of that."

But if John Corporon had his way, Young probably wouldn't have worked with Snyder. The veteran news exec was courting the high-energy newsman and interviewer for the upstart Independent Network News with its flagship at WPIX.

"We had conversations. He did a terrific job at Channel 4. I thought he would have been a terrific national anchor, but he wasn't interested," Corporon admitted.

Snyder is getting his due with a documentary in the works by his daughter Ann Marie and her son, as well as a companion book that is in the works.

"He was so important in terms of freedom of speech and journalism," Snyder says of her father. "He had a relationship with the viewer, a trusted voice that you could listen to."

He was such a force in the industry that former *NBC Nightly News* anchor Brian Williams devoted nearly two minutes for an obituary montage, saying Snyder was "born and built for broadcasting."

Williams said in the July 2007 newscast that Snyder had a "towering presence" in the style of "performance art."

Ron Powers of the *Chicago Sun-Times*, and first TV critic to win the Pulitzer Prize, wrote of Snyder at the height of his career (and later reposted as part of the newspaper's obituary) that he was "the greatest local newscaster of them all . . . a TV journalist of unquestioned credentials, the definite electronic newsman . . . a nationally known interviewer . . . a skilled reporter . . . and a personality of almost mythical proportions."

Tributes also poured in from late-night comics David Letterman and Jay Leno, who said Snyder was a "bit of a rebel, one of those guys who liked to tweak authority figures, especially NBC executives."

But the former *Tonight Show* host said his reason for missing Snyder was somewhat selfish thanks to that signature laugh.

"He was probably the best audience a comedian could ever have," Leno recalled.

Perhaps the best tribute to Snyder came from Snyder himself, decades before his death.

"I think I am the best anchorman in the television news business today," Snyder said. "I think Jim Jensen is superb. I think Roger Grimsby is just fine. I think that Bill Beutel is excellent. But I think I'm better than they are. I think

I can beat them…I don't say it in terms of being vain or having a giant ego, although I admit to having some. But I think I'm awfully good at what I do."[6]

Snyder wasn't just nationally known for the interviews. He was already established as a "newsman" from his time in Philadelphia and Los Angeles before taking New York City by storm.

"I think it was an honest and successful attempt at journalism that we saw from Dad," daughter Ann Marie Snyder says.

Young says the humor flowed from his direction also. "He was a funny guy."

Field added, "When Tom went to the commercial, he would regale [everyone in the studio] with off-color comments and had them on the floor. He was our Don Rickles."

When Snyder wasn't playing to the staff, he was showcasing his innate skills. One time on the *NewsCenter 4* set, Snyder led the newscast with breaking news from City Hall. However, as the newscast started, the producer told him to stretch as the mayor's announcement and reporter on the scene were delayed.

Field was sitting opposite him, watching this anchoring clinic, assuming Snyder was reading off from a script.

"The prompter was blank. Tom was talking man to man to our viewers without a pause and without a prompter. Cued finally to throw it to City Hall, he did, sat back, and lit a cigarette to thunderous applause from cameramen, control room, and writers," Field recalled in wonder. "That is the only time I ever experienced that in my fifty years in the business."

Equally as impressive, Snyder had excellent breaking news chops. Viewers saw the best of Snyder during a *NewsCenter 4* telecast in 1975, the year he moved to New York. A plane crash at Kennedy Airport just before airtime left Snyder to vamp for time and listen to a producer with his clunky earpiece. More than 100 people were killed. At times he was joined by (6 pm anchor) Chuck Scarborough, already showing his aviation acumen, and Frank Field to detail the weather conditions. Snyder at one point is told that Tony Guida is calling in on the "beeper phone" from Jamaica Hospital for the latest on survivors.

---

6. Magelof, Lustig, and Levine. *Anchors Away.*

While waiting for more information and reporters to gather live on the scene, Snyder interspersed other news from the day.

"Now back to the rest of the day's news, which is a hell of a transition," Snyder proclaimed. He promptly told a story about a different crash, involving a delicatessen truck and commuter bus in Midtown. No serious injuries were reported.

After doing a voice-over story using video from the scene, Snyder concluded, "I really can't get excited about delicatessen truck crashes at this point. We will continue after these announcements."

It was a classic moment for the abrasive Snyder, not afraid to take a jab at whoever made the call to drop out of the breaking news coverage. That was the style viewers could embrace and made management uneasy at the same time.

In New York, Snyder would anchor one hour of *NewsCenter 4* and then tape *Tomorrow*. He also got national exposure with the brief nightly *NBC News Update* and eventually *Prime Time Sunday*.

"It isn't like we're taking an hour of news division product and replacing it with *B.J. and The Bear*," NBC President Fred Silverman said.[7] "That hour will be in the schedule as long as I'm here."

In Los Angeles, he also anchored the 11 pm KNBC newscast along with the 6 pm and *Tomorrow*.

"He worked very hard," Ann Marie Snyder says.

"He could take poorly written copy because, let's face it, most of the copy is poorly written, and just rewrite it as he went along," former colleague Chauncey Howell said. "He could wing it, and he was always good at it."

As comfortable as he was in a television studio, it was only when there was a studio audience that he would be out of his element.

"I start thinking they're all here and they want to win a car and I don't have one for them," Snyder laughed. "That's the only thing that I've been frightened of is a studio audience, for some reason."

---

7. Shales, Tom. "The Prime Time of Tom Snyder."

Chuck Scarborough's presence doubled, as he added the 11 pm show to his duties. Even with Hartz at *Today*, he was still needed to anchor a portion of *NewsCenter 4* in the early evening. That's until WNBC found its successor in Snyder. A year earlier, the up-and-coming star started the *Tomorrow* show from Los Angeles. Now he'd bring it to 30 Rock and take over anchor duties at 6 o'clock.

"I came here because NBC felt that I could be of some value in the local news on Channel 4," Snyder said.[8]

Snyder's daughter was 10 years old when he was uprooted to the east. Her parents were separated, and she would remain in California with her mom and visit her father at 30 Rock during the summer.

If she'd be in town during the school year, the junior Snyder was forbidden from going near Studio 8H.

"Saturday Night Live was being taped upstairs. We weren't allowed to go up there because they were doing D-R-U-G-S. We couldn't have 15-year-old girls hanging around the eighth floor," she says.

Snyder's mid-1970s residence was a four-story townhouse on East 51st Street between 1st and 2nd Avenues, which was at one time owned by famed director John Ford. The original bed frame was still there due to the tight accommodations.

She has fond memories of her times with dad in New York, including one of the 1970s popular fads: roller-skating outings in Central Park.

---

8. Magelof, Lustig, and Levine. *Anchors Away.*

5

There's a New Girl in Town

Chuck Scarborough and Sue Simmons had a career together that most can only dream about: 32 years at the helm of WNBC/Channel 4's late newscast. The chemistry was legendary, but Dave Marash says it didn't compare to Sue's partnership with Jim Vance at WRC in Washington. (Vance retired in May 2015 after 45 years on the air there.)

"I don't think any of her anchor partners in New York, Chuck or [Jack] Cafferty, or whoever else she had, synergized her. Vance did. She had always been great on her own, but I don't think that she was greater because she was teamed up with either [Jack] Cafferty or Chuck. But when she was teamed with Vance, it was like, 'Fasten your seatbeat!'

"[She] was an original, was a very, very smart person, and an incredibly charismatic performer," Marash says. "She and Cafferty actually had more spark than she and Chuck. She and Chuck were like barbeque and mayonnaise."

"They had a special thing going, but it was a different kind of show," Berman says of the Simmons/Cafferty connection. "They were doing a lighthearted chat show before chat shows were big."

"I remember in the 80s, Chuck Scarborough did a sweeps series, *Is God Mad at Us?*, which looked at this earthquake and that fire and this hurricane, and pondered the deep question as to whether or not God had planned these things to send us a message," Marash admits. "That ain't news."

However, that three-part series, which aired in November 1985, did receive praise from the New York Emmy Awards the following year, netting Scarborough a trophy for Outstanding News Features. He shared an Emmy that season with colleague Pat Harper for Best Newscast.

Scarborough and Harper proved a winning formula for WNBC at 6 pm, chosen four years in a row by the Emmys as Best Newscast. Harper and Steve Bosh's *Action News* would also win in the late 1970s and early 1980s at WPIX.

Scarborough has received 36 Emmys (as of this writing) during his illustrious tenure at WNBC. His mantle includes the Governor's Award, the Emmy's prestigious lifetime achievement honor, in 2014.

Marash, a well-respected journalist, takes a diplomatic tack about his former colleague.

"I'm going to say, I've got absolutely nothing to say about Chuck."

But Rolland Smith has a different feeling about his former rival.

"I think he's a solid journalist. We both share a passion for flying."

As for Simmons, she's another key figure who joined the ranks of star anchor not long after her 1980 debut at WNBC. In fact, one of the seeds for this book was planted on Simmons's farewell broadcast in 2012. Al Roker, longtime *Today* weatherman and previous WNBC meteorologist, said in a taped clip that when the book is written about the history of anchors, Simmons will be remembered as one of the best.

"I understand why management didn't think sports was important, but for them to think Sue Simmons wasn't important . . . from what I understand, they've been in the toilet in the ratings ever since." Len Berman says.

And opposite juggernaut WABC with its early newscasts at 4 pm, Berman believes no one is tuning in to Channel 4: "I don't know why they bother. They should put on *Saturday Night Live* reruns; they would do better."

***

Whether recognized more for her passion or prowess on camera, Simmons is, indeed, recognized as one of the premiere anchors the city has ever seen.

When she returned home to the promised land of New York, she was 38, but a seasoned veteran with a stint in Baltimore before a memorable run in Washington that would put her on WNBC's radar.

Talent and well-placed connections helped Simmons break down the doors at Rock Center. Her news director at WBAL was Ron Kershaw, who would resurface at WNBC in time to hire Simmons. While still in Baltimore, Simmons asked about changing paths into sports, but Kershaw squelched it, telling the anchor it was too late.

"I dropped those dreams, because that was my original game plan when I got into news," Simmons says.

Kershaw kept in touch with his friend and former anchor while she blazed a trail in Washington until offered the gig at WNBC.

Despite growing up in Manhattan, Simmons was professionally the new kid on the block at Channel 4.

"My arrival was turbulent in the sense that management between Washington and New York were at war about it," she says.

Once at 30 Rock, Simmons felt more tension.

"The newsroom was waiting for this big new arrival because they had hoped that someone from within would have been promoted."

One of those people—a female reporter—later told Simmons she called out sick for a few days just to critique Simmons's performance.

"It was a little bit of a mess, but you're walking into New York City, the number one market in the country. It's going to be competitive," Simmons says.

She got the backing of her news director Kershaw, who took over at WNBC only months before she was hired. He was fond of Simmons from their time together in Baltimore.

Kershaw would become legendary in broadcasting circles for his innovative style. It's not hyperbole to call him a genius. He tore down the sci-fi-looking *NewsCenter 4* set of the 1970s and created the hugely successful *Live at Five*.

Simmons almost immediately had the 11 pm with Scarborough and *Live at Five* with Cafferty.

"[Sue] has great street smarts and a sense of humor," Cafferty says. "She speaks from the hip and is fun to watch."[1]

Kershaw, who died in 1989, was also famous for his tempestuous 10-year relationship with NBC News anchor Jessica Savitch.

In doing away with the tanking, traditional news at 5 o'clock, he chose to eliminate the "bad acts," such as advice columnists.

"How-to shows are very condescending to women," Kershaw told *New York magazine* in 1981. "They assume women have no other interests."

With his changes in place, including several segments totally abandoned and reporters terminated, Channel 4 went from last to first place within four months of Simmons's first newscast.

One segment was with Howard Stern when he was a neighbor at WNBC Radio. He enjoyed taunting Simmons on the air several times, like how many mistakes she could make in 60 seconds. But when he appeared on *Live at Five* July 12, 1990 to promote his new television show, there was Stern with a bouquet of flowers. He kissed her and placed his tongue in her mouth.[2]

Three years later, Stern was back alongside Simmons, this time to plug his new book, *Private Parts*.

"Did you hear about my radio show this morning?" he asked.

"Yes, I certainly did. That's why my legs are crossed," Simmons countered.

"First of all, you didn't wear a dress. Because I was supposed to run my hand up your dress," he said, putting his hand on her knee. "Do me a favor, give me a kiss?" Stern responded.

"No, because the last time you were here you wigged—the tongue came out," Simmons said.

---

1. Morgan, Daniel B. *Last Stage Manager Standing*. Page Publishing, 2015.

2. Lucaire, Luigi. *Howard Stern A to Z: The Stern Fanatic's Guide to the King of All Media*. New York, NY: St. Martin's Press, 1997.

"Al [Roker], don't you want to see her kiss me? It was ugly." Stern said. "Len [Berman], what are the odds she'll kiss me?"

"2 to 1," Berman said.

"Al, remember last time he stuck that tongue out at me?" Simmons said, while Stern moved to the edge of his seat as she held her hand out as a barrier.

"Just give me a kiss?," Stern said.

"I'm not giving you anything. Sit back. Do I have to get physical?" she said.

"I have a bet that I can get a kiss off of you."

"Well, you lost," Simmons said.

"Come on, give me a kiss hello."

The focus then switched to Chuck Scarborough's blonde girlfriend off camera, who was signaled to sit on Stern's lap.

"I wanna see what Chuck kisses," Stern said.

The woman, named Katherine said, "He does smell good." As Simmons went in for sniff, Stern lunged for a kiss and missed. Stern settled for pecking Scarborough's friend on the neck.

"I think Matt wants to get in on this," Simmons said.

"Matt wants to get in on this." Stern added. "Come on, Matt."

(It takes on a different feel when looking through the prism of Lauer's future at NBC. The *Today* host was fired in 2017 amid allegations of inappropriate behavior in the workplace.)

Stern joked about Lauer's limited broadcast experience before landing at WNBC/Channel 4. "He's hot, he's knowledge," Simmons admitted.

They finally started the interview properly, and Stern said that his book is atop the best-seller list.

"Come on, give the number-one author in America a little kiss," Stern said.

"No, no, I'm not."

"Why, will that ruin your credibility?

As they went to commercial before a second segment, Stern jokingly tackled her in the chair. Unrelenting, Stern returned to the same theme after the break.

"Give me a kiss to end this thing."

"No, let me just say goodbye nicely."

"You don't want to kiss me?"

"No."

"Why, what is the big deal?"

She said, "I don't know you. Howard, my darling, I hold your hand professionally as I say: 'Thank you for coming by.'"

Stern's fawning over Simmons went back to his radio show on WNBC a decade earlier. One time, in fact, he aired a parody song, "Sue Simmons Hair," to the tune of "Bette Davis Eyes."

Among the lyrics:

She sits each night with Chuck
They make a handsome pair
She'd never jive and shuck
She's got Sue Simmons Hair
Is she Jewish?
Is she Irish?
She don't know what she is
But she's stylish
Is she Afro?
Or mulatto?
She's got the IQ of a po-tat-o
Try an' guess what is she
If you dare
She got Sue Simmons Hair

***

Simmons had a huge fanbase, many wanting to date or meet the extroverted anchor, as former colleague Chauncey Howell recalled. He got to know the future New York icon sitting on the *Live at Five* set with her for nine years.

Howell claimed at times to run interference for her. "I'd pick up a phone and pretend I was her secretary," Howell said. "Well, I can't tell you those stories. They're just too raunchy."

"Ron [Kershaw] explained to me that Chuck was king, and that if I were to visit my personality too much, the viewers would see it as an intrusion, and disrespectful," Simmons remembers. "He instructed me to do or say whatever I wanted, as long as the camera was just on me."

In a camera "two-shot," Simmons could be personable, but would make sure not to step on Scarborough's toes. And so, for the early portion of the "Chuck and Sue" run that's how it went until Scarborough's agent stepped in.

"He asked me to tone myself down because I was trying to take over, or overshadow Chuck." That was a tough one for Simmons, never known for having a muted on-air style. "We did OK."

Sue Simmons and me, shortly after her forced retirement from WNBC in 2012. [Jerry Barmash]

Not anticipating the legendary partnership that would develop, Scarborough didn't want to share the anchor desk with anyone.

"He had been anchoring by himself. He was loving that, and in his mind he didn't want a co-anchor. But I think he adjusted to it pretty quickly, because I'm fun!" Simmons laughs.

Lou Young, a preeminent street reporter, who worked at the "Big Three" stations for more than three decades, says Simmons did more than simply hold her own with Scarborough.

"[She was] so good that she'd throw hand grenades under the desk and disturb the entire broadcast," Young says. "It was like everything was falling apart, but she was fine. She was hysterical."

"Somebody decided we better get somebody pretty to anchor with [Scarborough]," longtime WNBC meteorologist Dr. Frank Field recalled. "Sue came in—not with a great background, but managed to survive because of her beauty and her talent to talk."

Starting to place a female and/or minority opposite a tried-and-true white man was a work in progress for management, but an easy fit for viewers.

"It is family viewing for men and women. You want your anchors to reflect the community that watches the show. The stations want to communicate and integrate themselves into the family," The Paley Center for Media's Ron Simon says.

Simmons certainly was able to become part of the family like few others in history. As the daughter of jazz bassist John Simmons, performing was in Sue's DNA.

"She was one of those people who just shot from the hip," former WNBC colleague Pia Lindström says. "You never knew what was going to come out of her mouth."

"Pia Lindström used to laugh her ass off from Sue," Howell said.

The combination was, as Field put it, "a good-looking guy and his co-anchor was a beautiful woman." But the veteran weatherman said despite making a dent in the ratings, "It was always a struggle in the local news [for WNBC]."

Early in Simmons's tenure, a producer cautioned her, saying "no one in the newsroom is your friend."

"It was kind of an eggshell-walking experience, but I navigated OK."

The legendary anchor, hired for the 11 p.m. broadcast from the get-go, had no plans to walk away from her dream job, even when it got to be a nightmare. "This was my hometown and I didn't think I made a mistake at all," Simmons says. "I just knew that I had to be alert."

With a huge ad campaign welcoming Simmons "home," she was spending so much time taking calls from people she grew up with that she forgot to eat. In that day's local papers, readers were introduced to Simmons with the heading, "New York's Best Is Now One Better."

The caption gave readers (and potential viewers) a brief bio, "She's a great reporter, she's been a top anchorwoman in the nation's capital, and now she's coming back to New York where she was born and brought up!"

What viewers didn't see that night, however, was Simmons starving before her debut. Simmons was forced to grab a sandwich from the vending machine.

"I got that, ran downstairs, and put it on my lap to try and take a bite during a commercial break. Frank Field busted me on the air. He told everybody that I was busy eating while I was working," Simmons says. "I managed to explain myself to our viewers with food in my mouth. Great first impression."

Another initiation followed in Simmons's first days at WNBC as Scarborough fiddled with his pen.

"I read my first story, somehow the tip of his pen bounced off my eyebrow."

Simmons was also riddled with anxiety and self-doubt. "I was a wreck," she says. "I had stage fright and that churning in my stomach every time I put a mic on and sat down at that desk."

But she says her biggest pressure was doing a good job, until being reminded in articles about the torches she was carrying.

"What helped was that it was an era of partying after shows," Simmons admits. "We would go downstairs and we would hang out. I sort of alleviated the pressure. I was surrounded by people with the like goal and like ambition, who liked to have a good time."

Simmons walked into 30 Rock with two strikes against her: being Black and being a woman.

She had to "fight harder," as she told *Ebony* in a 1981 interview, not only as a minority, but because she didn't have a college degree.

"But there are ways around everything," Simmons told *Ebony*. "You can't be intimidated by credentials if you have a good brain."

Compounding that, when she started her TV journey in 1972, she says women in the industry only had a shelf life until age 40.

"Someone once told me, I think it was Jessica Savitch, 'Once you stop being a fantasy to the minds of the upper executives, you were toast.'"

Not having high expectations, Simmons's first WNBC contract was for four years, taking her over the 40-year-old threshold, with some guaranteed cash.

"My attitude was, if I couldn't get work elsewhere in the television industry, I'd have something good on a resume, so I could get a decent job."

Either way, she brought her unique style on the newscast. Sick of hearing the standard "Have a Nice Day" and "Have a Nice Evening," Simmons opted for the sarcastic, "Have a Mediocre Evening."

Following her opening night, *New York Post* columnist Earl Wilson said the new anchor was rude. She realized that her humor may not always apply, as Kershaw told her to think of New York as the many separate communities it is.

Simmons, hired eight years earlier through Affirmative Action, was a trail-blazing figure in the annals of broadcasting. But she didn't have any time for historical perspective. Simmons was too busy getting prepared each night in a fast-paced environment.

"I was just thinking about trying to survive with the current job and didn't care about whether I was Affirmative Action or not," Simmons says.

Taken right from the secretarial pool to reporter in New Haven, Simmons reached the career pinnacle without getting a college education. She kept legendary network anchor Peter Jennings in mind, whose education ended after high school.

"I just had to get by on grit," Simmons says.

6

The Chuck and Sue Era

With the rocky start in the rear-view mirror, Sue Simmons and Chuck Scarborough would establish an unrivaled presence in New York. From President Carter to President Obama, Chuck and Sue were the local news answer to Johnny Carson, seemingly always there to tuck us in with a smile while providing the latest information.

But when did the iconic anchor team officially become "Chuck and Sue?" When did they become something special to viewers?

Simmons gives credit to Marvin Kitman, the former *Newsday* TV critic, as the person who created the "Chuck and Sue" moniker. But when correspondents in a live report would occasionally twist their names into "Suck and Chew" that's when she "knew we pretty much made it."

They hit their stride with viewers during a transit strike in those early months, which cemented their chemistry.

"They began to inch up," Field recalled, "but it was always a struggle. This was a period where we had gone from just two stations that were tops. Our ratings were enormous in those days, because you only watched CBS or you watched NBC. ABC was a poor third all along until they went into the *Eyewitness News* setup and began to pull away the audience."

Chuck Scarborough and Sue Simmons were honored by the New York Emmy Awards in 2018. [Jerry Barmash]

"When it's a winning team, it's a happy team," Simmons says.

"It was fun working with Chuck and Sue," said Field, who caught a few years in person on set before switching to WCBS in 1984.

The first half of the 1980s meant viewers had their pick of the longest tenured anchor teams at 6 pm: Chuck and Sue on WNBC, Roger and Bill on WABC, and Jim and Rolland on WCBS.

"It was great to help somebody like that along. She'd sit there, read something, and obviously didn't understand exactly what it was. She'd turn to me, Chuck, or whoever was in," Field said. "She was getting an education on the air."

Len Berman says, "They were like a husband-and-wife team. They complemented each other beautifully."

After more than three decades of Chuck and Sue, the longest local anchor team in history, plenty of Scarborough rubbed off on Simmons.

The duo was so integral to each other's success that the New York State Broadcasters Association inducted them together as charter members in 2005. "Chuck is an accomplished journalist. I was a surviving one," Simmons says. "He brought one set of skills, I brought another. But I always watched to see what he was doing."

"She is one of kind. There will never be another Sue Simmons. Working with her for 32 and a half years was certainly one of the highlights of my 52 years in the business," Scarborough says. "We reported on New York through all the best and worst times in the city, side by side. It was a wonderful pairing, and I treasure those days with her."

Scarborough also admits that her personality made everyone better. "She was this singular personality. She has this extraordinary sense of humor, this ability to gain insight into people, kind of magically, and elicit things from them that they normally wouldn't divulge, simply to be this vivacious, unpredictable personality on television."

The Chuck and Sue era came to close on June 15, 2012.

Before playing a video tribute of Simmons's best moments, Scarborough said, "For 32 ½ years at 11 o'clock on NBC4, it's been Chuck and Sue. But that's as close as we're going to get to forever." Simmons exhales and holds back tears.

He called her "funny," "unpredictable", "dangerous," and a "very special woman." Scarborough would also call Simmons "one of a kind." Simmons, of course, could handle the stories of an urgent nature, but they weren't her strong suit. "Chuck and Jensen were the masters of [breaking news]," Len Berman says. "They would roll up their sleeves. There was no one better."

Entertaining and appealing for critics and clearly the, more important, viewers, former TV news executive John Corporon appreciated her work ethic, although it didn't mesh with his more traditional news values.

"She was not as serious as I like my anchors to be, and she would have some great missteps on air, but her audiences loved her," Corporon conceded that Simmons was successful, but "she is not one of my favorites." Corporan, a WPIX executive for more than 20 years, died in 2022. He was 92.

Despite her three-decade tenure at WNBC, Simmons was bounced in 2012 when station honchos opted not to renew her contract. A year earlier before the forced retirement, former colleague Carol Jenkins spoke incredulously about their on-air "stamina."

"I say to Sue, 'Haven't you guys made enough money yet?'" Jenkins laughs. "I think the answer is probably no."

As successful as Scarborough and Simmons were individually, it was as "Chuck and Sue" where they really shined.

"I was the straight guy in the comedic sense. I was the hard-nosed newsguy, 'givin' the facts, ma'am, nothing but the facts," Scarborough recalls. "She added the element of humanity to the broadcast. I think the yin and yang of the two of us was quite complimentary. And I think that's why it worked."

At the same time Simmons made her homecoming, WNBC landed another anchor—John Hambrick. He had a five-year stint at the station, primarily working opposite Scarborough on the 6 pm. His versatility was showcased by handling hard news and tongue-in-cheek fare with the same aplomb.

A 1981 ad showed a group photo of the three anchors (ironically, no Jack Cafferty), plus Dr. Frank Field and Marv Albert. Scarborough was listed as the "winner of numerous Emmy and Associated Press awards for journalistic issues," and "respected for his cool handling of hottest issues," As for Simmons: "Savvy and style tell you right away—she's a native New Yorker. With all the energy New Yorkers are known for."

Playing off the *Star Wars* frenzy at the time, the ad title was "May the 4s Be With You."

Jim Hartz, who died in 2022 at 82, was there for Scarborough's debut in New York nearly a half-century earlier, during the first few months of *NewsCenter 4*.

"He's a good, solid guy, who doesn't panic," Hartz said. "That's all you want to know about an anchorman in New York."

Scarborough was also a master of the conversational delivery. He had a knack for reading the teleprompter and yet, with a split-second maneuver of the eyes, would appear as though he was having an impromptu thought.

Scarborough, who commanded more than $3 million a year, made just a fraction of that salary in his early days at WNBC. A *New York* magazine piece said Scarborough made $98,000 in 1975, his second year at 30 Rock, a $20,000 upgrade from two years earlier in Boston. Scarborough had an inauspicious start financially in front of the camera, pulling in just $1.85 an hour in Biloxi.

1980 may not have been a watershed year, but it was key to changing perceptions. One female replaced another at WNBC when Sue Simmons took over Lindström's anchor role.

"I worked with her for many years. At first, I didn't understand it, but she's without guile," Lindström says. "[Simmons] is not mean. She just said what she thought."

Lindström, whose grew up in movie royalty as the daughter of three-time Oscar-winner Ingrid Bergman, says not knowing what Simmons would blurt next was part of her charm.

Unpredictability, that was her biggest on-air asset, Lindström thinks, and forced her to stay on her toes when alongside Simmons.

"She brought an element of risk – like playing with hand grenades – to live TV," Jack Cafferty said.[1]

"I got to handle her as well as I could when it came to the sports," Len Berman recalls.

From those interactions you knew Simmons enjoyed chatting about sports, especially the Mets, and could hold her own with Berman.

"I was more uptight," Lindström laughs. "It was fun, but a kind of fun you didn't know where it was going to go.

Aside from any bloopers, Simmons is using hindsight now, something she couldn't do in the heat of the action each night.

"It was just a process," Simmons says. "You're in there every day, just trying to do your job."

And, according to Simmons, chemistry is a requirement to survive as an anchor tandem for 30 minutes, let alone 30 years. "After the first year or two, we felt pretty comfortable."

It went to the next level for Chuck and Sue as their off-camera relationship came together.

Scarborough, despite being 18 months Simmons's junior, took on a fatherly attitude toward his co-anchor.

"He'd give me advice, and a little scolding here and there," Simmons says.

---

1. Cafferty, Jack. *It's Getting Ugly Out There: The Frauds, Bunglers, Liars, and Losers Who Are Hurting America.* Hoboken, NJ: John Wiley & Sons, 2007.

Although Scarborough wasn't her boss, Simmons jokes in her best announcer voice: "He was the lead anchor!"

Not wanting that to define their work together, Simmons eventually stood up for herself.

"I wanted him to know that he was looking in equal eyeballs. I wasn't a child," she recalls.

Perhaps out of that line-in-the-sand moment, the Chuck and Sue era was born. By her own admission, Simmons brought spontaneity and knowledge in sports and entertainment, areas that she says Chuck "weren't particularly interested in."

Simmons says he only became engaged in those topics once he had a son.

"But then he had zero knowledge, zero interest, except what was in the headlines," Simmons remembers.

With their chemistry prospering, Simmons remembers a news director taking over in the mid-1980s, pleasantly surprised by the lack of ego from his top anchors.

They cultivated the chemistry that most anchor teams could only fantasize about having, becoming close enough to have working dinner breaks together.

"We enjoyed the hell out of each other," she said.

It's trite, but the rest is history, with dozens of Emmy Awards for Scarborough.

If Al Primo had his way, he would have changed the course of history with the legendary anchor. The WABC executive made a series of overtures to the budding broadcaster. Before landing in New York, Scarborough got two years of major market experience under his belt in Boston. Primo made three trips there to woo Scarborough to WABC before WNBC came-a-calling in March 1974.

"He is a student of the business," Primo reflected. "I think he knew, between Roger and Bill together, and where we were, that was a fortress that was not coming down, nor was there ever going to be a place for him."

Although Primo didn't court Simmons, he liked her work, but not how her tenure concluded.

"I think that she was treated rather shabbily by NBC, but that's what happens when you get your salary up to 4–5 million," Primo admitted.

Early on, Simmons recalls technicians doing a test before going live—which Scarborough passed with flying colors.

"It's like the sun to him. He could tell if the lighting's not hitting him right," Simmons says. "I was oblivious to all that."

However, early in their partnership the experimenting with electricity persisted.

"Finally, it was revealed that they were trying to make me darker because they wanted the city to know that they'd actually hired a Black woman." Simmons admits.

7

"Do I Want to Play Catch with Mickey Mantle?"

While Tom Snyder was gaining his foothold nationally, Chuck Scarborough was establishing himself as the go-to guy on the peacock's local side. He was featured in a *New York* magazine article just five months after his debut in the big city. Because of Jim Hartz's *Today* show promotion, WNBC was now in the market for a much-needed on-air partner for Scarborough, its burgeoning star.

At the time, news director Earl Ubell was sifting through numerous audition tapes.

"Why not go out of town?" Ubell asked the magazine. "The rest of the country has always been a farm system for New York media."

But Scarborough wasn't making a dent in the ratings in those early days. Plus, Scarborough never spent more than three consecutive days in the city before landing the gig of a lifetime.

His blond hair and blue eyes did get him support from one demographic. "Women viewers respond to him," New York magazine reported in 1975.

Chuck Scarborough celebrated 50 years on the air at WNBC in 2024. [Jerry Barmash]

When the camera light switches off, Simmons says, "Chuck is a much softer, humorous person than most people probably think."

Within the broadcast: "We were pretty equal after a while. Where he stood shoulders above me is in breaking news. Because through the first part of my career when anything important happened in breaking news, it was given to the man. So I never developed those skills properly."

There were also times that Lou Young sat next to Scarborough during his four years at WNBC.

"The fact that I anchored with Chuck is absurd. The fact that you can say the words anchor, Chuck Scarborough, and Lou Young in the same sentence has to be an accident," Young jokes. "I can read out loud, but that's where my resemblance to Scarborough ends."

Young got his dream opportunity on the 11 pm thanks to a station rule at the time that no anchor, even the mighty Scarborough, could do a solo broadcast. Simmons was out sick and Young was in-house working on a future piece.

While nervous, Young didn't need much cajoling. "Do I want to play catch with Mickey Mantle?" he pondered.

He was informed, though, that Scarborough would handle reading the majority of stories that night, which didn't bother the inexperienced anchor.

"He can read all the copy. I will have no problem sitting on the set and watching him read," Young jokes.

Young, who dabbled in anchoring at WNBC and WCBS, says working with Scarborough was one of the smoothest broadcast experiences he ever had.

"I would wonder what goes on inside that brain of his that he's so well-organized."

When Young heading home to his apartment on 91st Street that night, the doorman congratulated the performance, but in an only-in-New-York moment he asked, "What, he couldn't do it alone?"

In the 1980s, Scarborough did double duty with network updates in prime time. For a time, you could also find him on weekends as *Nightly News* anchor. But, home was always the anchor desk at WNBC.

"I liked what I was doing and what better [place] is there to do it than New York City. I liked the stability of being here. This city is so complex," Scarborough told colleague David Ushery on a podcast.

To hear Scarborough reflect, he chose to stay put. Whether that's true or not about him and his contemporaries, they were commanding a big salaries as lead anchors at their stations.

"[It] was very profitable," The Paley Center for Media's Ron Simon says. "Obviously, it's always nice to have network exposure, but you're doing extremely well."

Of course, Snyder was the more well-known talent thanks to his late-night popularity on NBC.

"[He] had this desire always to be on television," Simon says. "So, that was a good thing for him."

John Huddy Sr. sums up the Snyder on-camera skills this way: "He was a great talent. He was unusual talent. He was an original talent."

Chauncey Howell, known for his long body of work primarily as a jovial street reporter, agreed—to a point. "He was very gifted [and] was a television wonder," the former WNBC reporter said. "He wasn't very literate. He would put out memos on the bulletin board and there would be lots of misspellings."

Howell recalled Snyder called him "chintzy" to his face, but Chauncey laughed it off, because he was impressed with the anchor/interviewer.

"Tom Snyder was different from all of them," Howell said. "When the red light came on, he'd lean in because he was so anxious and eager to greet his viewers."

Howell got a taste of anchoring. In a pinch, he needed to tell viewers about an incident in midtown. No other talent was available at that moment, so it was Howell in the newsroom, where he would report breaking news. Howell's so-called natural style impressed many viewers, who called WNBC requesting more anchor opportunities for him.

Howell said management actually held a secret meeting at a hotel to discuss it. The main reason he wouldn't get the high visibility was because he was "dangerous" as an on-air presence.

Primarily focusing on a "kicker" (a light story to wrap up the newscast), Howell showed his love of meeting people as he "kibbitzed" with them, and, of course, on the *Live at Five* set with Sue Simmons, who enjoyed the chance to show off her carefree attitude.

Back to the "traditional" anchors. Veteran Pia Lindström chimes in on Scarborough, "He has tremendous skills. It's just that they weren't sometimes apparent to people who didn't know what it takes to do that year after year after year."

She adds, "Your life can be in upheaval and things are happening, but you never show that. And you somehow maintain this level of performance for years. It's really a skill."

Scarborough's professionalism was a key trait to his success. But his demeanor didn't waver off-camera either. He was equally pleasant and cordial whether speaking to executives or the floor manager.

"I never saw him lose his temper," Lindström recalls. "There were other people who would ignore some of the crew and yet be subservient to the president of the company. I never saw that in Chuck. It was wonderful. It was a great example of endurance."

Looks and knowledge aside, Scarborough could appear stiff, especially opposite the demonstrative Simmons. But one night on set the classic anchorman showed a different side. Frank Field was doing a report on a premature baby who survived.

"To demonstrate the size and weight of the infant I held up a small apple and showed it to Chuck," Field remembered. "As soon as the film and my voice-over began, I bit a chunk of the apple and handed it to Chuck. I believe that was the only time in all my years we worked together that I was able to break Chuck up."

So, a gregarious personality wasn't why viewers kept watching.

Scarborough's own reason for a record-setting tenure comes down to a word: trust. As he told *The New York Times* in 2010: "It takes years to earn and can be squandered in an instant . . . I have no one to thank but you, our viewers. Had you not tuned in and given me time to build that sense of familiarity and bond of trust, I wouldn't have lasted very long."

"I never thought he'd last that long," Former cohort Jim Hartz said. "[It's] not that he's not any good, but that's just a long time to keep doing the same thing over and over again."

In marking his 40th anniversary in 2014 as the face of WNBC's news division, the station produced a short video about the legendary anchor.

"Frankly, I think the ability to stay here, that I've been blessed to be able to stay in this market is so remarkable—for this length of time," Scarborough says. "It just doesn't happen that people stay for 40 years in one job in television news. It is notoriously iterant. People come and go all the time. The fact that I've been able to, with all the vagaries of the ratings and management changes, still stay in the anchor chair at the head of the news operation here in New York has been breathtakingly, first of all surprising, completely unexpected. Mainly, I'm just grateful that I was able to do it and there was enough of an audience watching us for me to maintain my position throughout the years."

Technology progressed by leaps and bounds during Scarborough's five-decade stretch at 30 Rock. For example, when he arrived at NBC in the mid-1970s, they used 16 mm color reversal film that had a magnetic stripe for sound, before ushering in the convenience and quality of videotape.

"But the big transition that really changed what we do, and changed the environment in which we work, was the digital revolution," Scarborough said.

"We went from linear editing to non-linear editing . . . We can edit with much more speed now."

Furthermore, Scarborough's easygoing, yet professional attitude connected with viewers, sending his likability levels through the roof.

"He was very cordial, and very polite, equally to every single person," Lindström remembers. "Under that is something else. He's got a very strong core."

But Scarborough, who is racking up years like a pilot (which he also is) logs miles, knows he's the oddity.

"Frankly, I'm astonished that I'm still here. This is not normal. This is not typical," He said in a 2014 interview. "This is a very itinerant business. I'm exceedingly grateful that I was able to last this long and continue to last. I've got a couple years left on my contract now, so I'm not out of here yet."

As the "Lou Gehrig of local anchors," Scarborough is the one constant each night, a throwback to five decades earlier. However, as his legendary run kicked off, Scarborough had bigger aspirations.

"There's really only one other step to go, and that is to be on a national program doing what I'm doing now," Scarborough said in 1976.

He had a minimal presence at the network. "[When] they run out of all other souls, they come and get me," Scarborough admitted. "Obviously, somewhere down the line, I'm not trying to hurry anybody out of his position mind you, I would like to take the reins of one of the evening broadcasts, hopefully NBC's, long after John Chancellor and David Brinkley have decided that they don't want to do it anymore."[1]

Hartz said, "[Chuck's] a good guy. He's still at it, Lord love him. If he wants to do it, who am I to say don't? I just don't think I could do that every day anymore."

"He could do it," Lindström praises. "I just felt that I wanted another life. I think I like beginnings; I don't like endings so much."

Scarborough is "semi-retired" as of August 2019, anchoring only the 6 pm newscast. He was taken off the late newscast in 2017, while the popular Ernie

---

1. Magelof, Lustig, and Levine. *Anchors Away.*

Anastos lost the 10 pm at WNYW/Fox 5 in 2014. Anastos stepped away from the TV grind (sources say not by his choice) in 2020 to attend classes at the Harvard Business School.

They took different routes to longevity, of course. Scarborough logged his hours at one station. Anastos was less stable, but equally popular in his 40+ year career in New York.

"That is not the case in network news, where everything has undergone a radical transformation," Ron Simon, Curator, Paley Center for Media, says. "In local news... so many of the shows are passed on from generation to generation, so it's a good thing that you do have an individual like Scarborough or Anastos who can sort of carry on the tradition."

Anastos, Scarborough, and Simmons are members of the New York State Broadcasters Hall of Fame that was established in 2006. Unfortunately, through 2023, the organization passed over Beutel, Grimsby, Jensen, Jorgensen, Roland, and Snyder for inclusion. Retired WABC anchor Diana Williams is among the luminaries, along with WNBC's David Ushery and the late Gabe Pressman.

Melba Tolliver, a one-time colleague of Scarborough, isn't all that enamored with his amazing on-air longevity.

"I don't think about it," she chuckles. "Good for him." Tolliver says this was first time she was asked about Scarborough's historic run. "It certainly is a *Guinness Book of Records* detail," Tolliver adds. "But, so what?"

That record hit another milestone on March 25, 2024, when Scarborough commemorated an unprecedented 50 years at NBC. The company showered him with a luncheon at Rockefeller Center's famed Rainbow Room. He also lit the Empire State Building that night in blue (for the NBC peacock) and gold (for the anniversary).

"I'm touched beyond belief and it's an honor to work with you," he said to the large crowd of current and former colleagues, including Simmons.

Tolliver was surprised to learn that Scarborough authored a couple of books earlier in his career. "I just never saw him as a very thoughtful person, but what did I know?" Tolliver admits.

As for interactions on the behemoth *NewsCenter 4* set, Tolliver says Scarborough was a "pleasant, friendly guy."

8

"Oh Man! God, It Was Rampant!"

While at WNBC, Melba Tolliver made her own history, believed to be part of the first female anchor team in New York when she teamed with Pia Lindström in 1978.

"The ratings were poor," Frank Field admitted. "Pia and Melba failed to draw."

Tolliver, who was already in her second decade of TV news, had broadcasting mentors—all Black. Longtime WNBC reporter Bob Teague and Gerald Harrington, who had a brief stint at the peacock, helped shape her career. She also credits Mal Goode, the first African American reporter in the country, when ABC hired him as a United Nations correspondent in 1962, for molding her journalistically.

Back at WNBC, Lindström wasn't overly thrilled about the plan. "I enjoyed hearing men read the news."

She said the groundbreaking move was simply done to have "one Black, one white. I suppose they thought that was like bookends."[1]

---

1. Marlane, J. (1999). *Women in Television News Revisited: Into the Twenty First Century*. Univ. of Texas Press.

General Manager Ray Timothy came to WNBC in 1975, and he had Field in his sights.

"[He] asked me to lunch at the Rainbow Room. We were chatting in generalities when he suddenly asked me if I would be willing to anchor the 5 pm news," Field said he was placed in high esteem.

"Ray, who was promoted from KNBC in Los Angeles, said that his father considered me to be the local Walter Cronkite," Field said, recalling the offer. "I thanked Ray and said 'No thanks.' I would rather continue with the security I found as science editor and meteorologist and was unwilling to change and test the revolving door of anchors."

Even though women were in the TV news minority, Lindström didn't recognize sexism in San Francisco or New York.

"I didn't experience it, or if it happened, I didn't hold it against anybody. Maybe it was just my nature," Lindström admits. "I was always paid less.

"I don't feel like that I suffered because men were running things."

However, recalling in *Women in Television News Revisited*, Lindström said she and her female counterparts were in a tough spot. The spotlight was on them, and not necessarily on the air. She wasn't able to pass on assignments, get mad, or use bad language. Lindström also felt women in TV news, early in her career, had to work twice as hard as her entrenched on-air talent with the X and Y chromosomes.

For Lindström to break out in the industry that was dominated by men, it was important to balance dominating without people hating you.

"Or let them hate you, and you don't mind as long as they do their job. It required not being loved."

Carol Jenkins, who spent more than two decades as an anchor at WNBC, was always in the shadow of male counterpart Chuck Scarborough. When she ultimately left WNBC in 1995 for WNYW/Fox 5, it was apparently due to a blowup because of her making quite a bit less than Scarborough, even though they put in almost the same time at 30 Rock.

New York magazine reported at the time that Jenkins had a verbal altercation with then-news director Bruno Cohen, who told her that audiences related better to Scarborough.

"Fuck you," Jenkins was overheard shouting to Cohen.

At the time, Scarborough commanded $2 million a year and was apparently stunned to learn only an hour before airtime that he was flying solo.

"Apparently, I'm not one of her intimates," Scarborough told *New York* magazine.

Salary disparity among genders was a serious concern for Rose Ann Scamardella when she started her TV career with an $18,000 annual income at WABC, well below established male stars Roger Grimsby and Bill Beutel.

But she's quoted in the book, *Women in Television News Revisited* that her ending salary was in the high six figures. She credits Barbara Walters for allowing the contracts to finally become gender neutral.

"When she got that million dollars, everybody's salary escalated," Scamardella says. "That's when the animals took over the zoo. We were all making big bucks."

Initially, and for many years, Scamardella was subordinate salary-wise to Grimsby and Beutel. Popularity among viewers was always a prime negotiating ploy—even for women.

The ladies of TV news, including Jane Hanson, a young, attractive reporter/anchor at WNBC, were not only on the short end of the salary stick, they also dealt with sexism reminiscent of the '60s *Mad Men* era.

"Oh man! God, it was rampant!" says Hanson, who was hired in 1979.

While not dismissing it, she claims sexism was not unique to newsrooms or even New York. Now, as women are on heightened sensory alert since the #MeToo movement, Hanson says she lived through it all, but decided early on about her career.

"It happened to all of us, but we had to learn how to deal with it," Hanson recalls. "Unless it was really, really bad, you said, 'OK, let's just move on [and] figure out how to deal with it.'"

She had to take her skills to another level, proving she belonged in the New York market and a focus on breaking the glass ceiling.

Hanson, a personable twenty-something when she landed at Rockefeller Center, says plenty of the alpha-male personalities permeated parties and press conferences.

"It came with the territory," Hanson admits. "We had to deal with it, because frequently we were the only girls around. In today's world [that] would never fly . . . It was an interesting place. Was it a boys' club? Of course. But I had a great time."

It was lewd and even discriminatory, but Hanson makes clear nothing rose to the level of criminal behavior.

"I'm not saying that someone raped me, and I looked the other way," Hanson said.

After being unceremoniously dumped by her home of 27 years, Hanson was given another lifeline at WNBC when she was named co-host of lifestyle show *LX New York* in 2010.

"I'm a woman over 50, and women over 50 are not necessarily welcomed on television," Hanson admits.[2] "I honestly thought this may be a really nice signal for women out there that you don't have to be 35, or you don't have to be 25. You can be over 50, go back on the air and actually have a voice."

That quote remains timely in the television news landscape.

In 2019, five Spectrum News NY1 anchors and reporters got plenty of media attention for a bombshell lawsuit alleging sexism and ageism. The talent, ranging from ages 40–61 at the time, put forth a class action suit as aggrieved former employees. They all were still employed when they filed the legal papers. Each woman claims they were pushed from a high-profile on-air slot for a man or a younger woman. The group included Roma Torre, the first on-air anchor at the 24/7 cable channel in 1992.

---

2. Barmash, Jerry. "Marking First Anniversary With LX New York, Jane Hanson Says 'We Are Now' the 'Go To Show.'" *Ad Week*, March 7, 2011.

As founder of the Women's Media Center, Jenkins led the charge for more females in newsrooms. "When we started there were no [female] anchors," Jenkins said in a 2011 interview. "We didn't have Katie Couric, Candy Crowley, or Rachel Maddow. We waged quite a persistent campaign, both online and meeting with big executives at all the networks."

Her next focus was balancing women in high-profile anchor roles.

"There's been a huge loss of representation in newsrooms and people of color." Jenkins said a lot of work remained.

Jenkins, who joined WNBC in the early 1970s, saw that misrepresentation firsthand. "It really didn't include, for years and years and years, any women or any people of color," Jenkins said. "I think it's taken a gigantic effort to adjust to that transition."

As late as the 2011 interview, Jenkins claimed it was still rare for a Black woman to break the glass ceiling. While this book highlights advances women of color have made in the ultra-competitive world of TV news, Jenkins said she wouldn't be happy until a network gig goes to a Black woman.

For example, when Couric left her brief tenure at the *CBS Evening News*, she wanted the successor to be female and of color, but that position ultimately went to Scott Pelley. His short stint led to Anthony Mason as interim anchor, and Jeff Glor with just two years at the helm of the broadcast.

CBS did return with a woman in 2019 with Norah O'Donnell, but not of color. The only female minority was Connie Chung, ill-fated co-anchor with Dan Rather from 1993–1995. You could also count Barbara Walters as a minority for being Jewish. She co-anchored the *ABC Evening News* in the mid-1970s with Harry Reasoner.

Lester Holt became the first Black man to anchor a regular network newscast when he jumped into the chair at *NBC Nightly News* in 2015.

ABC, as CBS did three years earlier, promoted a blonde female to the anchor desk in 2009 when Diane Sawyer took over *World News Tonight*.

A main reason for the lack of Black females, Jenkins intimated, was that the "benches are so weak." She said the networks didn't establish a deep talent pool that included African American women. It was not that they deserved the positions simply because of their skin color. They need the experience, Jenkins said, which she knows something about from a 30-plus year career in New York.

"There were people ahead of me, like Norma Quarles [former *NBC News* reporter] who was already at the network . . . I can't quite claim first generation," Jenkins says. "But that next generation, and the fact that I managed to have a long career of 30 years, was trailblazing in that regard."

Quarles, who started at WNBC in 1970, was a reporter and a substitute hostess for a women's show. It was only three weeks, but management took notice, and she earns the distinction as the first woman to co-anchor a newscast in New York City when she joined veterans Gabe Pressman and Sander Vanocur on the *Sixth Hour News*. Quarles was positioned alongside Pressman in the center of the set with Vanocur seated on an angle at camera right.

The New York City native did one year of training through NBC in the mid-1960s, as pressure was building to hire more minorities. That led to a job at the Cleveland affiliate before WNBC. In 1977 she started a four-year stint at WMAQ in Chicago.

"You have to be willing to constantly learn and grow," she said in a 1971 interview with *Ebony* magazine. "Most of all, if a person wants to be in this business, she has to love it."

After being a New York correspondent for NBC, Quarles, who turned 87 in 2023, joined CNN in the late 1980s. She was inducted into the National Association of Black Journalists Hall of Fame in 1990.

Joan Murray is another vital link to the past, believed to be the first African American reporter on American television when she worked at WCBS in the mid-to-late 1960s. Murray had been in the network's publicity department, handling events such as the Kennedy/Nixon debate in 1960, the first man walking in space in 1961, and the initial broadcast of *CBS Evening News with Walter Cronkite* a year later.

She left CBS in 1963 for NBC, where she was a writer and occasional on-air commentator on *Women on the Move*, a daytime show hosted by Kitty Carlisle. After the show was canceled in 1964, Murray contacted CBS about her desire to become an on-air news broadcaster. She was granted an audition and interview with WCBS where she would be hired as a correspondent for the 6 and 11 o'clock broadcasts.

Her pioneering efforts included appearing on the station's public affairs shows *Two at One* and *Opportunity Line*.

And then there is Carole Simpson, who was the first African American woman to anchor a network newscast. She started at NBC, working primarily out of the DC bureau, but it was her two decades at ABC that are part of the annals of history. Along with the weekend anchoring, she had another "first," as a woman and a minority, when she moderated a presidential debate in 1992.

"Women can do the impossible ... if you want something, you'll do it," Simpson told ABC News in 2021.

9

NewsCenter 4

Eyewitness News kicked into high gear in the early 1970s with the full complement of reporters and, of course, Roger Grimsby and Bill Beutel at the helm. It was clearly now the station to beat night after night.

Steve Bosh anchored briefly with Jim Jensen. Bosh's wife Cindy says the *Eyewitness* shop actually didn't appeal to him and others because their news operation was radically different.

WCBS was in the best position to battle for second place.

That left WNBC to pick up the crumbs, usually as the last-place finisher with its sleepy production values of the *Sixth Hour* and *Eleventh Hour* broadcasts.

"It wasn't the eleventh hour. It was the 23rd hour," Former anchor Jim Hartz deadpanned. "You know television; they'll do whatever seems appropriate."

Something had to give at 30 Rock as WNBC, a top-flight news organization in the previous decade, couldn't find direction in the 70s. You could call them the Yankees of local news—great numbers in the 1960s and turmoil in the early 1970s.

"I think there were times we had 50 and 60 shares," Hartz recalled about Channel 4 in the mid- to late 1960s.

Part of the reason for WNBC's dominance in those early years, he claimed, was the two-station field in New York during that time.

"WABC wasn't even in the game," Hartz reflected. "They were really awful. It's only when they went to *Eyewitness* that they hit the jackpot."

But from the late 60s to the *NewsCenter 4* era, WNBC was sputtering.

Frank Field was there starting with the leanest days of the 1950s. "Early on, it was just a period of chaos," Field said, reflecting on the WNBC news operation in the 1960s and early 1970s. "It was just constant changing of anchor people looking for a magic bullet."

He's right—it was a revolving door, to be sure, when the clock struck 6 pm. This was when network talent brought viewers local casts, including Robert MacNeil (long before teaming with Jim Lehrer on PBS), Frank McGee, Lew Wood, John Palmer (later the *Today* news reader), and Sander Vanocur. Hartz followed next, and was then replaced by the combo of Carl Stokes and Paul Udell. Hartz stayed on for the 11 o'clock show.

At 24, Hartz was the youngest correspondent hired by the network, which included anchoring WNBC evening broadcasts. When he debuted in 1964, McGee was anchoring the late news, which was truncated due to *The Tonight Show*'s 11:15 start time.

A 1965 *TV Guide* listing gave a sense of how local news was being broadcast. McGee was on at 11 pm opposite WCBS's Jim Jensen and WABC's Bill Beutel. Tex Antoine, with his "Uncle Wethbee" persona had a separate weather listing at 11:10. At 11:15, Hartz had the local news. Similarly, WCBS had Frank Gifford with a separate sports heading at 11:25 pm.

At the height of WNBC's doldrums, Gabe Pressman bolted. The longtime political reporter (and brief anchor in the 1960s) moved to WNEW-TV, citing Channel 4 was opting more for entertainment than hard news.

Pressman wrote station VP and GM Arthur Watson about the importance of having more investigative reporting, stating, "I do not believe that NBC is the best milieu for the kind of local journalism that I think the times call for."[1]

---

1. Krebs, Albin. "Pressman Quits WNBC for Channel 5." *The New York Times*. June 8, 1972.

The letter received a swift reply from NBC VP Reuven Frank, who claimed the station was committed to hard news and investigative work, which was where the pleasantries ended.

"The latitude we gave you—including your own program, your own staff, and (forgive me) your own chauffeur—attests to that commitment. Because we share your belief that investigative reporting is vital to television journalism, we hoped to see more of it from you than we did."

Late in his remarkable career, Gabe Pressman (and I) appeared at the 2015 Folio Awards on Long Island. [Jerry Barmash]

Pressman made no secret that he thought the newly created *Sixth* and *Eleventh Hour* sets were "ghastly," despite having been designed by Robin Wagner, who created the look for Broadway's *Jesus Christ Superstar*.

He also appeared uncomfortable with the on-air small talk, perhaps directly going against the *Eyewitness News* winning formula. It didn't work for an old-school reporter.

Hartz, who considered Pressman a close friend, wished him well at his 1972 departure. "I know Gabe was unhappy with a lot of things, including the new set, but that matters little to me. You could do the show under a shade tree, and it wouldn't matter."

Pressman joined WNBC in 1956 and was an occasional New York-based correspondent for the network, including that November day in 1963 when President Kennedy was assassinated. He took to the streets of Manhattan for immediate reaction. He was back at Rockefeller Plaza to resume his NBC career in 1980, and stayed put until his death at 93 in 2017.

Pressman was also part of an early-evening newscast with Bill Ryan in 1963. Produced by NBC News in that era, Ryan was familiar to viewers nationally. He was the first person on NBC to go on the air when Kennedy was shot and was part of the network's extensive coverage for three days with Frank McGee, Chet Huntley, and David Brinkley in Washington.

The *Pressman-Ryan Report* was the first 30-minute broadcast in the city (25 minutes, technically). The duo was scrapped in 1965, but the idea of extended newscasts was not. They were replaced by a 6–7 pm newscast led by Hartz, who was taken under Pressman's wing upon his arrival from Oklahoma for impromptu training about New York City.

He was introduced to the mayor and the two flew to Albany to meet Governor Nelson Rockefeller and other state lawmakers.

"Introductions, pay your respects, get to know somebody, and get some phone numbers," Hartz recalled.

On the airplane, Pressman asked if he covered the legislature in Oklahoma. Hartz replied in the affirmative. "Albany is just like Oklahoma only more money," Pressman told Hartz, who said they were friends ever since.

By that time though, WNBC was suffering from steep competition and poor viewership. In 1971, NBC switched correspondent Vanocur to *Sixth Hour* anchor. The announcement was made jointly by the network and local brass. Vanocur, who died in 2019 at age 91, had numerous journalistic accomplishments. He is probably best known as one of the panelists for the 1960 Kennedy/Nixon debate. He was at NBC for more than a decade when he landed the local assignments.

Vanocur got the WNBC anchor role from a survey asking people to identify faces that they recognized on television. He was rated highly.

At this point, WNBC was no longer delivering a top-rated newscast, stuck below WCBS and WABC. Struggling at 6 pm locally also meant the evening news at 7 suffered in the lead-in. NBC's popular *Huntley-Brinkley Report* went off the air in July 1970.

Vanocur only stayed at WNBC for five months, unable to make a dent in the ratings before leaving the network.

"NBC is last at 6 o'clock because it is too structured and self-important," Al Primo told *New York* magazine in 1972. "They put Sander Vanocur on as the embodiment of their news organization and he was rejected by the audience."

He would go on to work for the *Washington Post*, PBS, and had a 14-year stint at ABC News.

Prior to making gains with *NewsCenter 4*, famed sportswriter Frank DeFord was asked about on-air work. He wrote for *Sports Illustrated* in 1974 that "WNBC is a very sickly competitor in the six o'clock news ratings."

He mentioned Carl Stokes as the anchor (though Hartz was also an anchor). "WNBC is so low in the news ratings I think it has minus ratings," DeFord wrote.

Stokes, the former Cleveland mayor, was personable, but not media ready. "He didn't know a goddamned thing about reading news," Richard Wald, NBC News VP, recalled. Instead, Wald said Stokes's understanding of current events made his reporting engaging for audiences.

WNBC couldn't find the right formula to fix its tanking viewership.

"When Grimsby was hitting his stride, Channel 4 was coming up with zero ratings," former WNEW and WPIX news executive John Corporon claimed. "It was the darkest days in the life of Channel 4."

An explosive turnaround once Primo was brought in from Philadelphia changed for the folks at "Circle 7," as he developed *Eyewitness News* in 1968 and the Grimsby/Beutel team two years later.

As WNBC began to the turn the corner, Hartz in 1974 gave up large amounts of viewers when he got hired by NBC's *Today*.

Hartz said, "There were more people in New York, New Jersey, and Connecticut who watched me at 11 o'clock than all over the country at 7 o'clock in the morning."

Hartz was at WNBC through the strong, early years, the poor ratings, and when the viewers, finally, returned. WNBC, like the other local flagships, was concentrating on the network level, using their own reporters at the anchor desk for the five owned and operated stations, including the WNBC flagship. The local broadcasts were not a high priority in those nascent days—just 10 or 15 minutes for the late news.

"At the end of every broadcast at 6 and 11 pm in New York, we ran the snake," Hartz said.

It was a three-second logo with an intertwined N-B-C saying that NBC News produced and is responsible for the content.

"It was like Trump's walls: They made WNBC pay for it," Hartz laughed.

It wasn't until the mid-1970s when Arthur Watson, later head of NBC Sports, would wrestle the O&Os from NBC by building an empire as the stations became independent of the network.

***

It was an early 1960s newspaper strike that led to WNBC's expansion of its on-air news product. McGee and Hartz briefly split time at the desk as newscasts reached 30 minutes. More primitive than a few years later, Hartz took over for the second half with local news. McGee, who would go on to *Today* in 1971, left WNBC as Hartz did the newscasts solo for a decade. He'd also have a continuing network assignment. His role was the space beat for Gemini and Apollo launches.

"I was doing coverage on the moon flights at the same time I was doing local news in New York," Hartz recalled.

One perk of working at 30 Rock in the sixties was doing news across the hall from *The Tonight Show* in Studio 6A.

"I'd take a break about 4:30 and listen to the band rehearse," Hartz remembered.

Frank Field was a frequent guest when Johnny Carson was in New York; they had offices next to each other on the sixth floor. Like David Letterman would do years later with his *Live at Five* neighbors, Carson would barge onto the set to playfully disrupt Field's forecasts.

"We had a lot of fun," Hartz said.

Once *Eyewitness News* found fame for WABC, it was time for NBC to make its own inroads. It would take some creativity, expanding its news presence, adding another anchor, who would ultimately join the legacy list of all-time greats.

Richard Wald as president of NBC News was the first to plant the seed: news production expansion on the local level. He told Hartz in 1972 or 1973 about his vision for turning NBC News into a 24-hour service.

"We're not anywhere near geared up to doing anything like that, and besides who would watch," Hartz replied.

At the turn of the next decade CNN debuted, and the rest is history. NBC News would ultimately go 24/7 with its own cable outlet when MSNBC launched in 1996.

Lee Hanna was Vice President of News at NBC Owned & Operated stations, but his focus was New York City. He already swayed Earl Ubell from WCBS as news director. Now Channel 4 faced a double-edged dilemma, needing viewers to tune in and keep them coming back for more.

"We were going to be the guinea pig on this two-hour extravaganza," Hartz said.

Frank Field was prominently featured wearing both hats effortlessly, meteorologist and health and science editor. "[The] change meant more on-camera work. I was given the task to present more weather segments and in addition health news packages, including live reports from hospitals and research centers."

NBC did, however, have a blueprint from creating a two-hour news block in Los Angeles. "When we were behind there, and it worked," an unnamed executive told *The New York Times* in February 1974. He added, though, the WNBC version would be vastly different from the format and style at KNBC.

For WNBC, a triumvirate executive committee of Hanna, Wald, and Arthur Watson, president of NBC owned & operated stations, led to the future of local news in a futuristic way. As for the daily preparations, Hartz was on the committee representing the anchors. He also took part in constant dry runs, while remaining skeptical.

"We probably spent a good six months with meetings, probably three times a week, on how it was going to work," Hartz, keeping his slight Oklahoman twang, said.

Hanna spent time in LA, likely getting a first-hand assessment of the on-air product. But his trip served another important purpose: hiring a Hollywood set designer to create the famous, albeit ridiculed, studio look. *NewsCenter 4* was known for stretching news content, or at least recycling it. But it also gave viewers an over-the-top set—you expected Captain Kirk to transport in any minute.

The spacious set, built in California, was shipped by truck to New York, where it was assembled. It got to Midtown only days before the scheduled launch.

The *NewsCenter 4* set was so big, they needed to take over Carson's old *Tonight Show* studio, 6B. All the seats were removed and the giant sci-fi looking pieces were hauled in.

Once installed, a serious problem was discovered.

"There was no room for the cameras," Hartz said.

The reason for the major mishap was that the set designer, Fred Harpman, was used to taking out a wall to shoot a reverse angle, putting it back in to get the master shot for movies.

Harpman was known for his work on *Deliverance* and *Beneath the Planet of the Apes*.

Needlessly to say, those options don't exist for live television news. No camera trickery is possible.

So the carpenters made a killing, forced to fix the faux pas all weekend. They had to cut into the set so the cameras could actually fit and move around. Four cameras were positioned to show the giant monitors and staff, in what appeared to be a sprawling five-area set.

Studio 6B was large enough for the WNBC news operation. What is old is new again, as Jimmy Fallon's version of the *Tonight Show* moved into the studio audience-friendly 6B.

WNBC finally did a week of test shows, not for broadcast, getting out the kinks, in addition to the third-floor commute for the actual newscasts from Studio 3A.

Hartz recalled, "It had a lot of glitches in the beginning, but I guess finally in the end it worked and set the stage for everybody else doing huge expansions."

The set, though, was a costly venture for NBC, as Hanna said it came at an "astronomical" price.

"We couldn't believe when we saw [it]," anchor Pia Lindström recalls. "We thought we were hot stuff."

Tom Snyder, never one to hold his tongue, told *The New York Times* in 1976 that WNBC's ability to deliver two-hour of news each day was "an impossibility, a con job."

But *NewsCenter 4* was more than just features and fluff. There were serious news stories from their journalists, and veteran anchor Jim Van Sickle as the headlines guy. Four times an hour, he delivered the latest update. More than a decade earlier, radio listeners would hear "James" Van Sickle on WNEW 1130.

Andy Fisher, a former colleague at 'N-E-W, remembers that fateful day in November 1963 when President John F. Kennedy was assassinated. "His style seemed to echo that of Lowell Thomas, but he would bristle if anyone openly made a comparison," Fisher told WNEW1130.com.

"What are we going to put on the air?" Lindström says. "Everybody had to do two stories. It was fun, like a real adventure."

To usher in WNBC's fancy new digs and the city's first 5 pm news, the station ran a print ad with Chuck Scarborough and Snyder side-by-side with the copy acknowledging, "no one could ever accuse [them] of being two peas in a pod. In fact, they are as different as two newsmen on the same news program could be."

It goes on to describe Scarborough as cool, smooth, and seasoned; intense, penetrating, bright, and brash are the descriptors for Snyder.

Field recalled, "The reception of [*NewsCenter 4*] was met with varying opinions by media columnists. It came before its time. The public wasn't ready for it."

Well, maybe so, but *NewsCenter 4* did introduce Scarborough to New Yorkers, and there's no denying that success.

"We had this mammoth set that we built. I'd come in here when the ratings had actually tanked to zero," Scarborough recalled in a 2014 interview. "I remember thinking after my first broadcast, after I got over the willies of going on the air . . . admiring the set but hoping that people would tune in for the set and me. Because it occurred to me that nobody ever walked away from a Broadway show whistling the set. I was hoping that I would finally be able to build enough of an audience in New York to get that news operation off the ground."

Scarborough's arrival from Boston in March was just weeks before *News-Center 4* debuted on April 29, 1974.

It was a visually stimulating set, but as Scarborough said, the news gathering was primitive. In an online interview marking WNBC's 75th anniversary, he pointed out they still used film in the field—16 mm color reversal film and those bulky "Mickey Mouse" cameras. Scarborough said the film magazines held 400 feet, or roughly 12 minutes worth of footage.

It was also an era before nonstop cable news and the online or mobile choices for news delivery.

"Everybody watched their news on a schedule. They knew the local news came on at a certain time every day, tuned in at 11 pm, they'd get the news of the day," Scarborough said. "It was a communal experience. Everyone watched one of the three networks [affiliates]. On the other hand, there wasn't quite as much competition for the audience." [2]

Despite being the 10-year WNBC veteran and three years his senior, Hartz says there was no mentor/protégé relationship.

"He didn't need any pointers," Hartz admitted. "He was alright. He had been in Boston, a big city. He handled himself OK."

It may seem like Scarborough has always been part of the WNBC family, and TV sets in New York. He predates Nixon's resignation, after all.

"I'm grateful to the National Broadcasting Company that they saw fit to keep me employed all that time and that I was able to do so many things that I wanted

---

2. Ushery, David. Broadcast. *The Debrief with David Ushery*, April 12, 2019.

to do, and they wanted me to do, to send me around the world covering stories, and to cover this metropolitan area," Scarborough said at his Emmy Awards Gold Circle induction with Sue Simmons on Nov. 29, 2018.

Chuck Scarborough hit the red carpet for another accolade from the New York Emmy Awards in 2018. [Jerry Barmash]

Another *NewsCenter 4* issue was the brisk timing getting from one story to the next. On opening night, Jimmy Breslin made reference to Senator Edward Kennedy and his two-minute appearance, saying, "I just saw Teddy Kennedy in the hall, and he said, 'Hurry up in or you'll miss your turn.'" Those who participated knew it was unique, but a breakthrough moment in local news—hardly.

"[We] were just happy that we could get the goddamn thing on the air that night," Hartz reflected. "We thought it was unusual and it was strange, but you never know what's going to happen. More shows get killed than survive on television."

Of course, WNBC took to advertising to spread the word for its new look. It wasn't just about the size and scope of *NewsCenter 4*; it was immediately different with its "Morse code" type of theme.

A May 27, 1974, full-page ad in *New York* magazine detailed what viewers could regularly expect to see.

It was called "WNBC-TV's 2 Hour Panorama of the News!," a template that would be copied by other stations going forward.

Then, to acclimate viewers, three columns listed exact times for each segment.

With a mix of local, national, and beyond, plus sports and other elements, "it worked out OK, much to the surprise of everybody who was there when it was born," Hartz recalled.

***

Here's how a typical broadcast might run as listed in a full-page ad at the time:

5:00 pm Index: *Chuck Scarborough, anchorman for the first hour, with a pictorial rundown of the entire two hours.*

5:01 pm Newsdesk: *Everything that's happened up to a moment ago. You can beat your neighbors to the news by an hour.*

5:10 pm Newsmakers/Newsbriefing

5:12 pm Databank: *Our computer tells you about traffic snarls, weather, sports scores, stock market closings, etc.*

5:14 pm LifeStyle: *Pia Lindström digs into people's lives.*

5:17 pm Children/Sidewalk Gourmet: *Marjorie Marjolies on children; Robert Potts with food from soup to nuts.*

5:22 pm Entertainment: *Chauncey Howell reports on everything from museums to musicals.*

5:25 pm Tonite: *What's up in Fun City, new openings, special events.*

5:26 pm Databank

5:30 pm Index *with Chuck Scarborough showing what's ahead in the next 30 minutes.*

5:31 pm NewsDesk: *Jim Van Sickle has the second edition of the breaking news. Totally fresh, totally updated*

5:35 pm Weather: *Not the usual meteorological razzmatazz. Dr. Frank Field brings you weather you can use.*

5:38 pm Comment: *A griping contest between our expert gripers: Jimmy Breslin, Edwin Newman, and William Rusher.*

5:40 pm Medicine: *Dr. Frank Field tells you if those cold pills work, or what to do about your aching back.*

5:44 pm DataBank: *The latest traffic delays to avoid.*

5:46 pm Sports: *Tim Ryan and Dick Schaap*

5:52 pm Action 4: *Betty Furness looks out for consumers to avoid getting ripped off.*

That completes hour one, followed by a reset for the second half as Jim Hartz takes over the anchor chair.

Some of the different features in the 6 o'clock hour:

6:10 pm CloseUp: *Scott Osborne and Norma Quarles add dimension to one of the day's top stories.*

6:15 pm Beat the System: *Carol Jenkins conjures up devious, but legal ways to get a good deal in New York.*

6:20 pm Five Minutes: *Jim Hartz face to face with the kind of folks you'd like to meet.*

6:39 pm Urban Journal/Neighbors *Carl Stokes: Survival in our cities; Tony Guida and Jim Collis roam our neighborhoods.*

6:43 pm Gene Shalit: *Movie review*

6:45 pm Sports: *Marv Albert (when not at Madison Square Garden to cover the Knicks or Rangers) is at Studio 6B with a live interview.*

6:50 pm Topic A: *Our daily cover story, like a fantastic voyage through the human body, or killer dogs roaming the streets.*

***

Despite those early growing pains, *NewsCenter 4* was named Outstanding Strip News Program at the Emmys, within just four months of launching. Scarborough and Hartz were given trophies along with the producers and executive producer Paul Friedman, who would have a long career in TV news. A year later, it was Scarborough and Snyder, who were recognized for *NewsCenter 4* as Outstanding News Show.

WNBC's futuristic set and synthesized theme paid off. WCBS would seize its own copycat version, having the anchors' desks in circular pods that, if the spotlights hit just right, would look like *Star Trek*'s transporters. Even the electronic theme was a knockoff of their pals at 30 Rock. Channel 2's music in the mid-70s had a driving, repetitive beat, almost a computerized sound.

NewsCenter 4 was the only place in town to find news at 5 pm, and by 1976 WNBC was successfully competing with WCBS and even market leader WABC. Occasionally, it was the top-rated show, beating Channel 7's popular *4:30 Movie*, the *Eyewitness News* at 6 pm lead-in for years.

Despite the gains made by WNBC, it signaled a victory, of sorts, for WABC, even before gathering any ratings data. "It was *Eyewitness News* with a different name," Primo said. Channel 7, on the other hand, did not feel the need to jump into the two-hour news business . . . not yet, anyway.

Primo said, "The programming that we had in place was doing so well. In TV land, if you've got something that's doing well, you don't want to mess with it. [WNBC] did the only thing they could possibly do, which was the right thing to do, just to get some news on the air when we weren't competing with them."

But filling those two hours each night was a challenge. It wasn't fresh material for the entire broadcast—they would provide news updates every 15 minutes, and have an anchor take charge of each hour—Scarborough at 5 pm and Hartz at 6.

Aside from the news radio format of repeating the headlines, they were a clearing house for filed network reports that might not see the light of day otherwise. Stokes, (uncle to Lori Stokes, longtime New York City anchor), had his "Urban Journal." Recently hired Betty Furness headed the Action 4 consumer reporting unit, plus a behind-the-news segment called "Topic A."

In fact, Hanna told the *Times* in February that WNBC would use a staff "in excess of 200," making it the most expensive news program in the nation.

Hartz, with the station since 1964, would not stay as one of those 200 for long. He was exiting for the *Today Show*, leaving an empty anchor seat to fill. He was called on to replace his best friend McGee, who died of cancer in 1974. But when they had lunch less than a week before his death, McGee, as concern grew about his health, confided, "Jimmy, I'm telling you the truth. There's nothing wrong with me."

Even though the genial Hartz was already occasionally filling in for his close friend, when he died suddenly, a void was left.

"NBC did something I thought was really stupid," Hartz recalled.

It may have been the first reality show as NBC brought in a rotation of hosts for weeks. The only thing missing was a phone number for viewers to cast votes. Well, that's not exactly true. "NBC set up a viewer response survey. Viewers are telephoned in key markets around the country and asked about [the] substitute co-hosts," author Cathleen Londino said.[3]

Hartz was propped up with NBC News colleagues Garrick Utley, Edwin Newman, Tom Brokaw, and Tom Snyder, among eight men alternating each week.

"All of a sudden it got to be the big contest, who's going to be the big winner?" Hartz said. "I thought, 'Jesus, this is not going to come out right. It's going to look like one winner and five losers.'"

Hartz got the "final rose" after the four-month on-air audition process and joined Barbara Walters for the next couple of years on *Today*.

"I felt kind of really sad, in a way, because I knew everyone else very well," Hartz admitted.

Snyder, however, a rising star for the network's *Tomorrow* show based in Burbank, couldn't parlay that overnight fame into the coveted morning slot. As the *Chicago Tribune* wrote, "Snyder's one-week stint was mediocre. There was a frightening amount of hostility between Tom and the show's production crew, and the chemistry of Tom and Barbara was strictly negative."

Snyder, though, was part of the final round of candidates, joining Hartz, Utley, and Brokaw. NBC was on a tight deadline, getting its anchor in place

---

3. Londino, Cathleen M. *The Today Show: Transforming Morning Television*. Lanham; Boulder; New York; London: Rowman and Littlefield. 2016.

before ABC launched *A.M. America*, the precursor to *Good Morning America*, with Bill Beutel, in January 1975.

Hartz believed the runners-up weren't informed about the bad news. But Hanna made the trip to the Catskills, telling him the good news personally during a softball event at Grossinger's Hotel.

The Hartz/Walters tandem stayed together until 1976 when Walters bolted for ABC and a mega deal to co-anchor the *Evening News* with Harry Reasoner. NBC used that excuse to make a fresh start, what would become the Brokaw/Jane Pauley era.

"I was never suited to that show, to tell you the truth," Hartz said. "I was a nighttime guy, and all of a sudden you're getting up at 4 in the morning. That show really needs a special kind of guy and I wasn't that guy."

Of course, he couldn't say no to the high-profile assignment, albeit with bleary eyes.

"It's one of those big jobs you don't want to turn down," Hartz said. "There are only two or three good ones, and that's one of them."

10

San Francisco

Before New York was introduced to Roger Grimsby, San Francisco already knew what the fuss was about. Grimsby was news director and anchor at KGO-TV. It was a successful seven-year run for the soon-to-be-famous anchor. Pia Lindström, an accomplished reporter/anchor in her own right, spent more than 25 years in New York, the majority at WNBC. But first, she worked for Grimsby at KGO.

She had no formal journalism experience. "But then, I don't know anyone in the business who went to journalism school," the veteran news person says.

In 1966, she was fired from the station's morning show. However, not wanting to wait on the unemployment line, Lindström inquired about other work at the station. Perhaps it was fate: KGO was looking to expand the newsroom by adding a woman, a progressive idea for the mid-1960s.

With a salary already sliced in half to $150 a week by the time of her firing, Lindström joked, "Where is the newsroom?"

This was coordinated through the general manager, not Grimsby, who had no interest in a woman in the news department.

"If he had to have a woman, he certainly wanted to choose her himself," Lindström recalls. "And not have somebody who lost her job on the morning show."

That set the stage for a prickly start between Grimsby and Lindström.

For Lindström, it was a trial by fire. There were no how-to books for being a TV reporter. In the dog-eat-dog, sexist world of 1960s broadcasting, her colleagues refused to give her pointers.

The first assignment Grimsby gave her was a mother and daughter topless act. So Lindström's first time out of a studio called for coverage of a provocative subject.

"I didn't know how to interview them. I tried to show them from the head up," Lindström laughs.

In another "titillating" story, she interviewed a woman who was dancing naked, or at least that's what police claimed. The woman, however, fought that complaint by wearing a bandage.

"I shot that in long shot, far away, then I held a Band Aid, and said, 'Is this clothing?'"

Both stories, however, were left on the cutting-room floor.

Lindström says her boss's personality and style would become a staple for New Yorkers in a few years—not to mention his inebriations.

"There was a bar across the street [from the station]. Our scripts had to be approved, so you would go and find him," Lindström says. "He would be sitting in the back. There'd be a candle on the table. I remember picking up the candle and trying to read the script to him. It was different."

Mara Wolynski picked up the baton with Grimsby in the 1980s when they were at WABC. Admittedly, there was still a lack of gender equality, especially in the newsroom. As was the case with Lindström, it didn't bother Wolynski. "I always like a man's club better than a stupid woman's club," she says.

At the height of the #MeToo era, Wolynski was critical of the worldwide Women's March a day after President Trump took office in 2017.

"I wanted to puke," she said. "Men are hard wired, and if you want to get what you want to get, you better know how to do it." She said everything she got professionally was because of how she presented herself, not being "an aggressive, nasty person."

Despite that, Lindström says Grimsby was a product of the times.

"Everybody drank in the newsroom. They had bottles in their desks," Lindström recalls. "Everyone was smoking, drinking, and had pictures of nude women around. I loved it!"

She enjoyed the environment, even if she was the only female, and being subordinate to a crusty Grimsby to boot. "I didn't mind him throwing papers on the floor."

Thereafter at WNBC, she confided in Chauncey Howell about wanting to have a relationship with anchor Tony Guida. In a moment fresh out of high school, she asked to find out if he'd date her.

Howell, in one of the final interviews before his death, opened up about some of his male colleagues being "fuckable" for legions of ladies.

"I know who could be a star, because women come up to me and they tell me who they want to fuck on our news show," he recalled about longtime WNBC and WCBS reporter David Diaz.

Howell also placed veteran New York anchor Jim Ryan in that category at one point in his career.

As for Scarborough: "That goes without saying," Howell laughed.

11

Roger and Bill

To usher in a new format in 1968, Al Primo needed a new theme that would bounce off the screen.

Primo and his director Marty Morris "spent hours at the ABC Music Library,"[1] where they discovered a 10-second segment from *Cool Hand Luke* that fit the bill. The film's pulsating sequence would get looped for extended air play on WABC and the network's other owned and operated stations for decades.

Composer Lalo Schifrin earned an Oscar nomination for the *Cool Hand Luke* score in 1968.

"I laughed all the way to the bank," he told the Archive of American Television about the *Eyewitness News* request.

Schifrin also made it big on the small screen with the *Mannix* and *Mission: Impossible* themes.

They were one of the first anchor teams that most New Yorkers saw. Roger Grimsby and Bill Beutel joined forces to form a common cause in 1970 at WABC's *Eyewitness News.*

---

1. Primo, Albert. "Eyewitness News — A Retrospective By Albert T. Primo." May 31, 2019. nyemmys.org

Eyewitness News was a collection of characters, molded after New York's melting pot: reporters featuring a Puerto Rican (Geraldo Rivera), an African American (John Johnson), and a Jew (Milton Lewis).

"You'll watch local newscasts now; there's a lot of people who look good, sound good, but they don't jump through the screen," says former WABC producer Mike Archer.

"*Eyewitness News* was kind of, at the time, viewed as 'of the people,'" veteran reporter John Johnson says.

Rivera, interviewed by WABC for the *Eyewitness News* 50th anniversary in 2018, said it was the genius of Primo that made the brand successful.

"There was a recognition that the news team should reflect the community that it seeks to serve."

Keeping them all in check: a classic anchor duo. Like the Smith/Marash tandem, one half was the more refined Bill Beutel, with the other with a gruffer exterior, and off-the cuff, Roger Grimsby.

Grimsby had been teamed with Tom Dunn, later of WOR-TV, and previously at WCBS.

But Dunn didn't pan out, primarily because of legal matters involving bad business decisions, and he was fired.

Executive producer and creator of the *Eyewitness News* format (first in Philadelphia), Primo started the search again. Given Grimsby's caustic nature, the right counterbalance was needed, or it could get ugly. (The phrase *Eyewitness News* actually predated Primo at a Cleveland TV station in 1961.)

Primo recalled matching several people in the anchor chair with Grimsby. But "Roger was so strong that the people sitting next to him really became just like him in terms of their presentation."

"As I used to say, 'I tried to soften Roger Grimsby, and I wound up getting two Roger Grimsbys,'" Primo admitted. "No one's gonna watch that."

So WABC doubled down its efforts to find the best fit for Grimsby and take *Eyewitness News* into the 1970s. Primo wanted someone who could be a soothing, professional presence opposite Grimsby. That happened and, along the way, the face of Channel 7 news would be cemented for the rest of the century.

"[Grimsby] liked pulling the chains of executives," Melba Tolliver recalls. "He was sarcastic."

Richard Sloan, an audio engineer for more than 17 years in *Eyewitness News*'s heyday, saw the anchors regularly, if only from a distance. But, well enough to observe that "Roger was a strange dude."

Bill Beutel was already "in the building." He started at ABC News in 1962 as a reporter and anchor of WABC's first incarnation of evening news, a newly created one-hour broadcast called *The Big News*. He left the local duties in 1968 as the network offered him full-time London bureau chief.

Beutel's WABC news director in the mid-60s was Ed Silverman, who compared Beutel to Peter Jennings, the future face of the network's *World News Tonight*. "Neither one was a brilliant, seasoned reporter. They were kind of superficial," Silverman recalled. "Bill was not a guy of great depth. He was a nice guy, smart, but was not when he began. Jennings was the same way."

Beutel would add layers to his personality and skill set, however, with the overseas stint for ABC. "When Bill went to London and he really became involved in international affairs and field reporting on important stories, he matured, developed, and became much more of a whole man than he was when he was at WABC being the boy next door," Silverman said. As for that first stint at the Channel 7 anchor desk, he said, "Bill always thought he knew more than he did." Silverman said his anchor would overreach for projects and interviews, although he scored some top subjects, including Malcolm X.

His greatest asset in those early days? "Being pleasant," Silverman said. "I'm not talking about it as a knock. Those are virtues."

But Beutel was also a dedicated newsman. He cut his reporting teeth with a trip to a 1960s war zone. "We were the first New York station, one of the few local stations in the country, to send a film crew to Vietnam," Silverman recalled before his death in 2019, at the age of 94.

There was a cordial relationship with Silverman and Beutel, still married to his first wife at the time.

Beutel would have four marriages, and Silverman says he was reserved with his family from his upbringing—a lack of affection shown. "His father never hugged him. His father might shake his hand, but he would never kiss him on the cheek or hug him. That's the way it was. It's not that he didn't love Bill, but you didn't express it. And Bill was the same way with his children."

"I was really intrigued with the fact that he was once the anchorman for Channel 7 and didn't really make it," Primo said.

Beutel got a tryout as co-anchor, doing a trial week with Grimsby. Primo knew instantly he had the winning combination.

"The two of them hit it off like magic," Primo said.

When you have chemistry of classic proportions, WABC VP of News Kenneth MacQueen said in 1975, "the viewer identifies with the anchor people."

Former producer Mike Archer says, "You probably couldn't take an hour of Roger by himself or an hour of Bill by himself. But together they balanced each other, and they made it work."

"Their chemistry worked as long as he could be the eager young beaver to Roger's curmudgeon," Lou Young describes their success. (Grimsby was, in fact, only two years older than Beutel.)

They were both known for their journalistic prowess, but of course, Grimsby brought another set of skills to the desk. His acerbic delivery, for one.

"He wasn't a phony," Sloan said. "If he didn't like something he would let somebody know about it." But Sloan said you'd never see Grimsby yelling or getting demonstrative toward anyone.

Grimsby, though, was low key, almost to the point of aloof, with many in the newsroom. "He only related to people on the crew if they were drinking buddies," Sloan admitted. "If you weren't one of that crowd with the other reporters and those engineers, you felt a little bit out of place with him."

"Al Primo will no doubt take credit for having foresight to put together Roger's bad boy irascibility and Beutel's school boy charm, and I will say to you, it was poor dumb luck," producer Alan Weiss claims, "because if it were that easy there be would teams like that all over the place."

Weiss believes no anchor team in the country has ever shown such an immediate and strong chemistry. He says arguably the most famous NBC News duo of Chet Huntley and David Brinkley only worked well due to separation, with one man in New York and the other based in Washington.

Chemistry aside, these were driven men who were competitive even about their time off. When Grimsby wasn't working, Beutel was asked to slide into his anchor seat.

"Bill would give the same answer every single time," Weiss recalls him saying. "There is no difference between the left chair and the right chair. If I sat in Grimsby's chair, it would make it look like that's the lead chair and Grimsby's the lead anchorman. We're both equal."

However, Grimsby would take another angle.

"How do people read?" he asked Weiss. "Left to right, or right to left?"

When he answered "the left," Grimsby followed-up with, "What's the most important part on the screen, the left or the right?"

In warm weather, unbeknownst to viewers, Grimsby would frequently sit at the desk in shorts and sandals after walking the block from the newsroom to the studio.

One time, when they were using a larger studio, either for an Election Night coverage or remodeling the regular, small studio, Sloan recalls Grimsby and others playing an impromptu game of handball.

While they kept the same seats throughout their run together, Grimsby and Beutel weren't above boosting them.

On one particular night, Grimsby, who was shorter than Beutel, raised his seat to make himself appear taller. Beutel noticed, lifting his chair higher than his desk mate during the commercial break.

During a taped report, Grimsby countered with more high school high jinks, taking the upper hand again. Beutel responded, raising his chair one more time.

"Grimsby is undaunted," Weiss says. "He pulls out a phone book that he brought with him. Beutel runs off the set during the commercial break and finds a pillow.

"By the end of the show their knees were almost over the desk," Weiss says. "It was the funniest thing in the world."

Grimsby was usually a staid persona, albeit with tongue firmly planted in cheek, and viewers were not aware of much behind-the-scenes frivolity.

Reporter Tracy Egan had her own Grimsby-induced moment. One time on the 6 pm broadcast, she says Grimsby "made the mistake of playing floor manager," telling Gloria Rojas to take a seat on set for the next story. However, the actual floor manager had a different idea, wanting Egan in place as they came out of a commercial break.

"Gloria jumped under the desk. I jumped into the seat and Roger was trying not to laugh," Egan recalls. "I had no idea what the story was about, but I had to read the introduction and close while Gloria Rojas's head was basically in my lap."

Egan says Grimsby and she hit it off from day one because of her work ethic.

"I don't think he knew much about me at all other than every time he saw me on the air, I was doing a good job," Egan says. "He could ask me any question; I would have the answer or know why the answer wasn't available at the time. He wanted people to be able to hold their own."

Not only did the venerable anchor respect Egan, but she also admits there was light flirting—on and off camera. No line was crossed, though. "In no way was it harassment, but it was fun." Egan said. "I would make him laugh, he would make me laugh, Very often when we were on the air, we were holding back laughter."

They were close enough that Egan got Grimsby to visit her upstate New York farm. "I remember driving him around in a rainstorm in the back 40," Egan recalls. Despite a nice rapport with Grimsby, Egan didn't play favorites among the anchors, and stayed friends with Beutel until he died.

Egan arrived at Channel 7 in 1979 as *Eyewitness* was already a news operation juggernaut. She says the laid-back atmosphere went beyond taking jabs on camera. Perhaps it was their invincibility or cockiness, but she recalls early in the next decade staffers flying paper airplanes at targets in the newsroom.

"They'd grab a radio and do a conga line around the newsroom when they did really great on a story," Egan says. "Everything was just fun." By contrast, she remembers late news director Ron Tindiglia referring to WCBS as News for the Dead and WNBC as the Chief Imitators.

"Grimsby was the franchise; let's put it that way," former WABC reporter Mara Wolynski says. "I always got the feeling that [he] thought Beutel was a little bit of a dope."

Lou Young, another 1980s reporter at *Eyewitness*, says Beutel brought a different set of skills to counterbalance.

"Bill wasn't as quick as Roger," Young says. "He was more affable and traditional."

But not everyone could be Beutel, when it came to working with Grimsby.

Warner Wolf, a longtime sportscaster in Washington, came to WABC in 1976 after work on the network's *Wide World of Sports* didn't last. His Channel 7 dreams, though, almost came crashing down before they started. Wolf was hired by ABC Sports president Roone Arledge, and in his first encounter with local GM Ken MacQueen he met president of the Owned and Operated Stations, Dick O'Leary, who asked if he had any questions.

"Whose idea was it, and why do we have to wear these Channel 7 pins on our lapel?" Wolf pondered aloud. Unfortunately, Warner's question was to the man responsible for talent wearing the logo.

"The guy explodes. He starts screaming at me," Wolf recalls.

MacQueen stepped in, breaking up the meeting. "It was the first time in my life I thought I was going to see a guy hired and fired the same day," MacQueen later told Wolf.

Wolf didn't get the special privileges like Geraldo Rivera, sporting a leather jacket or long hair.

"I thought it was redundant. You're on Channel 7; they're watching Channel 7, why do you have to wear a logo?" Wolf admits.

Now on board, Wolf's "Circle 7" pin brought him face to face with the biggest stars at the station—but that wasn't always necessarily a good thing.

Even though he would become known for "Let's Go to the Videotape!" Wolf's initial Channel 7 reports lacked intensity. However, as Weiss recalls, Grimsby rubbed him in the wrong way. It all started with a less than encouraging toss from Grimsby to Wolf.

But in short order, Grimsby lost the 11 pm newscast, which inadvertently breathed new life into Wolf and his sportscasts.

"Warner kind of lilted a little bit, and just plowed through his sports," Weiss says. "It was really Ernie Anastos who helped Warner become the 'Big W' that he became."

Wolf gives a signature hearty guffaw about working with the stalwarts.

"Well, it was different. Grimsby was kind of tough," Wolf admits. "He'd give you a tough time."

But offering a diplomatic tack, Wolf says he built on those awkward exchanges. "I considered it a great training ground. If I could get along and survive this guy, I could get along with anybody," Wolf says.

When Grimsby was fired from WABC in 1986, many staffers gathered to say goodbye after his 18 years of service. Despite the farewell, former colleague Lou Young says the legendary anchor wouldn't let Anastos inside the restaurant to wish him well.

"Roger would get his hackles up about some people, maybe because he didn't believe they deserved to be doing what they were doing," Young says. "He would simply just shut some people out."

Channel 7 held the "Happy Talk" label, but the popular sportscaster says there wasn't anything happy, and hardly any extra talk, with Grimsby.

"Jensen would be more interested in what you have to say," Wolf points out. "Grimsby, I felt, if he was interested, he never asked you anything on the air. I think that was the biggest difference."

However, Wolf had no plans to exit WABC in May of 1980 for WCBS. He did try to negotiate for a larger salary when a member of the sales staff showed him the ratings and claimed he was a big part of *Eyewitness News*'s late 1970s success. He wanted to double his salary. Management said no chance. With that news in the pipeline, Channel 2 was an immediate suitor, and Wolf accepted their offer with a handshake agreement.

Back at Channel 7, though, realizing they'd lose their high energy, high-priced talent, they'd acquiesced. Wolf refused, saying he already gave his word to WCBS.

It turned into a legal matter, as ABC sued Wolf for breach of contract. A judge, however, ruled in his favor.

The success of Wolf at WABC started to take shape with Larry Kane, despite his brief stay in New York. Actually, Wolf credits the former and future Philly star with first calling him the "Big W" on the air.

"That's when things really started to hit," Wolf recalls. "Then Ernie came in and picked it up when Larry left,"

Wolf fed off of Anastos's exuberant personality leading him to become one of New York's top sportscasters. "That's all he needed, like a flower needs water," Weiss says. "He just blossomed."

Grimsby, instead, played his ego games and nearly damaged Wolf's career. "[Grimsby] was a kingmaker, to some extent, or a king breaker," Weiss says.

Even though Ed Silverman made way for Al Primo as news director, he has strong views of Beutel's return to Channel 7 with Grimsby. "I thought he was intelligent enough to mature," Silverman reflected. "Bill was dedicated." On a personal level, Silverman said Beutel was a "wonderful guy," who he loved. That decency sat opposite Grimsby for more than a decade, and was no manufactured trait for viewers. It was pure Beutel. "I don't think he ever made an enemy in his life, or said a cross word to anyone," Silverman said.

Tolliver didn't socialize with either of the top-tier anchors. But she certainly got her fill of Grimsby and Beutel. "Bill was very different. He was like Mr. Nice," Tolliver states. "He made corny jokes."

Retired cameraman Mark Abrahams adds, "Bill was much more the straight man and very professional."

With her cubicle near the men's room, much of Tolliver's banter with Beutel came during his bathroom break.

John Johnson, who knew the anchors well while at Channel 7 for more than 20 years, says they needed each other for *Eyewitness* to succeed.

"I thought when Roger ultimately was no longer there, it just was different," Johnson says. "I definitely think Beutel was the straightlaced guy and Roger had been through a lot and didn't take himself seriously."

"[Beutel] was a gentleman," Alan Weiss says. "I just loved working with Bill. He was a terrific guy with a heart of gold."

John Corporon was an indirect competitor as news director at WNEW's *Ten O'Clock News* and then at rival independent station WPIX.

"Grimsby was very good at what he did, very effective and successful, but he's not my style of newscaster. It bordered too close on stunt news," Corporon recalled. "I admired Beutel mightily. [He] was more to my taste."

Negotiations, however, almost fizzled before nailing down the dream anchor team at WABC. Primo offered $80,000, the same amount already given to Grimsby. Beutel's agent balked. His client wouldn't accept less than $100,000 a year, presenting an early challenge in the Primo tenure.

"I had to rip up Grimsby's contract to give him $100,000 because I wanted to be fair to everybody," Primo said. "You would think [Roger] would be grateful."

Instead, Grimsby harbored dark feelings about leaving the management side at KGO.

"He would be watching all of my moves very carefully and translating them all as to how it affected him and his life," Primo remembered about his star.

"If Roger hadn't been as difficult an employee as he was, in the way he dealt with management, he wouldn't have a gone the way he did," Lou Young says.

Primo got Grimsby and Beutel to coexist famously, but Bob Lape, the long-time Channel 7 correspondent, says it worked because of Beutel.

"Bill was a pro. He was coming in after a ton of experience," Lape recalls. "Roger respected that. He was amused by Bill, and vice versa. They appreciated each other's strengths."

"Bill was a good communicator, [and] a gentleman," Young says. "But not anywhere near as adroit or sharp as Grimsby, and he paid for it with many humiliations that Roger heaped on him over the years."

Grimsby recalled late in life, "We had a mutual respect for each another, and I think that showed."

"They were as different as night and day, in real life and on the air," Tolliver says, who didn't have a preference between them.

Archer somewhat concurs. "They needed each other and they were the reason for the team's success, but I don't think they were best buddies at all."

Young says, "Roger was a journalist who was delivering the news and subverting the format while he did it."

"Roger was a case," Abrahams recalls. "But he was a brilliant man. He was an old curmudgeon and a lot of fun to be around."

Unless you were not part of his clique.

"It was a strained relationship," Richard Sloan recalled. "It was very weird. He was the only one who was like that. Everybody else you could easily shoot the breeze with. He was just an oddball in that regard."

ABC News Radio colleague Gary Nunn says, "He's one of the standout people in my career as a journalist. Some of his social habits I would not want to emulate."

WABC-TV Anchor Bill Ritter flanked by longtime colleague Liz Cho and former sports anchor Scott Clark. [Jerry Barmash]

It was appointment television on the 6 pm broadcast for 16 years. In fact, Roger and Bill had the longest running newscast at WABC until Bill Ritter and Liz Cho broke the record in July 2019.

"Bill is good. He's got his own style, and he sticks to it," Abrahams said.

But, of course, they'd need to double that output together to eclipse the all-time New York mark set by Scarborough and Simmons. (Ritter turned 74 in 2024, making it highly unlikely that they'll have a chance to reach that milestone.)

A genuine respect was clear between Grimsby and Beutel, but the competitive juices came first. One night, Grimsby forgot the name of Secretary of State

Henry Kissinger, going into full deer-in-the- headlights mode. Beutel whispered it to his partner.

"Just loud enough so the whole world heard it," Grimsby would say later. "I sat there and swallowed my tonsils."

"I thought that was a precious moment," Beutel countered. "I wish it was on tape."

Co-workers weren't above jabbing Beutel on set as well. One night leading into Warner Wolf's sports report, the anchor said, "The big worry is whether the subways will be running in time to get people up there to Yankee Stadium on the subways. What do you think about that, Warner?"

Without missing a beat, the veteran sportscaster replied to the confusing intro, "What did you say?" causing instant laughs from everyone, including Grimsby.

But if you want a "blue" blooper, look no further than the infamous Sue Simmons 2008 line. It was a live tease for the upcoming 11 pm cast, airing during a local commercial break in prime-time programming.

The 15-second cut-in showed her and Scarborough in the studio, followed by Simmons narrating about one of the lead stories. Scarborough, apparently, missed his cue and fell silent.

"What the fuck are you doing?!" Simmons raising her voice off camera at her legendary colleague. For his part, Scarborough didn't respond as viewers watched another five seconds of video without sound.

Simmons later apologized for her on-air tirade. She called the incident an "unfortunate mistake." But that moment just endeared her even more with the public. It was another example of Simmons proving that she's relatable to her audience.

"That was common for her," Chauncey Howell recalled. "Her favorite word was 'cunt.'"

He said Simmons would jokingly refer to her colleagues by the "C word."

Howell recalled that was only a glimpse into her "naughty" personality.

Ernie Anastos got caught in 2009 with some controversy, too, though in a greyer area. Coming out of meteorologist Nick Gregory's segment, Anastos said, "It takes a tough man to make a tender forecast," a reference to Frank Perdue.

In rapid fire, Gregory replies, "I guess that's me."

Anastos shocked co-anchor Dari Alexander with what happened next.

"Keep fucking that chicken," is what Alexander and most people heard, although it seems that Anastos actually said, 'keep plucking that chicken.' Alexander's jaw-dropping stare may have forced management's hands. Anastos had to give the on-air mea culpa, saying he "misspoke" and apologized to anyone who may have been offended.

Months later, Anastos admitted he was certain it was plucking and not the f-word, but "If you keep saying, 'I didn't say that.' It doesn't sound right," he told *The New York Times*.

While viewers were usually invited to watch any digs, barbs, or innuendos, occasionally Grimsby would give a special off-camera performance. For example, one night as the newscast was in a taped report about Richard Pryor freebasing, Grimsby offered an in-house homage to the comedian by opening and closing his thick lighter several times.

"All you had to do was turn that news on and you knew this is not somebody you want to watch," Primo said. "He wasn't from New York; he wasn't that handsome of a guy. You needed relief from that. You liked a little bit of his strength. But too much is too much."

Alan Weiss producer of the 6 o'clock newscast during the peak of *Eyewitness*, says, "[One of the] most cherished, high points of my journalistic career was producing Beutel and Grimsby. They played off each other perfectly."

In the time before Beutel's reemergence at Channel 7, Primo and Grimsby arrived on the scene. This was a stopgap period at WABC.

Featured in the *Eyewitness News*'s 40th Anniversary video, Grimsby opened up about his early days at WABC. "I preceded Al Primo by a few months [at Channel 7], but a year before, I had been asked to come to New York. I took one look at that newsroom and the program it produced, and said I'm really very happy in San Francisco."

News director Ed Silverman interviewed Grimsby for the anchor position, but the two already knew each other from working at several events and on assignments. "We used to play poker together," Silverman said. "We had a casual relationship."

Once Primo took over the daily operations, that card game was immediately halted, but not before a connection was in place between Grimsby and Silverman, who called each of them mavericks.

"I had a lot of respect for him," Silverman said. "He was my kind of guy."

Former *Eyewitness News* producer Mike Archer says professionally he was in the Grimsby camp. "Roger was the better pure news guy than Beutel. "I think Roger's writing was a little tougher and harder. Bill was a little more flowery," Archer says. "Roger would find a way to say things in fewer words. Which is what made them work. They were different."

Frank Cipolla is a veteran New York City broadcast journalist and disciple of anchors past. "Grimsby was doing Jon Stewart's shtick before Jon Stewart," Cipolla said, referring to the former *Daily Show* host.

One time in 1978, Grimsby was wrapping up an international segment with the story of a prostitute in Tel Aviv who applied for insurance coverage.

"She'll now be covered for maternity leave, child support, and work-related accidents," the last part causing a smattering of chuckles. He tossed to Beutel, who tries to get the last word or one-up his co-anchor: "Off the streets and into your heart, here's Warner Wolf."

A year later, while undergoing renovations in the studio, the newsroom hosted the 6 o'clock broadcast with Anastos filling in for the vacationing Beutel. A brief moment of dead air hangs as Anastos finishes reading his next story. You can hear a producer say, "Over to you, Roger." But when we see Grimsby, he is abruptly moving the phone from his ear to receiver.

"My mother calls me all the time," Grimsby says without missing a beat, adding a playful smile, and once again laughs ensue.

In late 1973, Grimsby was attacked by a woman with an ice pick. The 24-year-old had accused Grimsby and Beutel of saying unkind things about her on the air. However, this appeared to be more mental illness-related than an indictment of snarky anchors. Grimsby called her rationale a "fantasy" and said that the woman had previously kicked Beutel in the groin.

Viewers not only had the familiar faces in Grimsby and Beutel for more than a decade and a half, they had something to draw their attention.

Every newscast opened with the powerful theme from *Cool Hand Luke* and "I'm Roger Grimsby. Here Now the News." It ended with the famous outro: "Hoping your news is good news. I'm Roger Grimsby."

Beutel would close the show, but his own "Good luck, and be well" would evolve over time.

Even though it's been decades since the zenith of Grimsby's career, he's still remembered fondly. Today's budding broadcasters are too young to have watched him live, but luckily we have YouTube and the Internet.

Grimsby got a new found "identity" on social media, when an @Roger-Grimsby Twitter (X) account emerged, complete with a vintage headshot of the famed newsman.

The satirical, since-defunct, account had thumbnails from some online clips and imagined Grimsby quoting present-day events.

"I created it because I wanted that wry attitude which I identified within this business growing up," the faux Grimsby (and anonymous broadcaster) says. "I feel like the business has become sanitized and all that matters—to executives and to shallow viewers—is how you look."

Grimsby, and anyone who sits in that high-profile position, has the ego. But vanity wasn't one of his traits. It was just "what you see is what you get" from Grimsby.

"I admire that confidence, which has seemed to have gone by the wayside," he says. The journalist since dropped the homage account, focusing on his own social media and TV news career.

As for the real Grimsby, he was eventually cajoled into the cross-country change of venue.

When he landed at WABC, Grimsby was flying solo at 11 pm, while John Schubeck, who would go on to a thriving anchoring career at several Los Angeles stations, briefly led the 6 pm newscast. Schubeck, who joined WABC in

1967, predated the *Eyewitness News* format by a year. He stayed with the station until 1971, although the anchor stint ended by 1969.

"He was great looking guy, terrific voice, wonderful dresser," Bob Lape says about Schubeck. "[He] never worked very hard, except to play golf and chase women. The others were perhaps a little more journalistically inclined."

Depending upon your age bracket, Lape is either remembered on the politics and crime beats from the early days of *Eyewitness* or as the food critic who would sit down at eateries across the tristate to sample several courses.

In the halcyon days, Lape would regularly team with Grimsby for special political coverage.

"He'd do some of the harder stuff, and I'd do some of the softer stuff," Lape reflects.

There's one particular night that Lape recalls didn't make it to air. "In the Miami convention, [Roger] chose the wrong night and got tear-gassed," Lape deadpans. "I was happy that he made that decision for me."

Like his counterpart on Channel 2, Jim Jensen, Grimsby portrayed a gruff exterior to viewers.

"He was a tough guy in a lot of ways," Lape says. "But he was a dedicated journalist who really believed in it. He wanted to be just right. If you did it well, he was your friend for life."

Primo felt that Grimsby's top asset was his wit, usually as dry as his martini.

"I had a cavalier attitude toward some things that other persons held sacrosanct, and I was willing to exploit that, perhaps to a greater degree than I should have in some cases," Grimsby said.

One of the many examples is Grimsby talking about Britain accepting the 1980 Moscow Olympics invitation. "Earlier, France and Austria indicated they will ignore the U.S. boycott. Now if West Germany attends the Games, the U.S. athletes will be left, pretty much, to play with themselves."

"Those quick one-liners were brilliant," former WABC reporter Lou Young says. "But he knew exactly what he was going to say and when he was going to say it. He could see the play coming."

Mara Wolynski, who had her YouTube moment decades before its creation, enjoyed working with Grimsby, albeit from a distance.

"He was very decent guy, and funny," she says.

"Roger was a great news writer. He was incredibly terse," former WABC producer Richard Reingold remembers.

But Reingold says Grimsby could be difficult, so much so that years later the anchorman told him, "I was too tough on you."

Grimsby made up for being a hard ass to Reingold, when Reingold used his former top talent as a reference for a job at WBBM-TV in Chicago. Upon his return to New York, Grimsby found a note from Reingold waiting for him: "Act normal."

"They had obviously called him as a reference, and he must have given me a good one, because I was offered the job," Reingold reflects.

Reingold, who worked closely with the type-A personalities of Grimsby and Jensen, wouldn't draw comparisons other than saying, "Roger had a much more sardonic point of view about life and the way he presented the news."

That formed Grimsby's signature style and helped transform *Eyewitness News* into a powerhouse throughout the seventies and beyond.

"That was something that had never happened before on local TV news," former *Eyewitness News* producer Mike Archer says. "As history tells it, it just took off."

As for the "horse's mouth" himself, in conversation with the late colleague John Slattery as part of a behind-the- scenes feature, Grimsby gave one takeaway from being so well known.

"There's a certain amount of ego massage attending it, having a high-profile position and that sort of thing," Grimsby said in an interview for a WABC feature.

But first, Grimsby would predate *Eyewitness News* with the lesser-known *Noisemakers* format at 11 pm. "Actually, a good bar bet is, who did Roger Grimsby replace when he came to New York? Nobody gets it," Grimsby said. "I replaced Bill Beutel."

Each personality was given a "Noisemaker" title, like Rona Barrett as the "Hollywood Noisemaker" and Jimmy Breslin the "All-Around Noisemaker." "Sports Noisemaker" Howard Cosell and "Weatherman Noisemaker" Tex Antoine also aligned with Grimsby on the set.

The July 1968 advertisement states it was the "most rambunctious supporting cast in television news today."

However, what an embarrassed ABC president heard was the word "noise." It was his impetus to hire Primo to urgently overhaul the news operation.

"[Barrett] didn't match what my idea was for creating an effective news operation. In an operation that was perfectly legitimate she might have added an element," Primo said. "But in the current shape of Channel 7 it was a big detriment. I wanted to signal to the audience that we were completely new and different."

"The 6 pm was so deep in the tank, you couldn't see it," Lape agrees.

So Primo immediately killed *Roger Grimsby and the Noisemakers*, but didn't drop Grimsby, whose skills shined through in whatever attempt WABC would put forth on the screen. Clearly, Primo needed to form *Eyewitness News* around Grimsby. He was a new member at WABC after his success as news director/anchor in San Francisco's KGO.

In revamping the newscasts, Primo overhauled every detail including the logo. The Circle 7 lapel pin would be famous for the on-air staff, devised on a napkin at Chips, one of the prominent taverns near the studio.

The precursor to *Eyewitness* was also fraught with technical mishaps, leading Grimsby to the cardinal sin of TV news, pointing out the foibles. It did help him attract an audience from the start.

"He thought that if people saw something was going awry on the air he wasn't going to pretend it wasn't happening," Tracy Egan, a 1980s *Eyewitness* reporter, says.

Still, having failed as a solo anchor, Grimsby had something in common with Beutel.

"Roger had a great respect for him," Primo reflected. "[Roger] didn't think that this is someone who was holding back his career. But rather, here is someone who is enhancing my career."

But that didn't always translate to confidence for the conflicted Grimsby. "I know what you're here for, you're here to fire me," Grimsby would cautiously tell Primo.

Primo attempted to reassure the crusty anchor, telling him that he wasn't going to terminate him, just "make him better" and create a unique broadcast for viewers.

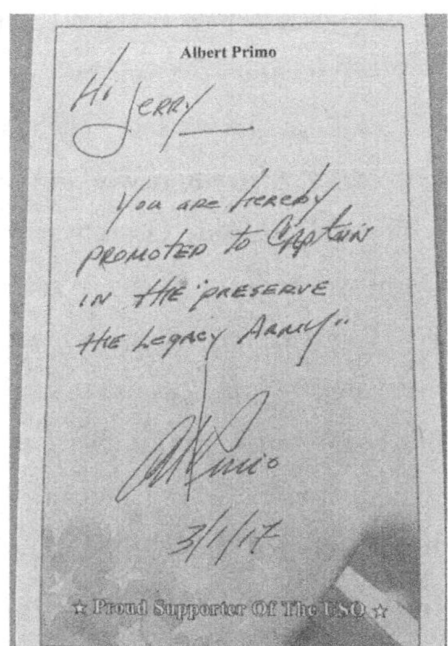

A personal note from Eyewitness News architect Al Primo. [Jerry Barmash]

"It took him a long time to believe that, particularly when I said, 'Roger, you're just too tough to take all by yourself. You look like the grouch in the box. I have to get somebody to work with you, somebody that's on your level.'"

But longtime colleague John Johnson says Grimsby's personality was created years earlier.

"[He] had suffered greatly during the Korean War, and I think that marked him forever."

Beutel's wit was a perfect balance to Grimsby's sometimes droll, if pointed, irreverent humor. If it was a nightly competition, Primo said, Beutel could hold his own in the writing department.

"That's the kind of the thing that a working relationship positively benefits the show, and the audience recognizes it," Primo said.

"They were incredible professionals," veteran producer Alan Weiss recalls.

Anyone who attempted to work alongside Grimsby saw his sardonic personality up close, and viewers were often lucky enough to catch it during the broadcasts as well.

"He was not the coziest guy to sit down next to," Lape says.

When it comes to Grimsby, there was no screwing around with the anchor. But Weiss says he was fair. "He had a great sign on his door: It's tough to soar with eagles when you're working with turkeys."

Shenanigans aside, Grimsby had a stoic exterior to many staffers. Archer says Grimsby was clearly known as the leading presence in the newsroom.

"He was an imposing personality that people just respected him and knew that Roger was the guy, more so than Beutel," Archer says. "Everybody liked Bill, but Grimsby was number 1 and maybe Bill as 1A."

Beutel, a fixture for decades on *Eyewitness News*, was a professional through and through. The longtime sound man for the WABC newscasts, Richard Sloan, said Beutel was a steady hand on the ship each night. "He always had it together . . . [he] knew how to work with Roger."

"They had a chemistry, no doubt about it, like Laurel and Hardy, Abbott and Costello," Sloan said.

Lou Young, a veteran New York reporter, retired in 2017. He spent the 1980s at WABC and that meant a front-row seat to Grimsby and Beutel, before staying for 23 years at WCBS. Young would become a good friend with Grimsby, but for now he simply was in awe.

It was an inauspicious welcome by the legends. Young, in makeup ahead of the 6 pm newscast, stumbled upon the duo.

"They both had beverages. I'm pretty sure it was gin and tonic or vodka," Young speculates.

He says Grimsby didn't like wearing makeup, save for light powder. But the neophyte newsman nervously sees Beutel and Grimsby in the chairs, looking in the mirror.

"Oh, look Roger, it's the new guy," Beutel says.

Asked his name, Young gives praise to his veteran tandem, saying he's excited to join *Eyewitness News* and that he has watched them forever.

Beutel shot back, "I'm sure you're mistaken about me, and I'm pretty sure Roger is tired of hearing that shit."

"Roger just grunted," Young recalls. "I left and came back later. They were terrifying, but they were also a lot of fun."

Young sealed a bond with Grimsby in the spring of 1982, rushing to the scene of murders of CBS technicians. He gave a live account before the broadcast ended that included the grisly sighting of dead bodies at a rooftop parking garage. The three victims had just left the Broadcast Center on West 57th Street when they were fatally shot. Two years later, Irwin Margolies was sentenced to 50 years to life for the murders of two women, which also led to the deaths of the three technicians.

That night found Grimsby at one of the local watering holes with advice for his protégé.

"Don't ever apologize to the audience. You started out saying 'we don't know a whole lot.' Then you went on to do the most amazing live report we've had on the air in quite some time," Grimsby told Young.

One of the few people to break through Grimsby's armor was close friend and reporter Roger Sharp. They privately used the term "Twinkie" for staffers not up to their standards.

Those forced to wear that scarlet letter, unbeknownst to them, didn't get much respect from Grimsby and Sharp.

"If you made it within the circle of not being called a Twinkie, you kind of felt something special."

Personally, Weiss, who started out as a young desk assistant, had a good working relationship with Sharp from overseas shoots. But he says it still took a while for Grimsby to trust him.

One of the nicest moments between Grimsby and the neophyte producer happened as Weiss was taking charge of the newsroom.

"I don't know why you want me to do this," Grimsby told him. "But I'll trust you. You better be right.'"

As for Grimsby's counterpart at the desk, Johnson says, "I think Bill Beutel was Bill Beutel. He thought of himself as an anchorman and walked around like that. I definitely preferred Roger."

Archer, who worked at WABC from 1974 to 1979, says, "Bill was a much easier guy to get along with."

At the height of their *Eyewitness News*'s popularity in January 1975, Beutel was plucked to anchor ABC's new morning venture, *AM America*. It only lasted 11 months as a precursor to *Good Morning America*, and Beutel fully returned to WABC. Beutel maintained a national presence into the end of the decade with weekend anchoring.

With the Roger and Bill respite over, the ratings bonanza resumed. The timing for great *Eyewitness News* numbers, especially at 11 pm, got a big assist from ABC's prime time schedule as Fonzie, Laverne, and Jack Tripper moved in. Grimsby and Beutel, followed by Kane, Anastos, and Scamardella, were the beneficiaries of the strong lineup.

You can track WABC's ascent with a sampling of the network's wildly popular prime-time programs:

1975–76

- *Rich Man, Poor Man* (Nielsen Rating #2)

- *Laverne & Shirley* (#3)

- *The Bionic Woman* (#5)

- *The Six Million Dollar Man* (#9)

- *Monday Night Movie* (#10)

- *Happy Days* (#11)

***

1976-77

- *Happy Days* (#1)

- *Laverne & Shirley* (#2)

- *Monday Night Movie* (#3)

- *Charlie's Angels* (#5)

- *The Six Million Dollar Man* (#7)

- *Baretta* (#8), tied

- *Sunday Night Movie* (#8), tied

- *Three's Company* (#11)

***

1977-78

- *Laverne & Shirley* (#1)

- *Happy Days* (#2)

- *Three's Company* (#3)

- *Charlie's Angels* (#5)

***

1978-79

- *Laverne & Shirley* (#1)

- *Three's Company* (#2)

- *Happy Days* (#3), tied

- *Mork & Mindy* (#3), tied

- *Angie* (#5)

- *The Ropers* (#8)

- *Taxi* (#9)

- *Eight Is Enough* (#11)

- *Charlie's Angels* (#12)

***

1979-80

- *Three's Company* (#2)

- *That's Incredible* (#3)

By contrast, WCBS was a ratings winner for its late news earlier in the decade. CBS provided its own good fortune, although with an indirect assist, as the biggest hits were on weekends.

1971-72

- *All in the Family* (#1)

***

1972-73

- *All in the Family* (#1)

- *Hawaii Five-0* (#3)

- *Maude* (#4)

- *Bridget Loves Bernie* (#5)

- *Mary Tyler Moore* (#7), tied

- *Gunsmoke* (#7), tied

***

1973-74

- *All in the Family* (#1)

- *The Waltons* (#2)

- *M*A*S*H* (#4)

- *Hawaii Five-0* (#5)

- *Maude* (#6)

- *Kojak* (#7)

- *The Sonny and Cher Comedy Show* (#8)

- *Mary Tyler Moore* (#9)

- *Cannon* (#10)

- *The Bob Newhart Show* (#12)

***

1974-75

- *All in the Family* (#1)

- *The Jeffersons* (#4)

- *M*A*S*H* (#5)

- *Rhoda* (#6)

- *Good Times* (#7)

- *The Waltons* (#8)

- *Maude* (#9)

- *Hawaii Five-0* (#10)

- *Mary Tyler Moore* (#11)

***

1975-76

- *All in the Family* (#1)

- *Maude* (#4)

- *Phyllis* (#6)

- *Rhoda* (#7)

***

Grimsby, who had one of the driest wits on TV, appeared to be a curmudgeon, a moniker that he rejected.

"He was very impatient guy [about] anything he thought was wrong," Lape recalls. "It could be technical stuff, bad written stuff; it could be film that wasn't cued up."

His short fuse could even be ignited during a broadcast, with last-minute change of direction from the control room. Grimsby was a perfectionist, as Lape recalls, who wanted 100 percent out of everyone, 100 percent of the time.

"He was a bad guy to be on the other end of the earphone with if you were producing that 6 o'clock news," Lape says.

Grimsby's boss gives some reasons why Grimsby wasn't always a favorite in the newsroom.

"[He] was an orphan. He was not in a happy marriage. He was reasonably successful in San Francisco with a reasonably successful news organization. Then [he was] brought to New York where there were a bunch of losers," Primo said, referring to the pre-*Eyewitness* days of WABC.

"When I did come, I came because I thought my marriage was breaking up and I'd get moved out of the house at company expense," Grimsby reflected years later.

His psyche was not helped by his arriving in the top market, where he was a stranger in the city. That led to Grimsby projecting a negative bent, Primo said. "He was suspicious of the management. He didn't like the writers. [Grimsby] didn't think they were on a par with him."

Whether it was his ego or shortcomings, Grimsby would constantly rework scripts in his style. "It was Roger versus the newsroom for a while, until they started to mesh," Primo remembered.

Grimsby had little admiration for the man who hired him. In some ways, he always subconsciously blamed Primo for putting him in a successful position. Instead of focusing on demos, Grimsby had demons to control him.

Prior to the *Eyewitness* era at WABC, Silverman says his lead anchor was the only staffer who didn't come to his office bad-mouthing anyone, pitching a story, or pushing for more airtime.

"He was satisfied with what his role was, and he thought it was treated fairly," Silverman recalled before his death in 2019.

But that comfort zone was short-lived for Grimsby, who not only worried that his days were numbered at WABC, Primo said, but also was concerned about his salary being cut or being deemphasized on the show. Primo said, "All kinds of spooky things were going on."

That was in the first few years at Channel 7, until Beutel pulled his weight and helped bring out the best in Grimsby. "Grimsby and I never set out to be funny," Beutel would say in later years. "I was there just kind of as the censor, saying, 'You don't really mean that Roger, do you?' Of course, he did mean it. That's why people watched."

The second half of Beutel's career was without Grimsby. He was either a solo anchor or with a female, primarily Diana Williams. Even though he was at *Eyewitness News* for decades, he wasn't always at ease.

"He was terrified of the management," Chauncey Howell, who worked at WABC in the late 1980s, contended.

In 1991, WABC boss Walter Hiss terminated Howell as a salary dump.

"Poor Bill was crying in his office to me," Howell recalled. "He was afraid that the audience would fall away if I wasn't there. That was flattering to me."

If Grimsby thought you were doing your job to the best of its ability, and not hurting "his" newscast, he put his claws in with his loyalty. "Loyal" could also describe the programs' viewers. After starting out in the ratings cellar, *Eyewitness* gained a strong following.

Within three years, WABC was the hottest news operation in town. Their marketing instilled this family unit with some classic commercials introducing the team in the early 1970s. Primo said those classic promos showed that his anchor team was on equal ground.

Tracy Egan, former *Eyewitness News* reporter, remembers hearing stories that single moms would enjoy having "dinner with Roger and Bill," who would act as father figures through the screen.

One promo shows the group playing a makeshift football game with Grimsby as the quarterback. Melba Tolliver, plucked from the steno pool, asks him to throw it her way. "You know I can handle a pass."

Another famous promo places the team at a Puerto Rican family wedding of Geraldo Rivera. "It's so funny," Rivera said.[2]

The seeming party crashers are introduced by Rivera before everyone opens up on the dance floor, especially Grimsby.

The voice-over ends with "The reason people like them so much is because they like people so much."

Jerry Della Femina is an advertising executive responsible for the *Eyewitness* ad campaign. Interviewed for the 40th anniversary video, he says the theme was simple, making them seem like best buddies. "They hated each other. But the fact is, we made them look like they were friends," Della Femina says. "What a scam. If there was truth in advertising, if it were a Nuremberg trial, I would be hung today."

Lifting *Eyewitness News* into the public's consciousness, the ads give off the impression of one big happy, albeit dysfunctional, family.

"[Viewers] don't want to see people competing against each other or fighting with each other, or being nasty to each other," Primo said.

"It was a circus of a train ride, not a train wreck," Lape says.

Channel 2, battling for eyeballs with Channel 7, had its own share of promos in the 1970s. One had a viewer watching at home, with the voice-over announcer: "No other anchorman is quite like Jim Jensen." Jensen ends his mock newscast saying goodnight. The female viewer responds to the TV with "Goodnight, Jim" as she kisses his face on the screen. The announcer concludes the promo: "See why weeknights on Channel 2."

Despite the early success of *Eyewitness News*, Primo worried that when breaking news happened, viewers would turn the dial to the familiar Channel 2 or 4.

"We had our worst moments when there was big news," Primo admitted. "We had our best moments when it was just like a regular day."

---

2. Labrecque, Jeff. "Forty Years with Geraldo Rivera: What a Long, Strange Trip It's Been." EW.com, September 3, 2010.

People came to rely on Primo's *Eyewitness* experiment as the station most identifying with New Yorkers.

One trick the trailblazing executive used to cover news: He knew that the majority of the Nielsen rating boxes were located in Brooklyn.

"Anytime we were going to do Man on the Street, I always pushed them to do it in Brooklyn. It signaled to that community we weren't the 'Bums' anymore."

12

Happy Talk

"Happy talk"—anchors chatting on set—was perfected by Al Primo, mostly bouncing off the weather and sports guys.

"It's a complete misnomer to have called *Eyewitness News* 'happy talk,' because it wasn't," John Johnson says. "It was good journalism."

Longtime producer Alan Weiss agrees with that assessment. "I never saw Roger or Bill ever do 'happy talk.' Yes, they made comments. Yes, they spoke to reporters. Yes, they debriefed them, and yes, Grimsby was famous for his one-liners, but they never said anything vapid."

In a 1973 interview with WNYC, Bill Beutel said: "People criticize my news program because we have a lot of fun on that program. When our program is at its best, we are reflecting the sadness and the happiness that is a part of real life. So, if we laugh on our program, it's because most people, unless they are very unfortunate, have a laugh during the course of a day."

Eyewitness with Grimsby and Beutel was well-established for more than a decade when Lou (then Louis) Young arrived at WABC.

"Roger didn't happy talk. Roger didn't chat it up with reporters on the set. Roger just delivered the news, really straight. 'I'm Roger Grimsby, here now the news.' How corny is that?" Young says. "It was a very staid delivery. It was a moniker with an allusion."

Mike Archer, a writer and producer, who was ultimately in charge of the 11 pm broadcast, says the set in those early days didn't even lend itself to happy talk. There was a staggered effect of reporters' desks positioned behind the lead anchors.

"Roger may have a comment, could be cutting or dry, but [he] would address the camera," Archer says. "He wouldn't turn around and talk to the reporter."

It wasn't necessarily happy talk, but like watching a home run hitter at the plate, it was must-see TV.

"You were always watching to see what the hell Grimsby was going to say about something, or what his reaction was going to be," Archer says.

Whatever you want to call it, Beutel got skilled opposite sportscaster Howard Cosell in those pre-*Eyewitness News* days. News director Ed Silverman recalled how Beutel would prepare retorts.

"They'd be one size fits all. There were times when Cosell wouldn't say anything, but Bill felt inclined." He said that showed the basic insecurities surrounding Beutel.

By contrast, Grimsby, dealing with his own personal foibles, was known to taunt Cosell, with lines like, 'Let's go to the president of the Howard Cosell Fan Club.'

While not in direct competition, perhaps there was just too much ego on the set for those two journalists. Even though *Eyewitness News* was thought to be ground zero for happy talk, Weiss says it's the copycats who should get credit for that label. "They couldn't do what Roger and Bill did, and they did a very poor imitation," Weiss admits. "You read about so many anchors who come in, pick up their scripts, read them, then go home. They don't really have a lot of depth."

Young concurs, "They exuded personality without stooping to that formulaic stuff."

Others, though, would go that route in forging the happy talk concept.

"People tried to emulate it by loosening up and just being really informal," Young says. "Other people happy talked, but those guys didn't."

During his second turn as WCBS anchor, Dave Marash criticized the banter, telling *New York* magazine in 1981: "If we fall into clowning around, it is at the bottom of the show. *Eyewitness News* goes wrong when the humor is mandated. When Ernie Anastos kids around with Rose Ann Scamardella, the whole rhythm of the show stops."

One print advertisement in 1972 hit that point hard. Seen in *New York* magazine, the full-page ad starts with the headline: "They can try to copy *Eyewitness News* but they can't copy Roger Grimsby and Bill Beutel." The large photo is an endearing view of the anchors, Grimsby cracking a smile in Beutel's direction while his colleague laughs. The text below the picture hammers home the theme that they are "talented newsmen" who are "intelligent, witty, and above all human." Addressing other stations trying to find the secret formula: "We've got that rare combination, the kind that just doesn't come along every day." The ad ends with "*Eyewitness News*. The news program the whole country is talking about."

For the smoothness under pressure, Grimsby and Beutel were in total control once the red light shined. They refused to wear earpieces that connected to the control room, a system known as interruptible foldback, or IFB.

"They had too many experiences where producers were yammering in their ears, and that drove them crazy," Weiss says.

Of course, this tactic drove producers like Weiss crazy as well. Whether it was an alert that a reporter's taped piece wasn't available or providing vital breaking news updates, Weiss was forced to communicate via studio phone.

"Unless we were in a commercial break or in a video, I could only talk to the anchor who wasn't talking on camera," Weiss says. "It was hysterical; fortunately, it worked because they were so unflappable. But it's a crazy way of producing news, I'll tell you that."

One day in the 1980s, the usual banter got an infamous boost, leading to a quintessential Grimsby moment.

Reporter Mara Wolynski is waiting to go live, in-studio, during the 5 pm newscast. As Rose Ann Scamardella does the introduction, viewers see a frustrated Wolynski making hand gestures to her producer, ending with her giving him the finger. She didn't realize her actions were part of a "two-shot" camera angle, with Wolynski visible in the foreground as Scamardella leads into the reporter.

While she doesn't recall a specific comment from Grimsby about her infamous blooper, she thinks it would have been something sardonic. But they didn't speak often.

"He was more like a guy's guy in the newsroom," Wolynski says.

But Grimsby enjoyed her finger so much that he "fell off his chair in the newsroom and rolled around on the floor laughing," Wolynski was told.

At the end of the 6 pm newscast, Grimsby added to his usual closing with perhaps his most famous line: "As Mara Wolynski would say, 'We're number one!'" The studio erupted in laughter.

News director, Cliff Abromats, though, didn't find the same humor in the incident and suspended her for a day.

Although there was no malicious intent behind her actions—just stress from the highly pressured world of live TV news—Wolynski expected to be fired.

"And I could have cared less," Wolynski says. "I didn't know I was on camera."

Furthermore, she didn't even have a desire to work in front of the camera. "I can think of maybe five times I didn't dread going into work," Wolynski says.

Wolynski, who was dismissed in 1985, two years after her infamous finger flip, missed the classic Grimsby ad lib as it happened, in a cab heading home. It managed to go viral—at least via word of mouth—within the station.

The faux pas is available on YouTube, something that Wolynski's daughter found one day and posted on her Facebook page.

It was a trial under fire of sorts for the former *Village Voice* reporter, making her maiden voyage in front of the camera. With an influx of robotic cameras today, a moment as loud as that is probably not likely.

"It was always fun to have live people in the studio," former WABC reporter Tracy Egan says.

While she kept the energy up during the live broadcast, Wolynski is remorseful—not for giving the finger, but for her story getting caught in the controversy. "The only thing I felt bad about it was I just did a whole story about the Black cowboys who had ridden in the west and were up in Harlem. It was a nice piece, and it got overshadowed," she recalls.

She had also missed the decade of Roger and Bill banter, as her family's choice for news was WCBS.

Still, Wolynski didn't hold any apprehension meeting the *Eyewitness* stars. Her stepfather was Net Hentoff, a columnist at the *Village Voice* for a half-century, whose articles were also published in *Playboy,* the *New Yorker,* and the *Washington Post.*

"I had already met Nobel Laureates. This was like nothing," she says.

Grimsby would rarely lose it to the giggles, but one broadcast in the early 1980s, he started to burst before airtime. It spread throughout the studio as *Eyewitness* hit the air. Grimsby is seen wiping the tears from his eyes as the announcer opens the newscast.

"We are live. Hoping your news is good news. I want to quit now!"

But the trooper that Grimsby was, he didn't walk off the set—although he kept cracking up while reading the first story about a tuberculosis scare. He didn't get through one sentence before completely stopping in his tracks, hand in face, laughter on full display. "Alright, composure." With those two words, Grimsby willed himself back into a professional stance.

Another time, Grimsby was interviewed for a behind-the-scenes feature on Channel 7, where he reflected on his most embarrassing moment. Ever the droll anchor, he said, "Yes, I mispronounced 'count.'"

Tom Snyder played that clip as part of his obituary on CBS's *Late Late Show,* which ended in hysterics.

There were enough Grimsby one-liners to fill a whole book. Here's another: Concluding a 1981 newscast with a profile of Tom Carvel's marketing techniques for his ice cream company, Grimsby says, "He's no dummy. He didn't pay for that one." Laughs are heard through his signoff.

"If something goes wrong, I'm inclined to underline it," Grimsby once said in a WABC profile. However, Grimsby was in stunned silence on the night of November 24, 1976, when popular weathercaster Tex Antoine turned the happy talk into a career debacle. Coming out of a story by Beutel about the rape of an eight-year-old girl, followed by a brief stock-market report to soften the awkward segue, Antoine made light of the unspeakable crime: "With rape so predominant in the news lately, it is well to remember the words of Confucius: 'If rape is inevitable, lie back and enjoy it.'"

Richard Sloan, sound engineer on that fateful night, claimed Antoine was fully absorbed in his maps for the weather report. "He was all business," he said.

The veteran weather anchor prepared the forecast knowing within seconds of how much airtime he'd have. "He wasn't aware of what the details were," Slone recounts. "It wasn't proper regardless of the age of the victim."

Antoine, as he had done often, quoted Confucius. This time, the shockwaves were stunning and instantaneous.

"You could hear a pin drop," Sloan recalled of the career suicide he just witnessed from the control room.

During the deafening silence, the studio monitors also told the story. While one screen showed the on-air feed of Antoine's weather report, another camera was positioned on Grimsby, who had thrown it to Antoine.

"Roger buried his head in his hands for almost the entire weather forecast," Sloan said. "Roger was acting as [if] Tex had just ended his career."

For all intents and purposes, that moment, only a few seconds in length, effectively did just that. News director Ron Tindiglia heard the remark and demanded an immediate apology before the newscast ended.

"If I offended you with the Confucius saying, I apologize," Antoine hurriedly said.

This did nothing, however, to stem the tide. Almost as fast as the controversial comment was uttered, Antoine was fired. Well, more accurately, suspended. He never appeared on the station again, removed before the 11 o'clock show that same night. The firing would officially have to wait as management opted instead to let his contract lapse in March. On December 18, General Manager Ken MacQueen lifted the suspension, allowing Antoine to assist his replacement, Storm Field, with forecast preparations. Field, son of legendary meteorologist Frank Field, was a trained meteorologist, whereas Antoine was not.

Five days after the Antoine ugliness, WABC found its permanent replacement in Storm Field. This time, Grimsby was back to his typical witty repartee for the introduction. (Ironically, the elder Field succeeded Antoine at WNBC years earlier.)

"Lie back, relax, and enjoy the weather with Storm Field," Grimsby would welcome Field.

Tom Snyder, working for rival WNBC, came to Antoine's defense. "The guy blundered and apologized," he told *The New York Times* a month after Antoine's professional meltdown. "What do they want? His total destruction? None of us are perfect. We all blunder at times. To pretend otherwise is sheer hypocrisy."[1]

The damage was done, despite many calls siding with Antoine. However, the Women's Anti-Rape Coalition held a rally in December. Despite Antoine being removed from the air, they wanted Antoine off the ABC payroll. That wasn't enough. They also demanded Grimsby be reprimanded for his flip remark in announcing Field's addition to the *Eyewitness* team. A spokesperson for the advocacy group said at the time: "We are concerned about a general insensitivity towards women at the station."

It was not the first time Antoine had made an off-the-cuff comment that necessitated an apology. In 1972, during the Munich Olympic Games, Antoine gave an opinion that ruffled feathers and smacked of insensitive at best, anti-Semitic at worst. He told viewers that more attention should be given to the many people killed annually in traffic accidents and not focus on the Israeli hostages.

Aside from a 10-month stint at WNEW/Channel 5 in 1978, a legendary 30-year broadcasting career imploded (justifiably) from that remark about Confucius.

---

1. O'Connor, John J. "TV View." *New York Times*. May 7, 1978.

13

"Hollywood Version of an Anchorman"

E ven the most astute *Eyewitness News* watcher would have no clue about any animosity. But WABC didn't miss a beat. Instead of reinstalling Roger Grimsby and Bill Beutel at 11 pm, Channel 7 went for an outsider as New Englander Ernie Anastos was welcomed in 1978, thankfully without any friction from the stalwart anchor.

"I don't think Ernie ever failed to get along with anybody," former *Eyewitness News* reporter Bob Lape says. "It's not in his DNA."

That is a feeling that most would echo about the legendary anchor.

"He was nice. Benign," Mara Wolynski says. "He didn't have a chip."

Meteorologist Frank Field worked with Anastos during his 1980s stint at WCBS. "Ernie is a congenial chap, and is a competent script reader," Field said. "Showbiz is his life." Those are also sentiments felt by many who had long associations with Anastos, a fixture on New York TV screens for more than four decades. Mark Abrahams, who worked with him during their time together at WABC in the 1980s, called him a "great guy," and said Anastos was the "first professional reader."

It was something of a backhanded compliment, however.

"Not a journalist, not a whiz-bang," Abrahams admits, "but a reader." Staffers would joke that if they changed the prompter to say, "'Good evening, I'm Harvey Schwartz,' Ernie would read it," Abrahams laughs. "He knew he was Ernie Anastos, but he would read it."

He agrees Anastos is a genuine decent person on and off the air. "It's not the most flattering thing, it's just true," Abrahams said.

Ad-libbing, a necessary component of the anchor's livelihood, was not his forte.

"Was he Ted Baxter? No," Abrahams suggests. "Ernie very rarely got rattled, so it was pretty easy with him as long as the script was there. He could tap dance for a few seconds and be able to cover, but if he had to really fill in or ad-lib, no. Forget about it. Then he'd switch over to Roz [Abrams]."

However, Anastos's colleagues Grimsby and Beutel were up to the task, no matter the situation on air.

I share a smile with Ernie Anastos (left) at an award ceremony. [Jerry Barmash]

"If you wanted something lighter, well, there's Roger," Abrahams said. "If you needed something heavier, there was Bill. The people of *Eyewitness News* were pros."

Former WPIX and WNEW news director John Corporon closely watched Anastos, whose career bloomed at *Eyewitness News*.

"[He] was the Hollywood version of an anchorman."

Warner Wolf, who shared the anchor set at *Eyewitness News*, and then at WCBS, agrees. "If you were going to pick a guy to have fun with on the air and laugh, you'd pick Ernie," he says. "We used to like to sing during the commercials."

Anastos stood the test of time after more than a decade at *Eyewitness News*. He added two stops at WCBS before closing his career at WNYW/Fox 5 with more than 15 years when he left in 2020.

As he was about to receive the prestigious Governors' Award from the New York Emmys in 2011, Anastos thanked his good genes for longevity.

One unnamed former colleague, however, begs to differ. "He looks the same as when I was young with black hair. Now here I am, a grey-haired guy, and Ernie looks to my eye exactly the same. Something's weird there."

Anastos teamed with Rose Ann Scamardella, one of the first female anchors at the station and in New York.

Scamardella, who's stayed under the radar since retiring from Channel 7 in 1983, married one-time WABC cameraman Mark Niedhammer. They have since divorced.

There was a joke in the newsroom when they were together: "Mark's not in today, he called out rich," veteran reporter Lou Young recalls.

In the early 1980s, WABC honchos paired her with Storm Field for the 5 pm broadcast until Tom Snyder came on board.

"He was not a particularly nice person," Wolynski said, as her only negative reaction toward any of the anchors, although Field is more associated with his weather forecasting than news-delivering skills.

"I didn't have much interaction with them," Wolynski said. "I couldn't wait to go home."

After more than 40 years, Anastos cemented his spot alongside the other New York anchor greats. His stretch of being his station's main anchor ended in 2012 when WNYW/Channel 5 removed Anastos from the 10 o'clock broadcast.

"He was extremely popular, and a friendly face," Sue Simmons says.

"Ernie loves being on TV, he just loves it," Lou Young says. "I'm pretty sure [for] Roger, it wasn't about being on TV."

When Anastos took over the early-evening newscast, a set was created with anchor's personality in mind.

Not the traditional feel, it looked like you were in his office, complete with Emmy Awards on a shelf in the background. Perhaps the perfect example of Anastos was his "man on the street" segment, where he posed a question generating the least-controversial and good-natured reactions.

Fittingly, Anastos also launched a "Positively Ernie" broadcasting brand.

"He was good at his craft," said John Corporon. "He did a first-class job."

14

"Lizards?! We're Leading with Lizards?"

Popularity notwithstanding, TV news is still a business first and foremost. Ernie Anastos was shifted from 11 pm in 1982 as WABC brought in Tom Snyder, who made his name as host of NBC's *Tomorrow* show. Anastos got a taste of national exposure when he was in line to succeed David Hartman as co-host on *Good Morning America* in 1987. He wanted that gig so badly that Anastos held secret auditions with Joan Lunden, with whom he previously worked at the local level. But as *New York* magazine wrote, WABC GM Bill Fyffe gave Anastos an ultimatum: *GMA* or *EWN (Eyewitness News)*.

"I did have a conversation with Ernie, to this extent: I told him he could fill-in on occasion for Hartman, but there was no way I'd let him go for good," Fyffe said. (Ultimately, Charles Gibson got the high-profile position.)

Tracy Egan was one of the reporters who made the transition to Snyder's show on WABC. "I think [Channel 7 brass] thought it would be a big get to have Tom Snyder on the air," Egan says.

On night one, Lou Young was told to cover an Yves Montand gala at Lincoln Center. But he balked.

"It's bullshit, we should be out doing news. This is Tom Fucking Snyder!" Young said.

The assignment editor didn't appreciate the tone and bounced Young from the broadcast—that was, until word came in that a pet store in Queens was abandoned from the economic downturn and dead animals were being removed due to fire.

"That was a normal kind of story for a Rose Ann and Ernie newscast to lead with," Egan says. "Snyder, having been a national news anchor, wasn't very happy with that."

Young was there to describe the scene, but no cats or dogs were seen. "I realize all of the animals they're carrying out are gerbils, mice," he recalled.

He pleaded with management not to run the story, but it was the lead. Snyder did a dramatic opening that "gave me goose bumps," Young said.

As the report plays, viewers and Snyder are staring at fish tanks and rodents being hauled away. Off camera, Snyder tells him, "Lizards?! We're leading with lizards?" Young ends his report, throwing back to Snyder who made no other reference to the story, and his initiation at *Eyewitness News* was underway.

That led to a write-up in *New York* magazine, as Young remembers being an "earnest, serious young reporter probing with his microphone demanding answers to the conditions of underfed gerbils and listless reptiles."

"[Snyder] said he watched Rose Ann and Ernie and wondered why he'd replaced them," former *Eyewitness News* producer Michael Horowicz recalled. "By the time he went to the five [p.m. newscast] he was already plotting his escape—two years and out."[1]

Although hired for his NBC cache, Snyder knew that was long in the past—even just a couple of years removed, joking with his friend and confidant Horowicz, "What are they going to do? Take the *Tomorrow* show off the air?"

That was day one, but the audience never gelled for Snyder. After six months, ratings failed to inspire management. The old-school solo act faded, and Kaity Tong was promoted.

---

1. Kaplan, James. "The Beast Is Back." *New York Magazine*, August 8, 1994.

Snyder was back on New York television in September, but by November his 11 o'clock newscast sunk in the ratings to an embarrassing third place. WNBC, with Scarborough and Simmons only two years installed, held the top spot in the late broadcast across the city with a 24-percent share of the audience.

Former WABC-TV anchors Kaity Tong and Ernie Anastos reunited at a New York Emmy Awards gala. [Jerry Barmash]

One night, when Tong was off, Egan moved to the anchor chair opposite Snyder.

"He was doing everything to throw me off, like slamming his hands on the desk really loudly right before I had to go on camera," Egan says.

The fill-in anchor says she didn't cave in to Snyder's shenanigans, but it was Snyder who seemed more focused on screwing up Egan than his own performance. At the end of their second segment together, he apologized; a line in the sand was drawn and respect was given to her.

Egan says Snyder's reason for the antics had nothing to do with a playful personality.

"He had said that if his co-anchor was off, he shouldn't have to work with anybody," Egan recalls.

The point would be moot soon enough. By the next year, he was removed from the more serious late news and moved to the lighter 5 pm broadcast. Snyder's interview skills were reestablished in an attempt to take the limelight away from WNBC's powerhouse *Live at Five*.

In 1984 he left, telling *The New York Times*, "Let's just say that I've had some philosophical difficulties with my format here."[2]

A decade later Snyder opened up again to the *Times*. "I hadn't realized how much the news had changed locally. It wasn't the news anymore. It was tabloid television. And after two years I got as sick of them as they were sick of me, and we parted company."[3]

"He made a big disruption—a lot of egos being bruised—and then he was gone," Egan says of her former colleague. "I think he really felt from day one that he didn't fit there. He certainly wasn't going to change to fit in."

Lou Young, another of the 11 pm reporters, says Snyder's second stint in New York failed from the get-go.

"They screwed that up royally. It was talent envy," Young says. "They didn't like paying Rose Ann and Ernie all that money...The thing went down the shitter."

Producer Michael Horowicz, who also worked with Snyder on his eponymous CNBC show, told the *Los Angeles Times*: "Those were bad times for Tom," and the feeling was mutual among many of the staff.

"Everybody thought he was a little strange," Horowicz said. "But it wasn't just strangeness: He also had the stink of failure about him."[4]

Chauncey Howell had a deep respect for Snyder's on-camera presence, despite constant ribbing on air. They met years later, just months before Snyder's death. The two newsmen's eyes met while walking on Fifth Avenue in Manhattan. Howell remembered Snyder's welcome as he screamed, "Chintzy, over here, it's me, Tom."

---

2. Associated Press. "Tom Snyder Leaving WABC." *New York Times*, August 20, 1984.

3. Meisler, Andy. "Tom Snyder Reconsidered: Everyman At 57." *New York Times*, May 8, 1994.

4. Kaplan, James. "The Beast Is Back."

But, as they briefly chatted on the street, Howell was surprised by what happened next.

"All of sudden he started to cry, and he said, 'You know I never meant those things I said to you, or said about you.'"

Howell, who died in 2021 at age 86, understood it was just his personality. "It was really most moving," he said.

"He had been away from New York long enough that I think the ABC audience really weren't aware of him," Simmons admits. "They didn't know who Tom Snyder was."

The *Eyewitness News* brand and the Tom Snyder brand were in direct conflict, setting the stage for his tumultuous, brief run. But the high-priced salary may have played the biggest role in his hiring and firing.

"He used to brag that he paid off Social Security by March," Egan says.

But Simmons, in her first years at WNBC, was scared upon hearing he would be the direct competition.

Channel 7 unveiled Snyder in 1982 in an effort to reintroduce viewers to him, rolling out an ad campaign with a curiously mixed message: "He's bold. He's brash. He's smart. He's arrogant. He's a windbag."

"It really turned out to be bad press for him," Simmons says. "I don't think that was his favorite time in New York, let's put it that way."

That late newscast with Snyder fell flat with a throwback solo anchor experiment. But management wasn't giving up instantly, feeling the broadcast was too male orientated, reporters John Slattery and Lou Young, plus meteorologist Storm Field and the sports anchor.

"They flooded the thing with a female presence, that was the term they used," Young recalls. The show now featured a handful of women covering stories, including Egan. It was the chance for weekend anchor Kaity Tong to gain new visibility, as an in-house reporter, meaning the look of co-anchor without being one.

"She was there for a segment and would banter with him a little bit," Young says. "It was just bizarre, like pretending she was the co-anchor."

Egan, though, just as she did with Grimsby, appreciated her time with Snyder, the one-time network hotshot.

"I like confident people," Egan, at *Eyewitness* from 1979 to 1986, said. "I can be myself, so I got along with him great."

Ultimately, management realized they had to make Tong the official co-anchor.

"You can't have a woman there just staring at Tom," Young laughs.

Even though the star power of Snyder took the ratings the wrong way after the success of Anastos and Scamardella, Young got a glimpse of his skills.

"He would find irony in my copy that I had not intended, and then tell everybody the joke as if I were a brilliant satirist."

One time, Young did a story about an amputee, when Snyder asked him if there were details regarding the loss of the man's arm. "Offhandedly, I don't know." While Young says it was a stupid line to say, Snyder thought the young reporter was clever. "He was convinced I did it on purpose."

Snyder would affectionately refer to Young as the "droll one."

"He took a liking to me," Young says.

Another time, in a moment reminiscent of the Mara Wolynski's infamous finger flying, Snyder flipped his own bird (in the same camera angle) while weatherman Ira Joe Fisher wrapped up his segment. Tong laughs at Snyder, who recalled the incident years later on his CNBC show.

"She knows I'm in the can," Snyder said. "Then, of course, Bill Fyffe, the legendary station manager, the most incompetent man I ever worked for in broadcasting, and a true son-of-a-bitch from start to finish, set me down. They suspended me for a week without pay."

Snyder acknowledged saying sorry to viewers at the end of the broadcast. A week after the on-air flap, WABC held a party, which Snyder attended with a bandaged finger.

"I got it caught in the camera," He teased.

Young says, "He would go to tremendous lengths for a joke. It was fun to be around him."

Snyder would occasionally hangout with his colleagues at the nearby tavern, but not often. "I guess he saw himself as a bigger celebrity. He *was* a big celebrity," Young says, "but he was accessible and a great guy."

Ending the opening segment on CNBC, Snyder said his former boss had moved on to a station in Green Bay, Wisconsin.

"It's the third station in the market, and he'll keep it that way," Snyder said. "Fyffe, I told you I'd get you one day for all the crap you did."

Jimmy Breslin would also have a contentious working relationship with Fyffe at ABC. When he moved the columnist's "People" to 1 am Mondays and 1:30 am Fridays, Breslin attacked his boss in his *New York Daily News* column.

"Bill Fyffe," he wrote, should "do the honorable thing and jump in front of a bus."

The general manager got into a mild controversy in 1983 when putting together the precursor to *Live with Regis and Kathie Lee*. There was a report circulating that execs wanted to avoid hiring those who "might have highly visible ethnicity" as hosts.

The memo indicated that WASPs were preferred for a show based in New York City, known for its melting pot of diversity. "Who knows why, but Jews, Blacks, Italians, Irish, Latinos seem to accept a WASP [perhaps] because of conditioning to the idea that this is 'American,'" consultants Ann and Bob Shanks and ABC-TV VP Beth Forcelledo wrote in the document sent to the Channel 7 production staff.[5]

Fyffe though said his hiring practices are linked to past performances. However, Regis Philbin, a white Roman Catholic, and Cyndi Garvey, a blonde, white woman, were selected.

Despite Fyffe's refusal, Anastos would ultimately find new life at WABC. The station had a "New York Loves Ernie" ad campaign to welcome him back.

As Egan remembers, it was a delicate balance for WABC management with their popular anchor during the Tom Snyder tenure. Anastos wasn't fired or even reassigned; he was left quietly in his office. Egan says he took the time

---

5. Churcher, Sharon. "ABC-TV Memo: Wasps Preferred," March 21, 1983.

to write a book, but throngs of viewers missed the star enough to make signs supporting their favorite anchor.

"They put up posters about bringing Ernie back all along the path that the General Manager Bill Fyffe took to work, so he must have thought they were everywhere." Egan says. "I think between Ernie being classy and having seen this outpouring of support from the Greek community, lo and behold, Ernie came back on the air."

Anastos's longtime colleague, though, would not return. "They asked Rose Ann to come back a lot," Young says. "When she left, she was done, to her credit."

"I really wanted to be a mother, and I was at the height of my career," Scamardella said about her 1984 exit, "so mothering was very important." [6] Her daughter, Vanessa, was an impressionable three-year-old at the time. She would juggle doing the 5 pm news and 11 pm broadcast, going home near the station for the family dinner break to "put her to sleep and go back." But Scamardella admits that once it got to the point where a choice was required between work and family, "I chose Vanessa."

Aside from the loss of the sizable paycheck, she has no regrets about walking away.

At the same time, Bob Teague, who was in the midst of a long run at WNBC as reporter (and occasional anchor), wrote a behind-the-scenes book. He uncovered one tidbit about Scamardella's look that WABC honchos wanted her teeth fixed before she was replaced by Snyder.

It was revealed in a taped WCBS interview promoting the book, but that portion was cut. However, Teague went to spill the "dental detail" in *New York* magazine.

"[That's] absolutely true," Scamardella told the magazine. "I have crooked teeth, and I didn't want them touched."

---

6. Marlane, Judith. *Women in Television News Revisited: Into the Twenty-First Century*. University of Texas Press, 1999.

Rosanna Scotto, the longtime WNYW anchor, is a direct link to Scamardella, as both are Brooklynites. "When I was growing up, we'd all watch her on *Eyewitness News*," Scotto says. "Rose Ann also happened to be a friend of my family's. I'd visit her at the TV studio, where she'd have me talk to some of the other reporters and anchors, like the respected Ernie Anastos."[7]

Scotto ushered her TV idol back on the air for a brief stint. In 1999, Scamardella did a two-part series about Albania refugees in Brooklyn on Fox 5/WNYW. Another link to the past, Susan Sullivan, news director when this aired, was an intern for Scamardella while in high school.

"Watching the tapes [of Scamardella], I think she's really back to who she was on the *Eyewitness News*, which was as a real person relating so well to other people," Sullivan said.[8]

While working for NBC in the previous decade, Snyder dabbled on the local news with Chuck Scarborough and Jim Hartz, who eventually would jump to the *Today Show*. During his time as *Tomorrow* host, Snyder also was an occasional weekend network anchor, and handled the one-minute NBC news prime time update.

On set with WNYW's Rosanna Scotto in 2009. [Diana George]

7. D'Arienzo, Camille. "New York TV News Anchor Talks of Life Off-Camera." National Catholic Reporter, May 15, 2012. https://www.ncronline.org/blogs/conversations-sr-camille/new-york-tv-news-anchor-talks-life-camera

8. Starr, Michael. "Ch.5 News Brings Back Scamardella: TV Legend Files Reports on Kosovo Refugees." *New York Post*, May 21, 1999.

"He was outstanding," Frank Field said of Snyder's talents. "When it was impossible to do something, he did it. He was just that great."

There were clearly reasons the audience tuned in to *Tomorrow*. His interviews, which ran the gamut from a Disney animator to John Lennon, showed a genuine curiosity.

"He could do the interview as a conversation," John Huddy Sr. says. "He could really go beyond what you would expect, to the nuance, the detail, to the inner soul of the person."

Interestingly, the former *Tomorrow* producer said, his on-camera chats were without preparation. Huddy assumed the job would entail discussing each night's guests.

"He never did do that," Huddy recalls. Instead, the veteran TV host opted for a first-time encounter, like meeting someone next to him on a plane. "Sometimes it worked. Sometimes it didn't work," Huddy admits..

One night it famously did work when Snyder went to California Medical Facility for a sprawling interview with Charles Manson. The episode, unsurprisingly, was a rating bonanza for the NBC late-night show.

Snyder had "extraordinary range," but Huddy declares this was "not his finest moment." He contends Snyder was fearful of the interview and the setting, but added that this was unwarranted. "The security was amazing," he said.

The other problem was that Manson himself was a rambling mess. Huddy called the convicted serial killer an "evil man . . . but he was also an actor." He put on a "performance," and, as Huddy says, "Tom didn't stop it."

As Snyder told Bob Costas on *Later* in 1989, "Manson is a nutcase. That was all that was learned from that interview."

Other times, though, his signature biting humor came to the surface. On one occasion, the film for a report he introduced was lost. Without missing a beat, he questioned, "Where is it? Over at CBS?" That was usually the type of Snyder retort you'd expect, although he'd play it straight with the serious stuff.

By 1977, with *Tomorrow* a success in late night, Snyder left the anchor desk, taking *Tomorrow* back to Burbank. *New York* magazine said Tony Guida was given the upgrade at WNBC.

That June, Johnny Carson asked him why he moved back to Los Angeles.

"It's a little bit easier to do television in Southern California, in this building, than in dear old Rockefeller Plaza," Snyder said. "I had a great time there. I went there not very wise. I think I came back a little bit broader, a little bit smarter. I exposed myself to different ideas and some different kinds of people."

Upon his return to the West Coast, Snyder said there was nothing asked about returning to the anchor desk for KNBC.

"I understand you didn't like to do it in New York, you wanted to get off the news?" Carson questioned.

"Suppose that you had to go over and do the news from 6 to 7, then run in here and do this." Snyder replied. "After three and a half years, it just became time to do one thing or the other thing. I think it's best for me to follow you. I'm very comfortable doing that program. I'm very happy doing it and I hope to do it for a long, long time."

Five years later (after *Tomorrow* added gossip reporter Rona Barrett) Snyder was fired and David Letterman started his illustrious late-night foray, but not before *Tomorrow* was revamped into *Tomorrow Coast to Coast* with a studio audience.

"It's not really worth talking about," Snyder told Costas. "It's a singularly unimportant event in the history of television, Miss Barrett and myself on the *Tomorrow* show. It's counts for zippo in the history of television."

Costas responded that no comment is a comment in and of itself.

"She's been everywhere with it, she gotten a lot of mileage from it. But I don't need that kind of mileage."

Snyder and Roger Grimsby shared a bond during their brief time at WABC. They had many similarities in their experience and their opinion of Barrett, who handled entertainment on the *Eyewitness* precursor.

"He really hated her stuff," Al Primo recalled, and Grimsby didn't keep it a secret from viewers.[9]

As for her time working with Snyder, Barrett recalled to the Archive of American Television: "From day one, it was almost a disaster."

Huddy was a producer of the *Coast to Coast* version of *Tomorrow*. He and Roger Ailes were in the meeting with Snyder when the changes were announced.

"We know you don't like the idea of having a co-host," Ailes said.

Snyder shot back, "She's not a co-host! She's a reporter."

But that wasn't the plan.

"You're the star, she's the co-star." Snyder was told.

"At that time, Roger weighed about 300 pounds, and you just didn't fuck with him," Huddy says.

Huddy cautioned Snyder to take the Barrett overhaul seriously, but in one episode, famed fashion critic Richard Blackwell was a guest with Snyder in New York. He happily told Snyder that his new co-host is on his best-dressed list.

Huddy, from the control room, could see the wheels in Snyder's mind moving. Ultimately, in a subtle way, Snyder took a jab at Mr. Blackwell, leading to howls from another new aspect of the show—a studio audience. However, the remark didn't go over as well in the control room, where Ailes punched the wall.

"He was really furious," Huddy remembers.

The Snyder/Barrett marriage was toxic from the beginning. Barrett appeared live via satellite, so the two hosts never had to work side-by-side in the same studio. Barrett spoke to Mary Tyler Moore from New York, which angered Snyder.

"Needless to say, that relationship didn't last very long," Huddy recalls.

For Barrett, it "turned into something that was really not nice, not good. I just decided I had to end this."

---

9. Waters, Harry. "The News — With a Dash of Dirt." *New York Times*, January 25, 1970.

As the gossip columnist would say, this was Fred Silverman's idea to reformat *Tomorrow*.

"But it's never turned into what I thought it was going to be or what my contract stated," she told UPI in 1981. Aside from being 3,000 miles away geographically, they were, in her words, "philosophically miles apart."

Snyder was also steadfast against the audience, hoping to keep the intimate set and puffs of cigarette smoke clouding the screen.

"That was the end of it for my dad," Ann Marie Snyder said. "That destroyed him. He hated it." She claimed NBC had it in for Snyder, and Barrett was the final straw.

"It was kind of a design to fail situation," she said. "It would be like if they brought in some woman to share the stage with Johnny Carson. How happy would he have been?"

We got a sense of what that might look like when ABC made a splash by luring Barbara Walters from NBC's *Today* show to co-anchor the evening news with Harry Reasoner. The old-school anchor did not enjoy sharing the spotlight. It was another trailblazing journalism moment for Walters as the first woman anchor on a major network newscast. But Reasoner, unfazed, was trying to make it as uncomfortable as possible for Walters.

Walters would say her only connection to Reasoner and the stagehands was talking about the Yankees.

"Harry wasn't mean," Walters told the Archive of American Television. "He didn't want a partner. He was unhappy at ABC and he was saddled with this woman. He would go every night across the street before the show and have, I guess, a couple of beers with the guys. It's an all-male club. They would all talk about how terrible I was."

It was Snyder's constant battle between being a newsman and showman, although Huddy looks back more diplomatically 40 years later. He maintains that occasionally having an audience was a positive for the show.

Snyder got little to no resistance from the network in early years of *Tomorrow*. Ann Marie Snyder believes executives weren't concerned about what the show delivered each early morning because no one would be up to see it.

But it was management, according to Huddy's recollections, who opted against continuing the cult following established by Snyder on the show.

"We can't afford the show," network brass would tell Huddy. "We need to rev it up."

Despite Snyder's skills and ability to adjust, "the show that was created was not something he wanted anything to do with, even though the ad ratings went up," Huddy says.

Clearly seeing the "marriage" was in disarray, Snyder, savvy about the economics of television, understood why changes were inevitable and, actually, necessary.

The final change came on February 1, 1982, when upstart comedian David Letterman would take the 12:30 a.m. slot after Carson. NBC was willing to keep Snyder, but push him back an hour, a move that would be repeated at ABC years later when *Nightline*, losing its luster, aired after *Jimmy Kimmel Live*. Snyder, already angered about dealing with the "Barrett era," would not stand for a later start. The last first-run episode aired December 17, 1981, while reruns continued until January 28.

"They kind of pitted them against each other," Ann Marie Snyder said. "They made it very hard for them to like each other."

Before YouTube and the viral video, a Snyder flub gained traction for several years. He related a story during a 1977 *Tonight Show* where a viewer asked him if he ended a WNBC newscast by saying, "Good night everybody, I've got to go take a leak."

"He and I used to do little shtick on the news," Snyder told Carson. "It's the oldest bloop in the world, and I swear to you (holding his hand up) I said, 'Now here's Frank Field to take a leak out the, er, look out the window and see how the weather going. By the time the whole thing was finished, I was being naughty on the air."

Field, whose mind defied his nonagenarian status, did recall that moment.

"No one will ever know if it was deliberate or not," said Field, 94 at the time of the interview. "It sure broke up the studio."

Field recalled another classic moment where Snyder played the mischievous boy on set.

As Field was doing his weather report, there was Snyder, hanging a rubber chicken on his three-foot map pointer. Ever the professional, Field kept going without a pause, while no doubt many yucks were filtering through the studio, especially from Snyder.

"Tom was irrepressible!" Field declared.

In recalling the NBC years on his CBS late night show, Snyder talked about filling in for Frank Blair as *Today* show newsreader. Knowing the going rate for talent was $500, management asked how much he'd need for expenses. He requested and got $2,500.

"I spent every quarter of it and more," Snyder laughed in his famous staccato delivery.

Later, his boss told him they needed to settle up the expense account.

"I forgot to tell you, I was robbed when I was in New York," Snyder said.

The boss asked if they took the money.

Snyder quipped, "No, they took the receipts."

***

Huddy got a close-up look at Snyder during the final 18 months of the reworked *Tomorrow*.

"[Snyder] was a heavy drinker," Huddy recalled.

In his roles at CBS, in both New York and Washington, families of staffers would occasionally tour the studios, but he would not permit any behind-the-scenes visits at *Tomorrow*.

"[You] would never do that with Snyder because he could be crude," Huddy says. "He could be very mean."

There was a shady moment at a birthday party for a staffer where a college girl was hired as a stripper, unbeknownst to Huddy.

While it was more of play acting, Huddy could tell the girl was embarrassed and "Tom did everything he could to ridicule her. He just was insulting, and I never forgot that."

That aside, Huddy could separate their personality chasm, including not being one for libations. So much so that when the opportunity presented itself for an anchor at the burgeoning CBS four-hour overnight broadcast *Night Watch*, Huddy jumped at the chance to bring Snyder on board as competition to upstart CNN.

However, Snyder told his former producer that he was no longer interested in that career path and they hung up.

News of their phone call quickly filtered to Ed Joyce, executive VP at CBS News.

"No way," Joyce empathically told Huddy. "I do not want that man in our organization. Under no circumstances."

15

Adult Beverage, Anyone?

As for the once-celebrated member of *Eyewitness News*, Roger Grimsby's professional life died nine years earlier when news director Bill Applegate and general manager Bill Fyffe did the once unthinkable move: firing Grimsby at WABC. Lou Young said he had firsthand information that the departure was connected to station research. Terms of departure included payments through June 1987, about $1 million in salary.[1]

"Although many people liked him, there were just as many people who were like 'I'd rather watch somebody handsome, affable, and who smiles more,'" Young admits. "If your research is good and your numbers are high, you can do whatever you want. If they're not, as soon as there's an excuse they'll kill you."

"There had been problems with Roger's performance for years," Applegate said.[2]

---

1. "Grimsby, News Anchor, Is Released by WABC." *New York Times*, April 18, 1986.

2. Ryan, Michael. "Channel 7's Eyewitness Blues." *New York Magazine*, June 23, 1986.

But if you were in the Grimsby camp, you were a loyalist to the end. One reporter in the same article even said, "You could look up to Roger. Can you look up to Ernie Anastos?"

Young: "He was very difficult, but he did it his way."

By the mid-1990s, WCBS had hired four former WABC staffers. When Grimsby passed, they gathered for the eight-minute obituary segment to reflect on the industry giant.

One of those reporters was John Johnson, who spent 14 years at *Eyewitness News* with the "exceptional" Grimsby.

"Roger was an extremely different man," Johnson said at the time, days before starting at WCBS. "He was keen-minded and had a great sense of humor."

Young, Magee Hickey, and John Slattery also joined the impromptu round-table discussion.

While working at Channel 7, Slattery did a 1982 profile that explored Grimsby's daily radio work. He anchored one newscast for ABC News Radio each afternoon.

Slattery asked him why a top local news talent, commanding big bucks, would need the extra gig?

"For me, radio is an imposed discipline," Grimsby replied. "I must be here. I have to write it myself. I have to read it myself."

Gary Nunn had a front row seat for Grimsby's radio days, as an ABC News Radio anchor from 1975–1980.

"He was probably one of the best writers that I have ever worked around," Nunn states. "I can't say enough good about how competent the guy was as a writer."

At the time, ABC had four radio networks. Both Grimsby and Nunn appeared on the Entertainment Network. It was also when the ABC's radio and TV divisions were within the same family—unlike today.

"He would take all this wire copy, throw it in the trash, and then write the stories," Nunn remembers. "That's the kind of guy he was. As far as I was concerned it was 100 percent accurate."

His newly written radio copy would join him at Channel 7 later that afternoon.

Grimsby, as pointed out in the Slattery profile, also used the radio gig as preparation for the evening newscast in front of the camera.

"He'd sit at my desk with about an inch-thick pile of paper," former *Eyewitness* producer Alan Weiss remembers. "He would start reading me all of the news stories that he'd already written and read for ABC Radio."

Grimsby's national and international story selection, though, always didn't pass muster with his supervisors.

No matter: Grimsby would swap out stories, reading a voicer on camera from memory, fitting into the exact allotted time of the discarded report, all the while confusing the newsroom.

"It's much easier just to read what's in front of you, but he cared enough about that to want to have his way and change it," Young says. "That's a real talent. Viewers never knew. He just gave the finger to everybody."

It was a classic, albeit subtle, jab for Grimsby.

"He was a low-key kind of guy," Nunn, who sat across from him, recalls. "It took a while to get to know him, but once you did, it was like a really familial kind of thing."

Family for Grimsby was lacking, having never known who his parents were. He was born in Missoula, Montana, and raised in Duluth. The orphan's upbringing was molded by a Lutheran pastor, Reverend O. M. Grimsby, who adopted the infant.

"Nothing on the written record of Roger Grimsby's life includes anything untoward, although he was obviously no saint," Jim Heffernan posts in 2013, based on his association with Grimsby as a youth.

In his blog post for The Zenith City, "The Great Grimsby," Heffernan includes his high school yearbook inscription: "Happy-go-lucky, witty and free, Nothing there is that bothers me."

"His mind always was really sharp, even in the worst of conditions," Nunn says.

In that Slattery report, Bill Beutel referred to his longtime on-air partner as a very shy man. However, Grimsby countered with "bashful, certainly not shy."

Shyness was definitely not a trait seen on the set, especially once comfortable with staffers. At ABC Radio, Nunn describes the newsroom more like a fraternity.

"That manifested itself in [Grimsby's] personality, the way he thought and the way he actually wrote stories," Nunn says. "He could tell the bluest of stories. It was just one of the guys."

That's before throwing some cocktails into the mix, which helped John Johnson describe Grimsby succinctly. "I credit him for his success with good writing—a lot of alcohol."

Former *Eyewitness News* reporter Lou Young adds to the inebriated legend of Grimsby.

"Roger had a refrigerator in his office and it was stocked with vodka," Young admits. "It must have been a case of vodka in there."

Partying alone or at the bar, Grimsby never missed a newscast. During the 1980s, as Grimsby's legend was growing (but his star slowly falling), GM Bill Fyffe created a contest for best attendance in the newsroom.

"Roger won it," Young laughs. "Fyffe wanted him to give the prize to some secretary who came in second."

However, Grimsby wouldn't relinquish the badge of honor, causing a rift with his boss.

"Not only was he making $10,000 or $15,000 a week, he took a free vacation from Bill Fyffe," Young remembers. "Fyffe was just beside himself. He wanted to drive his head through a wall."

In his 2000 memoir, *Larry Kane's Philadelphia*, the anchor reflects on multiple times he spotted Grimsby from his company-provided vehicle, driven by a former Pennsylvania police officer.

"We noticed him sprawled between garbage cans outside of his hangout, Chips Bar on Columbus Avenue," Kane writes. "We dragged him into the car and dropped him off at his home."

Kane added that the "rescue efforts" were never acknowledged by Grimsby.

That may be a reason why depending upon who you ask, you may hear a different interpretation of the anchor.

However, in 2001, Beutel gave this assessment to *The New York Times.*

"You'll understand I don't want to add to that issue," he said. "I don't believe he was a fall-down drunk. I spent a lot of time with him."

Beutel later told the reporter, "The thing of it is—not to be difficult—he was a friend. Were I in his position, I would hope my partner would not get into a discussion. You do not win in that discussion, no matter what you say."

"I've seen Roger have too much, but never on the job," Young says. "Never could you tell. He was rock solid."

Another former colleague recalls the complicated nature of Grimsby.

"He was outgoing to some people and a loner to others," Gary Nunn says. "It was a strange dichotomy of personalities."

John Roland, long-associated with the *Ten O'Clock News* anchor, sounded like he was delivering a joke when mentioning hanging out with the anchor.

"I was at a bar one time with Roger." Roland said. "God, he was a heavy drinker."

At the tavern on the West Side, also featuring Tex Antoine, the popular weatherman, Roland recalled a woman gushing over Antoine and asking his age, which he said was 52.

"Roger, without missing a beat, jumped in, 'That's Celsius,'" Roland remembered. "He was brilliant."

Before his death, Grimsby, a Korean War veteran himself, was an advocate for a monument honoring members of the conflict. It was dedicated just a month after his 1995 death, "largely because of his efforts," Roland said.

One veteran *Eyewitness News* cohort shares part of that outgoing persona.

"At the top of the newscast we would do our stories and then scoot under the building to the Café des Artistes restaurant on Central Park West," Lape reflects. "We would sit at the bar until it got to be about 10 minutes before signoff, at which point we would down our drinks and dart back through the tunnel underground and emerge at the rear of the set just in time to swarm in at the very end of the newscast, and schmooze as if we've been there all the time."

Mark Abrahams had a 43-year career at WABC, nearly three decades of which he worked for the nightly newscasts, primarily as videographer in the field. But in the early 1970s he got an initiation with the original *Eyewitness News*, visiting the studio with a friend who was a station page.

It was broadcast from the large TV-2 studio. He recalls it being freezing cold.

"And if you lit a match the whole block would have gone up," he said. "That's how strong the smell of alcohol in that studio was. It was mind-boggling."

But that was only the start of inebriation by broadcasters. Undoubtedly, it wasn't unique to WABC, but the station's close proximity to watering holes didn't help.

"There was a lot of stuff going on," Johnson admits. "I guess everyone went over to McGlade's after the show and had a few—whatever—and maybe Roger had one or two more than the rest of us. I think Beutel did his drinking at home."

"Roger might dip in there for a nip beforehand," Lape concurs. "Sometimes they'd have to go over with a rake to get him out of there for the 11."

While Grimsby was professional, and while viewers would not know about the earlier alcohol flowing, there were times he took it a step too far. "There were times that Roger had too much to drink," Richard Sloan said. "He pulled it off most of the time."

However, Sloan remembered one time when he was so wasted, "The producer of the show said, 'Take his copy away from him and give it to Bill. Have somebody integrate it with Bill's script and have Bill read it all.'"

Grimsby on this particular night "couldn't care less," Sloan said of his inebriated colleague.

McGlade's, Chips, or Dmitri's were all located across the street from WABC on West 67th and Columbus Avenue, so those wanting to cavort didn't need much incentive.

"If you wanted the cast or crew, that's where they were," Abrahams says, "almost to the minute, up until airtime."

Grimsby, Beutel, and Antoine led the stiff drinking, typically twice a day, lunchtime and dinnertime between the 6 and 11 pm newscasts.

"Obviously, Bill didn't have as much to drink as Roger did," Richard Sloan said. "Nobody did."

"It was a whole other era until later on when drugs started to enter the scene," Abrahams intimated.

That's likely one reason why Grimsby was ultimately yanked from the late broadcast. But it was rare for Grimsby's drinking to show through the camera, or even to colleagues.

"I never noticed it," Warner Wolf says.

Indeed, Johnson knows his former anchor was no stranger to sidling up to a glass.

"I didn't give him a sobriety test, but I would say that he could hold his alcohol," Johnson laughs.

Egan says she never saw him drunk or stammering on the air. However, there was at least one night, astute viewers may have noticed a drunk Grimsby and company.

The boozing had hit a crescendo in 1970 when management, on-camera talent, and other staffers gathered for the WABC Christmas party at an East Side bar. Grimsby and Beutel were part of the guest list that night, squeezed in before their 11 o'clock broadcast.

It took a call from the newsroom just an hour before airtime to start the frenzy. Lape says the *Eyewitness News* team finally left for the West 67th Street studios at 10:30 pm.

"I think we better go watch this newscast," Lape remembers telling a station producer.

It didn't disappoint. Lape said what ensued was "hilarious" and "priceless," as the veteran newsmen struggled to appear sober.

"Roger looked straight in the camera and said, 'Here Now the News,' and stopped dead in his tracks."

That brought Beutel to the rescue, who tried to get through stories while slurring.

"Then they moved onto sports, and [Frank] Gifford was half in the bag. Tex [Antoine], of course, was always half in the bag. He was three-quarters in the bag." There were no backups for these partygoers. "There were at least five people on that newscast that should not have been."

WABC kept a protection tape of all broadcasts, in case anyone sued due to content. This time the tape was gone by morning. Management hierarchy had no grounds to suspend or even complain about the performance.

"Primo and [GM Ken] MacQueen couldn't slap wrists very much because they were there," Lape contends. "They were the ones that should have been alerted long before anyone else."

Abrahams contends: "When you've got three bars across the street and a bat phone in there, you know that these people are drinking. And we're not just talking the talent, we're talking the crew, too. But, they'd get the phone call. They'd walk across the street. Do the show. Get done. Reassume the position.

"That's when it was fun. Now, not so much," Abrahams, who retired in 2020, says. "It's a denigration that I've watch happen over the course of my career. It's sad. It's the difference between pros and wannabes."

Despite solid ratings—usually number one across the board—Abrahams doesn't think the evolution of *Eyewitness News* was the best way to honor the historic past. Yes, the brand is in markets across the country, "But in New York, it's not a franchise, it's an institution."

***

While the 1970s were the indulgent time with booze, Bill Beutel maintained those pursuits into the 1990s.

When the Oklahoma City federal building bombing took place on April 19, 1995, Beutel struggled to correctly identify the location of the domestic terrorist attack from hours earlier.

In recording the tease for the 11 pm, broadcast, Beutel had to do multiple takes as the venerable anchor kept saying "Tonight, devastation in Atlantic City," Abrahams recalls.

After as many as 17 tries, he finally said Oklahoma City, but Abrahams worried that Beutel would do it live.

"Sure as shit, 11 o'clock comes along, they're tight on Bill and he goes, 'Tonight the devastation in Atlantic City.' They cut to the two-shot and Roz [Abrams] was mouth hanging open like a deer in the headlights," Abrahams says.

This incident led to a suspension for Beutel, according to Abrahams: "He was stone cold sober from that point on."

As Bob Lape remembers, Beutel was a "charming, classic guy, and a fine drinker, as were a lot of us."

Despite the libations, Beutel and Grimsby typically brought their "A" game, or at least their "A-" game to the studio.

Abrahams said people would wonder if Grimsby was high based on his smirks or his comments, but "that was just Roger."

Commemorating KGO-TV's 40th anniversary, Grimsby returned for the studio audience taping. The host said he'd occasionally enjoy a "friendly libation" with Grimsby and asked about a legendary drinking story from his San Francisco days.

"The story followed me to New York. It's followed me everywhere I have gone. I was so sloshed on the air that I fell off the stool. It's not true. It broke," Grimsby said to an eruption of laughter.

Readers know about the legendary partnership that Beutel had with Grimsby and later with Diana Williams, who actually worked longer with him. Susan Roesgen, though, not so much.

If the term is "wet behind the ears," she was soaking. Her first TV job took her to WABC and the anchor desk with Beutel. You might think he would turn this into a learning opportunity for Roesgen. But Beutel had other ideas, and they didn't include training inexperienced anchors, according to Abrahams. "Not ready for prime time," Abrahams says of Roesgen, who would go on to work for CNN and other local markets, including New Orleans.

But when she landed in the top market, a lack of on-air acumen kept Beutel from gelling with her, or even acting as the elder statesman at the station.

"Bill had a real hard-on for her, and did not make her life easy at all," he said. "He didn't cut her a scintilla of slack."

Abrahams said that was the only time he saw the *Eyewitness News* team fail to act like a team.

This was around the same time Williams would arrive at WABC, and she would occasionally fill-in for Roesgen.

"If it was Bill and Susie, I would have to go to about 72nd Street to get the two-shot," Abrahams jokes. "If it was Bill and Diana, I could put the lens on the desk and still get the two-shot."

For a decade leading into the 1990s, Greg Hurst was an early evening anchor, mostly with Roz Abrams. He's not remembered as one of New York's best news journalists.

"People like Ernie [Anastos], Greg Hurst, and Charles Perez: These were the Ron Burgundy of their time," Abrahams says. They, and others, had the main skill of just being able to read the news, and "were full of themselves."

At the end of each newscast Hurst would tuck his pen into his jacket breast pocket, reminiscent of Dennis Miller's *SNL Weekend Update* "I am outta here" close, where he scribbles on his script.

"I don't think you know how to write your name, what's with the pen?" Abrahams deadpans.

Hurst would go on to an 18-year run anchoring in Houston, leaving KHOU in 2017.

"These were a very lively group of mature people who were not youngsters," Lape recalls. "Most of us had pretty good experience behind us even before coming to *Eyewitness*. They weren't kids and they engaged in adult pursuits. The fact that some of them were flakier than others maybe elevated the bar there a bit."

WABC didn't own exclusive rights to enjoying the adult beverage. At the "Deuce," Steve Cohen remembers Channel 2 staffers gathering at a bar near the Broadcast Center on West 57th. Jensen and others could often be found at the bar with a few pops of scotch at the dinner break between newscasts.

"Everybody would take a deep breath and we'd come back and do the late show," Cohen says.

But the professionalism outlasted the alcohol.

"You would absolutely never know," Cohen recalls that once the red light shined, viewers always got the best of Jensen.

With such strong skill sets to get a newscast on the air, Jensen, and others of the era, could usually work on automatic pilot.

"Their ability to conceptualize a story, write the story and present it—they were so absolutely good at it that could come back half in the bag at 9 o'clock and they could knock out a program like that," Cohen states, snapping his fingers.

Pia Lindström, before lifting the curtain on her two-decade career at WNBC, had a two-year stint at WCBS in the early 1970s. Primarily out in the field, she had limited contact with Jensen, but recognizes he was serious-minded and "did a very credible job. But it wasn't something he was doing that I could copy."

Not only was Jensen credible, but viewers liked him. In 1975, WCBS was trying to stay at the top at 6 pm, but *Eyewitness News* was about to hit its crescendo in the marketplace.

At that juncture, Jensen was 46 and a pro's pro. The industry's internal Trendex rating for Jensen was 56, making him one of the most favorable.

"It would be a real mistake to get rid of Jensen," a rival executive squawked.[3]

His work ethic took a back seat to no one. That was evident in 1986 when CBS CEO Laurence Tisch decided to eliminate free delivery of newspapers in the newsroom, which didn't sit well with the "franchise." Jensen wrote the boss complaining about the decision, according to Ken Auletta's book *Three Blind Mice*.

Not to be left out, WNBC talent also had no problem enjoying themselves.

"The 70s and 80s were a period of excess," Sue Simmons says. "There was a lot of partying going on, and people relieving their stress."

---

3. Diamond, Edwin. "Anchorpersons Aweigh!" *New York Magazine*, August 18, 1975.

Back to Channel 7. With or without drinking, there was bad blood between Grimsby and star reporter Geraldo Rivera. It was based on a trip Rivera made to the Middle East, covering the war between Israel and Egypt for the Yom Kippur War. But Grimsby, a former medic in the Korean War, knew how incoming artillery should sound, which he claimed wasn't in Rivera's edited pieces.

Lape says, "He cast him as being a liar."

"At the time, this incident was a subject of intense scrutiny by critics alleging that it had been staged or misrepresented," Rivera wrote in his book *The Geraldo Show.*

He said that Grimsby gave that tidbit to a *Rolling Stone* reporter to "point out how miraculous it was for me to have survived a precisely targeted artillery strike just as the camera rolled."

That remark led to at least one confrontation between the strong personalities.

The *Rolling Stone* reporter, realizing how serious the charge would be, alerted Rivera, who was "in a rage."

"He worked 20 years to get where he's getting, and Geraldo worked 20 minutes almost to his level," Primo says. "There was a little bit of, 'Shit, life's not fair.'"

The clash of egos led to a dramatic exchange.

"Geraldo administered what appeared to be a double shiner to Roger," Lape says.

As Rivera details it in his autobiography, "I asked for some time with Grimsby during a dinner break one evening." They spoke in Rivera's office and when Grimsby confessed, "I started punching him, saying that I was going to kill him, until he fell to the floor, defenseless," Rivera wrote.

With Grimsby seemingly knocked unconscious by the multiple blows, the famed *Eyewitness News* correspondent worried he might have killed him. He visited friend and producer Marty Berman and they gathered waiting for the 11 pm newscast.

"I was enormously relieved to see Roger give his signature line," Rivera wrote.

Rivera said to his credit, as far as he knew, Grimsby never said anything about the incident.

Cooler heads would prevail, at least upon word of Grimsby's death in 1995. Rivera told the *New York Daily News* that the fisticuffs "never affected my admiration for him," and, "I never hated Roger, although I'm sure he hated me."

Mara Wolynski never worked with Rivera, and she's happy about that from everything she knows about him.

"I cannot stand Geraldo. He is just so pleased with himself," Wolynski says. "You're not working at the Rockefeller Institute on a cure for cancer, you moron."

Grimsby confided in Gary Nunn, who had brief chats with Grimsby during their five years together on the radio side, about his disdain for Rivera. It would go to another level when the popular correspondent would appear in the radio newsroom.

"Roger would almost attack him verbally. He just really disliked the man," Nunn says. "That's one of the few people who was on his list."

Wolynski says, "I'm sure there was no love lost. Roger wouldn't have liked him."

In 1972, as Rivera's star was soaring, *New York* magazine interviewed the former lawyer. While he didn't rip his anchor, a quick read between the lines sheds more light on the story.

"Roger and Bill used to butcher the name 'Geraldo.' They spit it out. They said it like a slur—We had this fire at . . . and we sent 'Ger-al-do Rivera.' I could have slid right in as 'Gerry,' but it was a conscious decision to be 'Geraldo.' I wanted to show them. My brother Wilfredo is 5 feet 3 inches with kinky hair and dark skin. He's a steamfitter. They would never have hired him on *Eyewitness News*. They hired me not because I'm bright or an attorney, but a Puerto Rican who's not too offensive looking and not too short. Racist motives put us here, but now there are 16 million people who know the 'g' is pronounced 'h' in Spanish."

"He was a charming, classic guy, and a fine drinker, as were a lot of us," Lape remembers.

***

A mutual respect for the veteran anchors shined through the screen. But like dysfunctional families, they could make fun of the other. For example, Grimsby would laugh at his colleague's nightly commentary to end the broadcast.

In 2019, Rivera posted a vintage *Eyewitness News* ad poster from 1972, with the team and Grimsby in the front and Rivera laughing over his left shoulder. "Awww, these were the daze." Rivera tweeted with the photo.[4]

"[They] were perhaps the most banal couple of paragraphs I ever heard on a consistent basis, never very much of anything in particular," Lape says. "Bill knew that. He knew that it was kind of corny. But he thought that was alright.

"Roger, on the other hand, thought it was funny as hell, because it never got better."

Another moment that viewers were unaware of, Lape says, involved Beutel briefly embodying Carol Burnett, giving on-air signals to his girlfriend or "wife of the moment." (Beutel was married four times.)

"At the end of the show when he was coming home, he'd give a slight tug to one ear." Lape says it was a tip-off, although he didn't know to what.

"Roger would occasionally tug at his own ear."

As Gary Nunn points out, Grimsby dated a Pan Am flight attendant and may have lived with her at his place, The Apthorp on 79th Street and Broadway. Nunn was invited to the apartment a few times.

"He could throw a wild party," Nunn says.

---

4. Geraldo Rivera (@GeraldoRivera), "Awww these were the daze. Welcome back to 1972 Eyewitness News NYC." Twitter, May 19, 2019, https://t witter.com/GeraldoRivera/status/1126480706652209152

Grimsby's Channel 7 heyday in 1978 also marked his 50th birthday party celebration at a Hilton penthouse in the city.

"It was like a parade of who's who in broadcasting and show business," Nunn recalls. "He was a household name around this town for a while."

16
An "Eyewitness" to Success

Aside from the milestone personal achievements, the perennial third-place news organization was getting better. At the height of their popularity in the mid- and late 1970s, *Eyewitness News* was now the one to beat. While the anchor desk was still filled with white men, the reporters had a better representation of New York City, Geraldo Rivera, Chee Chee Williams, and Gloria Rojas among them.

"Those were people who were more middle class," Lou Young recalls.

Another memorable part of the news team at WABC was former print reporter Milton Lewis, who persevered for years on the City Hall beat despite an unorthodox style (or maybe that's what made him so endearing).

It was during that time and into the next decade that the *Eyewitness* celebrity was at its peak.

"If you were from Channel 7, I guess you could just walk into Studio 54 at the time," reporter Tracy Egan recalls seeing Grimsby at the iconic club after his newscast.

But closer to the Columbus Avenue studio, Grimsby had his pick of a few watering holes, including John's. A story handed down from the tavern involves the anchor having a few too many.

"He tumbled backwards in his chair," Egan says. A concerned waiter asks Grimsby if he can help.

"Yes, get me a double."

"That was an all-star team [at] Channel 7," Warner Wolf, sportscaster from 1976–1980, says.

During that time, Primo landed sportscaster Dan Lovett. He writes about his experiences at WABC in the 2014 memoir, *Anybody Seen Dan Lovett?*

He recalls the first time sampling the station from the St. Regis Hotel, watching the acclaimed news team: "My sky-high self-confidence goes quickly into a tailspin."

Lovett recalls Grimsby jabbing gossip reporter Rona Barrett, segueing to her report after a story about the city's garbage problem.

"Speaking of trash, here's Rona Rooter," Grimsby said.

"Roger was a good solid newsman, who took no shit from anybody," former WABC news director Ed Silverman remembered. "From day one, he made it obvious on the air with these barbs as only Roger could."

Many times, Grimsby would give viewers a hint into the strained relationship with Barrett, barely introducing her by name.

"It took a lot of guts," Silverman said. "But that did not set him in good standing with management, and I backed him on that."

Lovett wrote: "Would it be that way in New York for me? How might Grimsby trash me?"

Lovett, who left Houston for the career advancement, says in his book that the prospect of working at WABC was "a bit overwhelming."

Within a year of his arrival, Beutel moved to mornings for a network gig, causing WABC to hire outsiders—Boston veteran Tom Ellis and Bill Bonds from Detroit.

With Beutel gaining a national presence on *AM America*, a print ad introducing Grimsby's new partners at 6 and 11 circulated. In typical Grimsby fashion, he revealed a sardonic, if uninterested, pose. WABC had the ad with Ellis and Bonds, separately putting an arm around the crusty anchor. Ironically, the text at the top says: "The Only Thing as Exciting as Our New Anchor Team at 6, [the second photo then shows] Is Our New Anchor Team at 11."

However, the two unknown commodities in the market smiled with teeth, while Grimsby was, well, Grimsby. "Both great. But in entirely different ways. For a new kind of excitement, watch *both* new anchor teams."

Watching, however, was short-lived. *AM America* and Beutel quickly fizzled, and he was back home with Grimsby at 6 pm, while Ellis and Bonds had a short stint together on the 11 pm broadcast. Their history in New York isn't long, as Bonds and Ellis were shipped back to their previous cities where they became broadcasting legends. Bonds was lead anchor at WXYZ into the mid-1990s. Ellis anchored at the three main Boston affiliates in the 1960s, 1970s, and 1980s.

Primo got a compliment from Ed Joyce, the former CBS News president and WCBS news director, who questioned in his 1988 memoir, *Prime Times, Bad Times*, "Why can't we be like *Eyewitness News*?"

"I treasure that quote," Primo said.

***

As the 1970s progressed, stations began transitioning from film to videotape.

"You looked so much better," Pia Lindström remembers. "You didn't see all the things people see now. Closeups look like they're terrifying."

There was no 5 pm news until 1974 when WNBC blazed that trail. Prior to the expanding news option, it was afternoon movies and entertainment for viewers. WABC had the popular, thematic *4:30 Movie*. Over at WCBS, the syndicated *Mike Douglas Show* was the lead-in for the early evening news show.

Movie 4 took the 4:30 pm to 6 pm slot once news was given an hour of programming, followed by the network's *Nightly News* at 7 pm.[1] The 11 pm cast went a half hour—no stretching for extra commercial time, unlike today.

Local news was just starting to become viable in the sales departments. For NBC, the two-hour slot was to help on two fronts: take viewers away from WABC while helping *Nightly News* with John Chancellor in its tight race against Walter Cronkite on CBS.

The 4:30 Movie, in the days before *Oprah*, *Ellen*, or *Judge Judy*, was a 90-minute showcase, usually featuring one genre each week.

It's no coincidence that the movie aired weekdays from 1968 to 1981, as *Eyewitness News* got started and grew into a force to reckon with, ultimately becoming the highest-rated broadcast once Grimsby and Beutel found their synergy.

Eyewitness News has been a regular ratings winner in most dayparts (the categorical blocks into which the airing day is divided), each sweeps period, for years. But it's not the same newscast on so many levels from a generation (or two) before.

"I think there's a lot from the past that could have been maintained, just in integrity, that would have held up the overall structure," Mark Abrahams said.

---

1. Adams, Val. "WNBC-TV to Modify Format to Give 1 1/2-Hour News Package." *New York Times*, April 13, 1965.

17

Moving On

For all their peccadilloes and eccentricities, the Roger Grimsby/Bill Beutel anchor team stayed together until 1986, when Grimsby was fired.

"I still don't know who fired me," Grimsby said.[1] "They haven't even given me a reason."

Grimsby did get compensation, with his salary being paid through June 1987—close to $1 million in total.

Financial considerations notwithstanding, the final years for the gruff broadcaster were underway.

Grimsby showed up doing commentaries on WNBC's *Live at Five*, but viewers saw a shadow of the former star.

"When he arrived, NABET [the National Association of Broadcast Employees and Technicians] went on strike and our forces were severely decimated," Sue Simmons recalls. "It just wasn't a good atmosphere for him."

Simmons, alongside her *Live at Five* co-anchor Jack Cafferty throughout the 1980s, knows Grimsby showed up as damaged goods.

"Getting released from *Eyewitness* was a tremendous crush to him," she admits.

---

1. Ryan, Michael. "Channel 7's Eyewitness Blues." *New York Magazine*, June 23, 1986.

She says Grimsby put on the brave face for his WNBC "columns," but 60 seconds of daily face time was a huge drop-off from 60 minutes.

Simmons says everyone at Channel 4 revered the crusty anchor, but acknowledges, "His time here [in New York] had passed, I guess. That's sounds harsh, but the chemistry never got going."

The glory days for the legendary anchor were in the rear-view mirror. After two years at WNBC, Grimsby was fired. The spotlight shined one more time as he anchored for San Diego's KUSI. That stint, however, only lasted a few months as Grimsby resigned over the station's direction of the newscasts.

Grimsby died of lung cancer in 1995. He was only 66.

Tom Snyder took time during his *Late Late Show* to honor his former colleague.

"He and I used to drink together. [Grimsby] was a hero and teacher to many people who worked in television news." Snyder said.

Then, as a montage of clips played, Snyder told viewers, "You may never have heard of Roger Grimsby, but he helped define the local television news that you watch today."

Aside from occasional drinking buddies, Grimsby and Snyder weren't close, but there was a respect.

"Roger didn't make fun of Tom, not like the way he did with Larry [Kane]," Tracy Egan says.

While Grimsby's time in New York ended inauspiciously at WNBC, the 30 Rock address proved to be a broadcasting pit stop for Dave Marash. Not everyone who worked with Marash, though, got to know him.

"One of the things lost to me when I came to a big market is the newsroom is so large, so segmented and clicky, that there [were] just certain people you didn't interact with that much, and he was one of them," Simmons admits.

Professionally, later years would be kinder to Beutel. He remained as lead anchor at WABC until 1999, when Bill Ritter assumed the 11 pm. Two years later, Ritter succeeded Beutel again, taking over the 6 pm newscast. For the next couple of years, Beutel gave loyal viewers a chance for a long goodbye, staying on with a nightly fixture as senior correspondent or commentator into his 70s.

"Sure, I miss it every day, because we had a great time," Beutel said in an interview for the *Eyewitness News* 40th anniversary. "Twenty-five percent of my life was spent with Grimsby. Can you imagine that, for God sakes? Most people couldn't spend 25 percent of a day. I loved every minute of it."

Beutel died of Lewy body dementia three years after retiring in 2006. At the time, his 37 years of service at WABC were only surpassed by Rafael Pineda of WXTV, who began his Spanish news anchoring in 1972. Chuck Scarborough became the longest-tenured English-speaking New York anchor in 2011.

Ernie Anastos fondly remembered his "special friend" in a 2021 Instagram post showing a vintage photo of the two broadcasters, where he said it was "many wonderful years with a real gentleman and beloved NY anchor."[2]

"He was a masterful reader," former WCBS and WPIX anchor, Steve Bosh, says. Although he never knew Scarborough personally, he did watch the competition during his years in New York.

"You pick up things from other people." Bosh says.

That, of course, meant the heavy hitters at Channel 7 too.

"They were really a great team," Bosh says.

In a special video tribute that ran at his funeral, Beutel was shown late in life talking with a frail voice about how he hoped to be remembered.

"There's never been a day when I didn't want to come to work. That's not to say that I wouldn't have rather gone fishing on a given day . . . I would hope that younger people can find the same kind of joy in this kind of work. With God's luck you can be happy doing it. I was."

The dapper anchorman also was shown saying he and Grimsby never set out to be funny and never scripted any of the banter.

In the throes of dementia, late in Beutel's career, Mark Abrahams recalls the sadness watching the venerable anchorman trying to track audio for one of his reports. It would take him multiple times to get it mistake free.

---

2. Anastos, Ernie (@ernieanastos). "I always admired my Ch 7 Eyewitness News special friend Bill Beutel." Instagram, September 25, 2021. https://www.instagram.com/p/CUPIkKyrvw1

"That wasn't the part that bothered me. The part that bothered me was that he was beating himself up about it," said Abrahams, who admired Beutel for decades. "It was sad to watch an icon, [who] you grew up with and had the honor of working with, to watch him really start to lose it." Beutel wasn't able to stay on the air much longer.

Beutel: "Liz and Dick getting back together. We'll tell you how and why."
Grimsby: "I can't follow a lead like that."

Perhaps ABC News longtime anchor Peter Jennings said it best about Beutel at his 2006 funeral. "It may be that Bill was just born to be a great local anchor person."

Even Donald Trump eulogized Beutel. "He would always treat you fairly. Sometimes maybe more fairly than you even deserved."

At a happier occasion marking the 10th anniversary of *Eyewitness News*, a giant cake with a frosting version of the anchors was displayed at the end of the show direct from the newsroom as the entire staff looked on.

Beutel: "You would never say it, Roger, but I'll say it. It's been fun."
Grimsby: "But why does it seem like 20 years?"

***

Before there was Chuck and Sue, there was simply Chuck.

Chuck Scarborough was the amiable, blond anchorman, who landed at 30 Rock in March 1974. He would become WNBC's face of a new look—*News-Center 4*. It was a futuristic newsroom set that took advantage of the newly popularized space craze.

The spacious set with oversized monitors was gone by start of the 1980s—also gone was *NewsCenter 4*, in favor of the newly branded *News 4 New York*.

The set would have more incarnations, including a "rear deck," as Len Berman called it. That would be the location for *Live at Five* and where the weather and sports anchors would sit while the news anchors stayed in the foreground at 6 and 11 pm.

Predating Scarborough was Carl Stokes, the former Cleveland mayor, who in 1972 was New York's first Black anchor. More lasting was Jim Hartz, a talented newsman, who anchored at Channel 4 for a decade until Scarborough's arrival. Farther back in the WNBC annals, Gabe Pressman was an anchor and reporter in the black-and-white era from 1960-1966. Pressman was one-half of an early anchor team with Bill Ryan, who was part of NBC News's coverage on November 22, 1963 telling the country that President John F. Kennedy was assassinated. Pressman died in 2017 at age 93.

The New York anchor, and the anchor writ large, came of age largely because of Scarborough.

"I remember when Chuck came to work, there was a lot of like, 'He's young, handsome, and blonde, a pretty boy.' Longtime colleague Pia Lindström recalls. "But, they don't keep you for that reason."

Despite that claim, women did "respond" favorably to Scarborough's blond locks and blue eyes, NBC News research found.[3]

Apparently, some of those women found other ways to respond "favorably." For example, as Chauncey Howell told it, there were a bunch of brownies sitting in Scarborough's office. He quietly grabbed one and Scarborough's secretary told Howell they came wrapped in a pair of panties from a viewer. He joked, "Did Chuck eat them? She told him I said that and he was pissed at me for a while."

Howell said Scarborough would deny this story, "Of course."

"He was a chick magnet. There was nothing like him," Howell said of Scarborough and his matinee idol looks. "He had so many women after him."

---

3. Diamond, Edwin. "Anchorpersons Aweigh!" *New York Magazine*, August 18, 1975.

Lindström thought that assessment was odd, as it's not why he was hired, nor why he became a New York institution.

"It's just apparent to those who didn't know what it takes to do that year after year," Lindström says.

"He's become an icon. I think he has a lasting quality," John Corporon said. "As far as bringing intellect to a newscast, he does a terrific job."

A Pittsburgh native, Scarborough was 30 years old when he answered WNBC's call. He was already well seasoned with anchor stints in two Mississippi markets, followed by stops in larger markets: Atlanta and Boston.

Two generations of WNBC anchor teams: Chuck Scarborough and Sue Simmons gather with Natalie Pasquarella and David Ushery in 2018. [Jerry Barmash]

"It's whatever combination of hard work and skills that I've acquired and storytelling ability and the audience appreciating what I do fundamentally," Scarborough said in 2014. "Without the audience and without the ratings being adequate throughout the entire 40-year span, I wouldn't have lasted. I'm grateful to the audience that I'm still here."

One former colleague said Scarborough's longevity is even more amazing when you consider what goes on behind the scenes. "Your life can be in an upheaval, but you never show that and somehow maintain this level of performance for years," Lindström says. "It's really a skill."

"I'm a real outlier," Scarborough told his WNBC cohort David Ushery on his Debrief podcast. "It's uncommon, especially to stay at one station for that length of time."

At WCBS, Jim Jensen had a long stint, taking over the anchor duties as early as 1965, when veteran CBS Radio correspondent Robert Trout stepped down.

"Three months before Jim came to New York, CBS put on an advertising campaign that was unprecedented," Former WABC news director Ed Silverman recalled.

Silverman estimated that the station paid between $250,000 and $500,000 to promote its future star, primarily in newspapers.

"By the time Jensen got to New York, I said to my friends, 'You know something, this guy's already number one.' He was presold."

Once established, and now at war with Channel 7's upstart *Eyewitness News*, Jensen and WCBS needed to get the word out. In 1972, Jensen was profiled in a full-page ad. The August 7 issue of *New York* magazine referred to Jensen's baseball promise with the Chicago Cubs: He had developed such a strong arm from a newspaper route that he was offered a contract. But as the ad stated, he turned it down. Broadcasting was already a passion, and Jensen settled for a $1-an-hour gig at a small CBS Radio affiliate.

The ad continues: "Nobody will ever know how well Jim Jensen might have done with a major league baseball team. But as an anchorman on a major league team, he's in a league by himself."

A 16-hour workday was the backdrop for another sports comparison.

"He could have had shorter hours playing baseball. But to him the news is a lot more fun."

The ad closes with a slogan: "You can't be the best unless you do it all the time."

So, it's no accident that Jensen led his station in athletic endeavors.

"Jensen was one hell of a softball pitcher," Former WNBC anchor Jim Hartz said. "He was almost like a professional pitcher."

"He was a notch or two from being a real softball player." Onetime colleague Steve Bosh says that activity was a key to their bonding. He recalls twice-a-week softball games across the tristate region. "A bus was rented, and we were all a team. That whole team spirit carried on right into the newsroom."

Jensen's longtime WCBS colleague Rolland Smith had brief national exposure after leaving "local" for the ill-fated *CBS Morning Show* in 1987. His co-host was actress Mariette Hartley, and comic Bob Saget was also the announcer and on-camera regular contributor. If the grouping wasn't odd enough, the studio audience probably was. The early-hours program couldn't survive a year, as the more traditional *CBS This Morning* premiered on Nov. 30. Seemingly doomed from day one, Hartley introduced her new friend, as a "newsman and journalist" but pronounced her colleague's name as "Row-lind." Before the applause dies down, though, Smith corrects her.

"Mariette, that's Rah-lind," he said.

Smith logged 18 years at CBS, ending with the doomed attempt to grab viewers away from NBC's powerhouse *Today* and ABC's *Good Morning America*. In less than 11 months Smith and Hartley were fired. One Smith was out and another was brought in as Harry Smith took over as co-anchor of a revamped AM news program on CBS.

It was a rare misstep for the veteran newsman.

Years earlier, before Smith was a fully formed star in the WCBS galaxy, news director Ed Joyce made a change that could have altered Smith's career trajectory.

"When I first arrived at WCBS, Rolland Smith was a weekend anchorman. I removed him from that role and assigned him full-time to feature reporting," Joyce wrote in his autobiography. "I was honest about my reason. He was so young and boyish and I thought he lacked credibility."

After exiting CBS, Smith, though, wasn't done with local news. A pair of stints at WWOR/Channel in Secaucus, New Jersey, would follow into the next millennium.

During that time Frank Cipolla got to meet and even co-anchor with his broadcasting idol a handful of times.

"It was one of the highlights of my career," Cipolla says. "It was phenomenal, and I'll never forget it." Growing up in Queens, Cipolla says Channel 2 was his news choice and Smith was his anchor to emulate. "In high school we did a mock television newscast, and I was Rolland."

He found chemistry was an easy lift on set with Smith.

"Rolland pegged me as somebody who was a potential news anchor," Cipolla recalls. "He took a liking to me, I think, because I knew everything about Rolland from the moment he began his career."

Shortly after joining WWOR/Channel 9, Cipolla was invited to dinner by Smith. Moments later, the news team technical staff also arrived at the restaurant.

"From that day on, I was treated differently by every single person in that newsroom," Cipolla says. "Rolland had figuratively put his arm around me. . . Just by the one action, it changed the entire dynamic for me."

While Smith is retired from TV, Cipolla is still amazed to call him a friend. "It's a dream come true."

When WWOR opted not to renew Cipolla's contract, there was Smith for encouragement at a farewell party.

"He was one of the most spiritual guys I ever met. There was something emanating from that night," Cipolla says. "I think he understood that I was on to another step in my career and he was wishing me well."

***

Smith gained some indirect national exposure when he was parodied by *South Park* more than 20 years after doing a newscast promo. The two-second bumper, or announcement, from 1978, which aired during a *Star Wars Christmas Special*, featured Smith saying the immortal words, "Fighting the Frizzies at 11."

Trey Parker, who embodies Smith (complete with the signature mustache) within the 1999 *South Park* episode, and co-creator Matt Stone were huge *Star Wars* fans, helping them find the memorable clip.

"I remember saying it, but I don't remember the story," Smith admits.

Beyond that, Smith doesn't know why it has sustained as an iconic piece of pop-culture history. That popularity isn't lost on his family, who've seen the clips on YouTube.

At the other end of Smith's decorated on-air work was being live in December 1980 as word filtered in about John Lennon's murder. Smith anchored the next night's broadcast, alongside Michele Marsh, called "A Legend Lost" as the city was in mourning.

***

As the *Eyewitness News* concept took hold, viewing habits, production values, and coverage of local news would change each night and forever. The competitors took notice, especially as WABC's ratings skyrocketed.

During this era of magnetic on-camera personalities, the anchor also was responsible for most of their own writing.

As Steve Cohen remembers, "You put your words on the page and an editor would do something with it. But fundamentally it was your language. We were very strict about how copy was presented and put together."

Despite being prepared with scripts, prompters, and earpieces, it was when technical glitches and breaking news took place that the anchor really proved himself.

"When Jensen and Rolland, or Grimsby and Beutel, just got the chance to go, they were extraordinary," Cohen says. "They were thoughtful. They had the right tone."

Mark Abrahams, who ran the teleprompter in-house and later was a videographer in the field for *Eyewitness News*, says you couldn't go wrong with Grimsby or Beutel when the pressure of live news coverage was on.

"There was nothing that got past them," Abrahams says. "Everything was just absolutely perfect. These were pros."

One standout memory for Cohen as WCBS executive producer was the death of former New York governor and vice president Nelson Rockefeller in 1979.

Smith and Jensen were at the desk for the sad story.

"That evening we were all in the newsroom. Rolland and Jim took the horns of that story. We had to start cutting film clips as fast as we could to create our coverage."

The Spring 1980 subway strike affected millions of people, and Cohen believes it led to constant anchor ad-libbing during the 11-day strike that April.

Cohen takes a jab at today's crop of anchors, saying it's hard to imagine any of them delivering that same repartee in such situations.

News-department promos are always showing the deep connection within the community. But in the 70s, it wasn't just a 30-second clip—these were real people connecting with their audiences.

Take Tony Guida, known for years to viewers at WNBC and WCBS. One night after a local event in Riverside, the Bronx, Guida escorted Cohen to the nearby block where his mother lived.

In an old-world moment, she peered out at the screen door, shouting, "Hey Tony!"

Cohen says that reflects why the anchors became stars.

"Everything that we were ever going to be in local news, and anything that anyone of us would be, was in the crucible of New York City, and that's what New York got. These folks were so much a part of their time and in sync with the audience's needs."

18

In This Corner: Larry Kane

Whether you called it hazing the new guy, or his ego and insecurities getting the best of him, Roger Grimsby infamously took some subtle jabs at the new man in town, Larry Kane, who spent a year commuting from Philadelphia to anchor the 11 pm broadcast in the late 1970s.

"I didn't have the same butterflies that others had," Kane recalls about his arrival in New York.

Kane's tenure on the anchor desk in New York was short-lived, but he was an important bridge of talent at *Eyewitness News*.

Kane was already a Philadelphia favorite for a dozen years before WABC courted the anchor. Choosing to keep his suburban home and not uproot his wife and two young children would hit a nerve with Grimsby.

"Roger would remind him that his limousine was waiting outside to take him back to Philadelphia," Bob Lape says. "He could make your life nasty if he didn't like you much."

On this particular night, Kane's commute from Philly was hampered by a blizzard and terrible traffic in the Lincoln Tunnel. While sitting in the elements, Kane called in a live report, and as Kane describes it, Grimsby concluded the reports by telling viewers, "That was Larry Kane reporting from his exclusive limousine on the way from Philadelphia."

Warner Wolf says, "Ernie, Jim, or Rolland would never do that, never try to embarrass."

As the alpha male feeling threatened by someone encroaching on his territory, Grimsby didn't have much of a relationship with Kane. "It was commonly known that he wasn't happy that I was there," Kane says.

A Coney Island native, Kane took Grimsby's shots in stride, admitting that he wasn't upset by the actions. "I didn't have any war; he did. And he made it as uncomfortable as he could for me there," Kane says. "It was just a cold atmosphere."

Comfort zone notwithstanding, he was rattled by Grimsby's thinly veiled attempts to get him to quit under lousy working conditions. So, Kane brought in management for help, but despite it coming from the rising star at WABC, his pleas fell on deaf ears.

"They can't legislate behavior. You can't tell someone to talk to someone," Kane remembers. "In a way, I may have been immature the way I handled it."

"Larry, I don't think ever made the full commitment, and I think the whole Roger thing probably affected his decision," longtime colleague Mike Archer admits.

Ultimately, his dream job was a nightmare, but Kane insists his choice to leave WABC had nothing to do with Grimsby and everything to do with his dual residences.

"In reality, it was a mistake. It's difficult to live in one place and work in another," Kane admits. "Although it was a fantastic career move, and probably would have put me in a position where I would go very, very far at ABC, it wasn't where I wanted to be."

"Mistake" aside, Kane is proud of leading ABC in New York to its highest ratings.

During his tenure of wearing the "Circle 7" blazer, Kane helmed newscasts during the tumultuous summer of 1977 as the Son of Sam targeted young brunettes. He grabbed the mic, hitting the streets for reaction to the death of Elvis Presley. Kane also guided viewers through the blackout. Channel 7 did not have a back-up generator, so there was limited coverage of the lack of lights or looting. WCBS and WNBC, however, had the equipment to broadcast.

"Larry and I wound up standing on the corner of 66th Street with Peter Jennings, talking about the blackout on the network," producer Mike Archer recalls.

It may have been brief, but Kane made the most of it by adding network anchor appearances to his demo reel, including as fill-in for the *ABC Evening News* "oil-and-water" team of Harry Reasoner and Barbara Walters.

Warner Wolf wonders, "What if?" about his former colleague. "I always felt bad that he went back [to Philadelphia] because I think he would have been huge in the New York market."

It could have been a different experience for Kane in New York. Two years earlier, *New York* magazine reported, Kane was close to signing with WCBS. In fact, all three stations had their eyes on Kane. As an anonymous news director told the magazine in 1975, "He's bright, fast talking and looks like he has a ---- nine miles long."

Exit Kane and enter Ernie Anastos on the late newscast. Anastos would become one of New York's longest tenured anchors. Initially, he was teamed with Rose Ann Scamardella.

"They were as friendly in person as they were on the air," Tracy Egan says. "They weren't surly individuals who pretended to be nice on the air."

The brief, bittersweet run at WABC/Channel 7 ended for Kane, who would go on to cement his standing as a broadcasting legend in the City of Brotherly Love.

"He had the art of making it sound like you were the greatest performer in television," Wolf says. "It was just a natural thing for him."

19

From Popularity to Pop Culture

E verything is bigger and better in New York. That's why it's so important, no matter the industry, to arrive in the city. But more urgent, is ensuring not to leave, despite the successful "Plan B" for Larry Kane.

New York is the home to television news, with networks holding their headquarters in Manhattan. All of the "Big 3" local affiliates are just floors away from their "daddy."

So it's no surprise that many of these popular personalities were granted exposure. There was Chuck Scarborough on the now-defunct nightly *NBC News Digest*, those 60-second updates during prime-time commercial breaks. Scarborough, in fact, did some weekend anchoring on the full broadcast. Jim Hartz, who predated Scarborough, got the upgrade to *Today*, until Tom Brokaw came along a few years later. Dave Marash, after bouncing between WCBS and WNBC, found a home as correspondent on ABC's *Nightline*.

At CBS, Rolland Smith didn't "double dip," but when he exited WCBS, the network was waiting for him to co-host their morning show. However, that attempt failed to generate any ratings against powerhouses *Good Morning America* and *Today*.

Kane didn't have a long career in New York, but made the most of it during that tempestuous summer of '77 with appearances on ABC News. Roger

Grimsby filed occasionally for the TV network, including the blackout of that same year. When ABC extended coverage into the overnight hours as Robert F. Kennedy was mortally wounded, Grimsby was brought in to assist in the wee hours.

Aside from the plum broadcasting assignments, you could find these anchors popping up in pop culture. For example, Scarborough is shown reading a story in the 1994 movie *The Paper*. He appeared briefly on some NBC prime-time programs and even the 2011 Matt Damon flick *The Adjustment Bureau*. IMDb lists Scarborough six times as an actor. He is also credited as a reporter in *The Corruptor* from 1999, where Mark Wahlberg plays a cop investigating drug trafficking and corruption (hence the title!) by immigrant Chinese Triads. Scarborough is credited as himself in the 2000 horror flick *Book of Shadows: Blair Witch 2*. In 1976, early in his WNBC popularity, there was Chuck appearing as audience member on *Saturday Night Live*. This was a cameo in the smallest form, unlike his former colleague Brian Williams, who hosted the show in 2007, a first for a sitting network anchor.

When Williams was demoted in 2015, Lester Holt moved into the *NBC Nightly News* chair permanently.

Decades earlier, Holt had a pair of WCBS stints, including weekend anchor duties. His national exposure, of sorts, kicked off when he arrived at CBS' WBBM in Chicago. Midway through his 14 years, Holt made a (very) brief appearance at the end of *The Fugitive* in 1993.

***

Grimsby played himself in a handful of films during his career, including *Bananas*, *Ghostbusters*, *Turk 182*, and *Nothing but Trouble*. He appeared on the small screen on CBS's *The Equalizer* in 1988, playing, of course, a newscaster. At the height of his *Eyewitness News* success, Grimsby took on soaps in back-to-back episodes of *Ryan's Hope* in 1975.

There was also *The Exterminator*, as himself, five years later. A description of the movie from IMDb: "A man's best friend is killed on the streets of New York

City. The man (Robert Ginty) then transforms into a violent killer, turning New York City into a great war zone, and Christopher George is the only one to stop him."

The phrase "straight to video" comes to mind.

Former WNBC and *Today* anchor Jim Hartz worked with Grimsby once, not on the news set, but a movie set. It was the 1986 Sidney Lumet directed *Power*, with an all-star cast: Richard Gere, Julie Christie, Gene Hackman, and Denzel Washington. The script called for two newscasters, Edwin Newman and Hartz. However, Newman contracted the flu and Grimsby was his "understudy."

It included a 40-second shot of the anchors covering a mock election night.

"My recollection is it opened and closed in one week in New York," Hartz said, though he would get residual checks ranging from pennies to a few hundred dollars.

Other than perhaps bumping into each other at functions, this was the only time Hartz and Grimsby spent any time together. "We were not buddies," Hartz said.

Hartz had more interaction with Bill Beutel, who had his own on-screen moments in movies such as *Turk 182* (with Grimsby) and *Hanky Panky*.

However, Hartz said there wasn't much socializing with talent from the other stations. "Everybody had their own drinking holes," he explained.

The year Jim Jensen died he was seen in Spike Lee's *Summer of Sam*. The year Jensen exited WCBS he appeared in Lee's *Girl 6* as "Newscaster Jim."

His longtime partner, Rolland Smith, had his chance in celluloid playing the newscaster in the John Ritter comedy *Hero at Large*.

Being in the media didn't mean you avoided the media glare. No one embodied that more than Rose Ann Scamardella. She appeared as herself in the 1973 drama *Badge 373* starring Robert Duvall, according to IMDb.

But her celebrity reached its crescendo thanks to a certain member of *Saturday Night Live*.

It was the late Gilda Radner who made the Channel 7 anchor/reporter from Brooklyn a national figure, even if the connection to Scamardella was unbeknownst to most viewers outside of the New York metropolitan area.

One of Radner's lingering characters on *SNL* was anchor Rose Ann Roseannadanna, inspired by the former anchor.

Scamardella, although not mentioned directly, was given new recognition in the 2018 documentary *Love, Gilda*, where her Rosannadanna character was prominently featured in the story about the comedian's life.

"God bless Glida Radner," Scamardella told *The New York Times* in 2008. "She was very good for contract negotiations."

The hometown girl turned TV star loved the characterization so much she kept a signed posted from Radner above her office desk with the timeless inscription: "To Rose Ann from Roseannadanna."[1]

Scamardella is known for keeping private and not granting interviews, especially during the *Eyewitness* years, and so it required digging deep to locate this one from the *Village Voice* in 1975.

"Ya know, when I first came to ABC they wanted to change me. They sent me to this lady named Lilyan Wilder who criticized the way I dressed, the way I wore my hair, how I talked," Scamardella told the *Voice*. "She gave me elocution lessons to clean up my Brooklyn accent. I was getting so paranoid about myself and my background! Well, the last straw came when she started making me sing 'April in Paris' at the top of my lungs. I thought, 'Is she kidding?' I stopped going."

She struck a chord with New Yorkers, but of course, none more than in her home borough.

"Everyone in Brooklyn loved [her]," Tracy Egan says.

New York also had a special place in its heart for Sue Simmons, a mainstay at the NBC flagship for over three decades.

---

1. Marlane, J. (1999). *Women in Television News Revisited: Into the Twenty First Century*. Univ. of Texas Press.

She dabbled in Hollywood shortly after her 2012 exit from WNBC, landing on three episodes of *Law & Order: Special Victims Unit* playing a newscaster. Fittingly, she would appear in an episode of *30 Rock* as herself.

Years earlier, there was Simmons as newscaster in the film *The First Wives Club*.

Ernie Anastos, referred to as "Hollywood version of an anchor" earlier in this book, got some newscaster fame on celluloid, including in *Summer of Sam*, *Independence Day*, and *The Sitter*.

20

The Ten O'Clock News

The Big 3 were competing for viewers' attention each night at 6 (or 5) and 11 pm. The late newscast on a given channel could track success directly with the prime-time performers on the network.

However, Channel 5 and Channel 11 were not buoyed by that.

At WNEW (today's WNYW), the independent station owned by Metromedia made a bold step on TV news landscape with the 1967 creation of the *Ten O'Clock News.*

Bill Jorgensen was a charter member of the anchor team. John Roland was a reporter in those early days, before moving into the studio for several decades.

Shortly after the Six Day War in 1967, Roland was dispatched to Egypt the same day. He got some advice from the late Peter Jennings, already a world traveler for ABC News. Roland was dating Jennings's ex-wife Valerie, who connected them. Jennings provided Roland with the name of a college student, who helped his assignment go smoothly.

"If it hadn't been for her, I would have been lost."

Ted Kavanau, hired as the first producer for the Channel 5 program, didn't have a news background. That would quickly change. Within three years he was running the newsroom, and in less than the decade he was instrumental in CNN's launch.

Kavanau went to John Kluge, Metromedia president, requesting he buy a building across from WNEW's East 67th Street studios, giving all staffers good deals on rent and have them ready to work at a moment's notice.

"He wanted everybody to work as hard as he did," Roland said. "He was just amazing."

While eyes were on *Eyewitness* and the other two stations each night, Channel 5 was finding its own niche at the earlier hour.

"Everybody watched the *Ten O'Clock News*," Roland said.

Especially commuters, who were tucked in before the 11 pm newscasts. So Channel 5 went for a heavy focus on Long Island.

"We had a solid reputation," Roland said. "When something big was going on, you turned on *the Ten O'Clock News*."

They also had virtually no competition. Only WPIX was a news option in that hour, but they were miles behind the Metromedia product.

"They were a blip," Roland said.

Before his historic run with WNEW/WNYW, Roland was on KNBC in Los Angeles (well technically "Beautiful, downtown Burbank"), working with Tom Brokaw. During the 1965 Watts riots, Roland was at the assignment desk when he was questioned a few times by an unknown person on the phone. Ultimately, Roland, overwhelmed by the hectic nature of the ever-changing story, told the man, "Get the fuck out of here!"

The next day he expected a pat on the back from his boss for their coverage. Instead, Roland was told the person at the other end of his expletive was Reuven Frank, a top NBC News executive.

"I was one the best assignment editors they ever had, and that is where I would be for the rest of my career because of what I said to Reuven Frank," Roland said. "What a small-minded son of a gun he turned out to be."

Knowing his on-air career was dead on arrival at NBC, Roland began to network. He connected with Marty Haig, who was looking to inject youth into Metromedia's Los Angeles base KTTV. Roland was hired and quickly made a name for himself, covering the Manson trial and on the scene as Robert Kennedy was assassinated.

His reports would incorporate newscasts on Metromedia stations in other markets, notably the biggest of the bunch, NYC. That meant Kavanau was seeing packages nightly from the budding reporter and a position followed.

"In those days, you had to work in New York," Roland recalled. "I packed my bags and I arrived in New York on December 26, 1969."

The fledgling *Ten O'Clock News* was only in operation since March of 1967. And with riots in various cities that summer, including in Newark, WNEW created an opening line for the broadcast that would become its signature for decades.

"It's 10 pm, do you know where your children are?"

If Mel Epstein, director of on-air promotions, was the man behind the phrase, Tom Gregory was the voice. Gregory was the baritone announcer who belted out the famous line for decades as sights and sounds from the city flashed across the screen.

But, Gregory and the iconic "Do you know where . . ." opening actually started with his anchoring *Faces and Names in the News*, a precursor to the *Ten O'Clock News*.

When Roland arrived in New York, he had no friends or family in place to ease the cross-country transition. Channel 5 put up their new street reporter at the Roosevelt Hotel.

"In those days we'd do four-five stories a day," Roland said. This was the era where not only was film time-consuming to develop, it was still black and white.

Roland's stock rose and he landed weekend anchor and co-anchor slots on the main show. In 1979, when Jorgensen bolted for WPIX, Roland assumed the lead role on the *Ten O'Clock News*.

Roland, a Pittsburgh native, died in 2023 at the age of 81. He would have a three-decade run at Fox (and pre-Fox) in New York.

"Ted was never a big fan of anchormen," Roland reflected. "He liked reporting and fast-moving news programs. He didn't want anchormen's faces on the air. He thought that we slowed things down and got in the way of the news. If he would have had his way, you would never [have] seen an anchorman."

Kavanau had a bittersweet relationship with Jorgensen.

"I was constantly having a war with [him]," Kavanau says. "He was a great anchor, but a very difficult guy. When he got on the air, he was perfection."

"Yeah, we had a lot of disagreements," Jorgensen admitted. "But in many ways Ted was very innovative."

One heated exchange led to a format change on the broadcast.

"Because I was angry with him, I actually decided to have four anchors," Kavanau says.

So Roland recently transferred from Metromedia in Los Angeles, joined Bill McCreary, George Sharman, and Jorgensen.

As the *Sunday Record* pointed out in a 1972 article, "Jorgensen said he makes more money at Metromedia than everyone except the chairman of the board."

It also said Jorgensen was forced to become incorporated; otherwise his tax bracket would allow the Internal Revenue Service to confiscate his paycheck.

Jorgensen, with his chiseled Norwegian looks, was a powerhouse at Metromedia's New York outlet. The *Ten O'Clock News* doubled to 60 minutes in those early days. During that time, Jorgensen said Sharman was hired as his backup, "in case I departed."

Jorgensen didn't consider his mid-1970s colleagues much in the way of competition.

"It can be considered sour grapes, I suppose," Jorgensen said at the time. "I frankly don't have a very deep respect for many of the people that are on the air here today. I think that many of them have prostituted themselves to the problems that are specific to New York and unique to New York."

He was so popular in Cleveland before going to New York, Jorgensen dropped a bombshell that he was offered to replace Walter Cronkite as anchor of the *CBS Evening News* in 1963. Jorgensen said the ratings were terrible in that first year for Cronkite, and network brass started searching for Uncle Walter's replacement. Jorgensen got a call from a VP of news at CBS. He said they wanted him for the high-profile job, but Jorgensen stayed loyal to employers at WEWS.

"Why would I ever want to go to New York?" Jorgensen admitted. "For six or eight weeks they were after me to come to New York, and I would not do it."

Of course, by November 22, 1963, no one was thinking about replacing Cronkite as his voice had led Americans through the trauma of the President John F. Kennedy assassination.

Don Hewitt, known for his long association with *60 Minutes*, is credited with first coining the term "anchor" to describe Cronkite. That might not be completely accurate. But it was the 1952 political conventions when Cronkite shined in a way the burgeoning medium hadn't seen.

In March of that year, the *Chicago Tribune* outlining plans for Cronkite, CBS's Washington bureau chief, labeled him as "anchor man of the CBS crew."

By July, ahead of the Republican convention, the *Hartford Courant* detailed Cronkite as "anchor man" who would be tasked with "coordinating switches from one news point or reporter to anchor."[1]

Unaware of how close Jorgensen came to unseating "Uncle Walter," their interaction years later would be tension-free.

"I tell my writers I want them to write like you sound," Jorgensen recalled what Cronkite told him. "I thought it was the greatest damn compliment I had heard professionally in a longtime." "The deal was, I had a guarantee that I would have at least 40 percent of the show every night," Jorgensen said.

Jorgensen was a journalist who did a lot of his own stories, especially the lead.

Ultimately, Jorgensen, who could be crusty with his bosses (or vice versa), was able to sever his Metromedia contract.

"I liked what I did, but I had a lot of disagreements with management about integrity," Jorgensen said. "[It's] a primary word in my life. I felt that they had done some things that were immoral or wrong."

The veteran anchor had a verbal agreement to leave Channel 5/Metromedia if he could be part of a TV network. A contract dispute expedited his departure in 1979. It wasn't a standard network, but Jorgensen headed to WPIX. He joined Channel 11 to become the cornerstone of their flagship *Independent News Network*.

---

1. Zimmer, Ben. "Was Cronkite Really the First 'Anchorman?'" Slate Magazine, July 18, 2009.

It was a homecoming of sorts, as *INN* hired John Corporon to oversee the same person who ran the *Ten O'Clock News* at its inception a dozen years previous.

The independent network got clearance for 23 stations when it debuted in 1980. It increased to more than 100 outlets before Tribune Broadcasting replaced Jorgensen, Steve Bosh, and Pat Harper in 1985 with Morton Dean on a rebranded *USA Tonight.*

While speaking on a low-budget show called *Personalities with Jessie Gray,* prior to the INN announcement, Harper said it was still speculation, but "they've talked about of it at quite some length, so I would suspect it's closer to being a reality than it was three or four months ago when we first did the initial programs for it."

Years earlier, Corporon put Harper and Harper together. The once-married Pat and Joe anchored in the mid-1970s, but he claims it was not a ratings ploy.

"I think they thought it was," Corporon said. "It never entered my thinking. I didn't care if they got [re]married."

But at the press conference to announce Harper and Harper, Corporon said, they mentioned (likely in tongue-in-cheek fashion) that they might reconcile, which kept extra eyes on the gossip column, not just their newscasts.

They didn't get back together, remaining friends, making their teaming like Sonny and Cher, who went from popular married couple to separated and finally bitterly divorced, all in front of millions each week. For the most part, they could fool the public about their personal strife. Occasionally, Sonny and Cher would play it up in the monologue, but like the chemistry of a winning anchor team, it worked.

Having already hired Joe, Corporon then added Pat to his team that included sportscaster Jerry Girard, who would become a fixture for more than 20 years.

"I thought she was the best woman anchor I'd ever worked with. She was a sensation," Corporon said.

However, Corporon didn't recall if he was actively seeking a woman anchor or if she was simply the best person for the job.

Although not a minority, it was still a trailblazing move for WPIX in 1974, and lifted Harper, who initially referred to herself as "Patricia," into the pantheon of first female anchors in New York.

Did Harper ever deal with sexual discrimination?

"Never," Harper said in an interview while still at WPIX.

Harper began her career in Philadelphia in 1959, and was up for the *Today* show writer/researcher gig two years later, which ultimately went to Barbara Walters.

"I wanted that job so badly," Harper said.

She thought her news experience would serve her well for the network opportunity.

"It didn't work that way," Harper would reflect years later.

Crashing the party of the old (or not so old) boys club of anchors made Harper a target, but Corporon said it wasn't much and didn't linger.

"There were some instances of hate mail and some crazy nut calls, but it was so minor we didn't even discuss."

Rather, he says the overwhelming majority of reaction was mostly positive.

"People really loved her," Corporon said.

WNBC management, seizing on that, poached Harper from WPIX/INN and sat her next to Chuck Scarborough starting in 1984. The 6 pm newscast would win five straight Emmy Awards. She was the first woman to regularly co-anchor that broadcast.[2]

"I thought they were a dream team," Corporon admitted.

She also won a trophy for famously venturing out on the street as an undercover homeless woman.

Corporon, her former WPIX boss, who stayed in touch, says she didn't like how that special series was portrayed.

---

2. Halper, Donna L. *Invisible Stars: A Social History of Women in American Broadcasting*. Armonk, NY: M.E. Sharpe, 2001.

"She resented that. She thought she had been exploited. Even though it was a success, it really bothered her that she had done it," Corporon admitted. "Although that's irrelevant. She did it and it worked."

In the first part of her news career, Harper said she was assigned to cover "fluff." She got to handle hard news, because management finally got creative.

"It was their imagination, their sense of theatrics," Harper said. "It was the ratings game."

Apparently, those interviewed by Harper on park benches and elsewhere were the ones really exploited in a 1987 week-long sweeps piece and a 30-minute special *There, but for the Grace of God.*

The Working Poor in America: A Sourcebook for Journalists says Harper's subjects were not told about the hidden cameras/microphones, thus violating their privacy and robbing their dignity.[3]

Despite her popularity and depth as reporter and anchor, it didn't move the needle in a big way for women, especially one with experience in the 50+ age group. Management decided that she was too old for viewers, a sentiment that would repeat in 2019 with a major lawsuit by NY1 talent.

After a strong start for the Scarborough/Harper tandem, the ratings began a steady nosedive. The *New York Post* broached the subject in 1991, saying that Harper became a target of five news directors during her time at Channel 4. The feeling was she didn't work hard enough, wanted to spend more time in her Spain home, and didn't want to get out in the field. So, the die was cast.

Jerry Nachman who hired Harper at WNBC, at or about her 50th birthday, told the *Post* that "TV men can age on-camera. They can be bald and fat, but women must remain attractive."

Harper and her $750,000 salary were parlayed into a $500,000 savings for the station with the hiring of Dawn Fratangelo, a much younger brunette.

A 1991 *New York* magazine headline made it clear that "Anchors Get Younger and Blonder."

---

3. *The Working Poor in America.* Washington, DC: National Academies Press, 1990.

The same *New York Post* blurb also highlighted another female anchor, Kaity Tong, who had a farewell party at WABC after much of the last decade there alongside Roger Grimsby, Bill Beutel, John Johnson, and Tom Snyder.

When Tong took maternity leave in 1986, there were internal rumblings that she wouldn't survive bad ratings and could be made the sacrificial lamb. The handwriting was on the wall four years before her exit. After a maternity leave, Tong says her boss Walter Liss admitted her 11 pm newscast was number one, but he wanted "a much bigger number 1," and discussed "his vision for what television should be and should look like for the 90s."

When the time came in 1991, Tong was replaced by Susan Roesgen, who worked in several markets but never clicked in New York, lasting just one year.

The group Coalition of Asian-American New Yorkers suggested that Tong's Chinese-American background was the cause for her exit.

Tong, 41 at the time, also made a $750,000 annual salary when she was cut loose. It was "strictly a business decision," meaning the company (Capital Cities/ABC) would get a bargain deal in the replacement.

In a letter to *New York* magazine shortly after the anchor swap, Timothy Tung wrote, "As far as viewers are concerned, what's the difference between Tong and her replacement?" He goes on to say that they are both competent newsreaders and pleasant to look at. "Since these replacements are usually younger and prettier, TV station general managers are making good business sense by replacing older anchors."

Tung concludes, "Though I am Chinese-American, I don't need to watch news read by a Chinese face that's worth $750,000."

However, by early 1992, Tong's iconic run was underway at WPIX and there was no let up in sight through May 2024. Recognized for more than four decades of anchoring in New York, Tong earned the prestigious Governor's Award from the New York Emmys in 2018.

Tong has the unique distinction of being linked with some of the city's top anchors: Grimsby, Snyder, Johnson, Beutel and Anastos at WABC, and Jack Cafferty for her first six years at WPIX.

***

Jorgensen, who died in 2024 at age 96, kept that familiar deep gravelly voice late into life, although distant memories took a bit longer to become words. Arguably, his most famous words would come at the end of each broadcast, "Thank you for your time this time until next time."

He estimated doing 6,484 live broadcasts, not to mention 35 movies, and his baritone sound was also featured in numerous voice-overs, including a few years as Tony the Tiger in Kellogg's Frosted Flakes ads.

"Ordinarily, news people are averse to doing anything commercial," Jorgensen said. "I broke the rule, my own rule."

One thing you never saw during Kavanau's tenure at Channel 5: a woman anchoring. He left the station abruptly in 1974, following a dispute with VP/GM Larry Fraiberg.

While Al Primo is recognized for creating the brash *Eyewitness News* format for WABC, Kavanau is on equal ground for his innovations at WNEW that would become staples.

He created the whip-around, where reporters in the field throw to each other, instead of directly back to the anchors in the studio.

"I put a camera in the newsroom. I think it was first newsroom camera in television."

It's a technique that enhanced breaking news coverage.

"He probably created some things that people will never give him credit for today," Jorgensen said.

"There were so many small things in production and coverage that we did," Kavanau recalls. "We were always trying to do something different . . . from the cookie-cutter ways newscasts were done."

He also enacted the first teases on a broadcast, showing a few reporters (usually taped) giving a few seconds of their story, name, and location.

Kavanau may not have created crime stories, but he put an extra focus on them in the nightly broadcast. Roland confessed to *New York* magazine in 1977, "I'm not sure whether that is good or bad."

However, Jorgensen had a less gray take on that topic. "It was disgusting to all of us because Ted's idea of continuity was to put a rape, next to a murder, next to a robbery—an entire violence section." WNEW news director successor Mark Monsky would cut back on the "if it bleeds, it leads" theme.

Still, the staff wasn't above staying protected.

"A lot of people in the newsroom had guns, including me and Monsky. Thank God we never had to use them," Kavanau says. "It probably would have been a disaster."

The pioneering *Ten O'Clock News* man, Kavanau also was behind the hire of Martin Abend—a name largely lost to time, who helped set the tone for Channel 5 in those nascent days.

Monsky, who died in 2006, told *New York* magazine in 1977 that Abend was the "voice of people who don't have a voice . . . 'I'm the one getting it in the neck, and I'm pissed.' Who's gonna speak for them? Eric Sevareid?"

Kavanau says it wasn't smooth sailing from the start for the controversial commentator. Kavanau, who was the producer at the time, had a connection to Abend while they taught at Ithaca College—Abend in political science, Kavanau in the TV department.

"A lot of people in the news department didn't like him, didn't like his politics," Kavanau says. "Other stations had commentators, but they were all liberal."

The battle lines were set in the sand, to the point that newsroom staffers actually created a petition to get Abend off the air.

A key player in the Abend crisis was Ed Turner, news director at WTTG in Washington and executive in charge of news at all Metromedia stations. Turner came to New York to see firsthand how bad the Abend firestorm was.

After a week or two, as Kavanau recalls, it was Turner's decision that Abend was vital for the newscast.

"He was a national treasure and should be advising in the White House," Kavanau says about Turner's over-the-top recommendation.

To quell the one-sided rhetoric, Sidney Offit was brought in to provide a liberal point of view as a counterbalance to Abend, marking one of the earliest political debates on a nightly newscast. In the 1970s, Kavanau says *60 Minutes* would "imitate" them with its Point/Counterpoint segment.

It would prove so popular that *Saturday Night Live* did a parody between Dan Ackroyd and Jane Curtin, leading to the famous line, "Jane, you ignorant slut!"

21

Melba, Martin, and John

Melba Tolliver is one of the more decorated and intriguing characters to appear on TV sets in New York. Her blog and once-planned memoir are titled *Accidental Anchorwoman*.

Tolliver got a foot in the door at ABC News as a secretary to an executive, Donald Coe. Truthfully, journalism wasn't on her radar in 1966.

"I took the job really because I thought I wanted to be a researcher, not knowing what researchers in television news did," Tolliver admits. "But it sounded like that would be something I would love to do."

Up until this point, Tolliver was a registered nurse. Her new career path did not include on-air aspirations.

"I didn't have a real master plan, I just figured, I liked reading . . . meeting people, finding things out, and researcher seemed like that could be a real interesting job," Tolliver recalls.

Tolliver, a 28-year-old at the time, says maybe somewhere in the back of her mind, getting on camera piqued her curiosity. But she claims that's not why she accepted the position.

In the next decade, Tolliver would become a trailblazer in local news, but as her book title indicates, it was a man's world, with her having no intention of breaking that glass ceiling.

"Come on, this was 1966," Tolliver laughs. "I just followed what comes next."

While she does recognize that she fits the definition of a trailblazer, Tolliver also admits she isn't comfortable using the label herself.

"It makes me sound like Davy Crockett," she jokes.

Happenstance and talent brought Tolliver to the eyes of viewers and a new look from management at ABC. In March 1967, members of the Screen Actors Guild went on strike, including Marlene Sanders, host of the daily afternoon show *News with a Woman's Touch*.

Execs scrambled to find a temporary replacement and Tolliver's boss suggested the extremely novice, pretty personality. She had done some modeling and took acting classes, which was enough to placate the network brass. After the meeting, Tolliver was alerted that she was the fill-in for Sanders—that night! When the red light went on, Tolliver had made history as the first African-American to anchor a network news program.

Tolliver, who turned 84 in 2023, never practiced with a teleprompter or even toured the studio. But that was about to drastically change.

"There wasn't anyone else to be found, because we were all secretaries," Tolliver laughs. "If the show was just called News at 2, or something like that, it probably wouldn't have mattered."

It was a five-minute broadcast with the non-politically correct title. And as you'd probably imagine, the content was slanted to the large number of housewives in the viewing audience.

The strike lasted 13 days, ending in time for broadcast of the Academy Awards that night. Despite a fortnight of fame, Tolliver says it was only a brief detour from her original TV path.

"This was a break in my plans, which was to become a researcher," Tolliver says.

She also admits that first time news anchoring was scary, but a great learning experience seeing how the show was produced. However, union rules forbade Tolliver from writing her own material for the broadcast.

Despite its title, *News with a Woman's Touch*, which aired at 2:55 between *Dream Girl of '67* and *General Hospital*, brought a pedigree of serious journalism to the afternoon.

"*Eyewitness News* was the breakthrough in local news reporting," Tolliver, interviewed for a 40th anniversary video of the newscast, said. "Prior to that you had the sole, white anchorman sitting in the studio telling people about what happened."

***

Sanders, the mother of author and former CNN legal analyst Jeffrey Toobin, notched many firsts for females in television news. She was the first woman to anchor at night for a network. Serving as correspondent in Vietnam was another milestone moment for her.

Sanders spent more than a decade at ABC before being named VP of the news division, another female first in the business. Prior to joining ABC in 1964, Sanders was a writer, producer, and reporter at WNEW-TV.

She ended her broadcasting career at CBS News, before becoming an adjunct professor at New York University. Sanders died in 2015.

Even the previous anchor of *Woman's Touch*, Lisa Howard, had the legit journalistic chops. A career change from acting led her to reporting for radio, including the Democratic National Convention in 1960 and being the first American to interview Nikita Khrushchev.

At ABC she was the first woman hired as a correspondent, and in 1963 she was given top billing when *News with a Woman's Touch* was created. At the time, *McCall's* magazine, showing the juxtaposition, called her a "dead-serious reporter," but also "bright, buxom, and bumptious."

That same year, she traveled to Cuba for a special with Fidel Castro. The story is largely lost to history, but the White House took notice of Howard's ties with Castro and Cuba. Top-secret documents from that time speculated about a "physical relationship" between Howard and Castro.[1] There was also concern that she would use her position at the network to break the story about Washington's secret talks with the Cuban dictator. However, shortly after Lyndon Johnson moved into the White House, her clandestine liaison role was over. Howard leapfrogged the White House to back-channel discussions with the UN ambassador, and former presidential candidate, Adlai Stevenson. Concern grew that Stevenson's involvement would mean more media attention and scrutiny the news of the back channel leaked.

Sadly, her career and life spiraled thereafter. With her Cuban connection dried up, ABC News cut her position. The dominoes would keep falling for the reporter who had powerful friends.

Her 1964 participation in the "Democrats for Keating," a group of liberals who opposed Robert Kennedy's senatorial bid, caused ABC to suspend her. She was fired after the election.

After suffering a miscarriage, she took her own life on July 4, 1965, with a barbiturate overdose. She was 39.

***

As for Tolliver, she remains conflicted about the *News with a Woman's Touch* title.

"It wasn't about baking or cooking," Tolliver recalls. "It was a deliberate appeal to women who were home."

Yet, it was a lucky break for the burgeoning journalist. The civil rights movement was heating up in the south, but she faced no opposition there or anywhere else in the country. Tolliver says viewers just reveled in her Cinderella story and not the color of her skin.

"I personally never got any backlash," Tolliver says.

---

1. Kornbluh, Peter. "'My Dearest Fidel': An ABC Journalist's Secret Liaison with Fidel Castro." Politico, April 20, 2018.

While initially she was content with resuming a behind-the-scenes career, Tolliver says she felt compelled to become a stronger voice for Blacks as the country was in upheaval.

"It was the year of the long, hot summer, the rioting, [and] the subsequent Kerner Commission report," Tolliver says.

The class system for African Americans with high rates of poverty and unemployment came to a head with riots in prominently Black cities such as Newark, New Jersey and Detroit, Michigan. Protesting became violent as (the seemingly always topical) police brutality became another defining cause (and effect).

The oppression started to boil over in 1964, with a white police officer shooting a Black youth in Harlem. Violence bubbled up in the next couple of years. However, as an unfortunate bookend to the Summer of Love, 1967 is when the racial divide ripped at the seams. More than 150 American cities saw major uprisings, with over 100 deaths.

In 1968, the assassination of Martin Luther King Jr. led to another round of rebellion in dozens of communities.

All parts of society were making changes, including the news media. ABC took steps to create a news internship for minorities, and Tolliver was again in the right place at the right time.

After completing a training program at New York University School of Journalism, she was hired as a news reporter in October 1968. The talents of Tolliver burgeoning, her duties included weekend anchor and public affairs host.

The one-time nurse at Bellevue Hospital, would launch her television career at the height of the country's civil rights unrest. For Tolliver, that meant her personal and professional life would be display in the most public way.

Tolliver grabbed a regular reporter spot on *Eyewitness News* with occasional anchoring. Her star was rising among the rag-tag, if talented, broadcasters.

She reached her zenith professionally when assigned to cover the wedding of President Nixon's daughter Tricia to Edward Cox at the White House in 1971. It was a line-in-the-sand moment for Tolliver and her bosses. She gained national attention as she opted to change her hair to a natural look. That one move changed her entire career, as she became an instant celebrity. Management ordered her to straighten the locks on her head, or Tolliver would lose valuable airtime. She would be removed from studio appearances to discuss the wedding if her hair stayed in an Afro style. But Tolliver refused to change back to the less confrontational look. She wasn't suspended, but her live reports were scrubbed, and even taped pieces almost didn't air. If not for a *New York Post* article explaining her follicle folly, Tolliver believes WABC would have gotten rid of her without much groundswell.

"I didn't think they would be jumping up, saying 'Oh, it's so beautiful!' but I didn't expect them to have as drastic a reaction as they had."

Despite that, letters from viewers were, largely, accepting. There was one exception she recalled, as a person who identified himself as Black called Tolliver's dramatic hair change, "a disgrace to Black people."

While taking the stand was important personally, Tolliver was mostly trying to do her best, filing assignments on deadline.

She received only positive feedback in the newsroom, although Roger Grimsby did deliver an off-the-record comment on the hot topic. Tolliver was told secondhand that he said her hair looked like a Brillo pad. When Tolliver confronted him years later, he denied making the racially insensitive statement.

That remark aside, she was never harmed personally by any on-air jabs from the late anchorman.

Tolliver used her on-air style to address the late 1960s tumult facing African Americans, considering the camera and microphone her best tools to tell the much-needed story. It was her version of being on the front lines.

She did claim that the move to allow her original hair style to show wasn't premeditated and certainly wasn't done with any malicious intent.

"This was something I wanted to do for quite a while," Tolliver admits. "This wasn't taking anything about ABC or WABC into consideration."

Any thoughts of being a trailblazer were quickly dashed, as she says her reasons were selfish.

Once ABC management cooled down and restored her on air, primarily due to viewer outrage, she used it as an opportunity for a special show called the *African Influence on American Style*.

Honchos at the Alphabet Network were criticized for the stance, even by people who didn't like her new look. She recalls one such letter saying the ABC bosses had a hell of a nerve telling her how to wear her hair.

The late Gwen Ifill, from the *PBS NewsHour*, said her role model was Tolliver.

"[She] was the only African American woman I'd ever seen on television. She had a big Afro, and when we turned on our black-and-white set, there she was," Ifill said in a 2014 interview with *Explorations in Black Leadership*. "I never met her, but she left a very big impression on me. I didn't want to be on television, but here was a Black woman asking the questions."

For Tolliver, that is the legacy she is most proud of.

"That was just incredible. I was an admirer of hers."

The Peabody Award-winning journalist, Ifill, died in 2015.

While Tolliver enjoyed her victory with the fans and the network, a former colleague says she should have done more.

"She would have a good shot had she sued them," John Johnson says. "I think something more should have been made of it in the courts."

Johnson successfully sued ABC for civil rights violations—after working for the company.

"You can make a statement, but unless you do something that codifies in law and makes it a statement in law, nothing in the long run will happen," he says.

Tolliver did take legal action during her time at WNBC. Although not a lawsuit, the anchor went to arbitration.

After taking a one-year sabbatical for a fellowship from the University of Michigan, Tolliver was back on TV as co-anchor with Pia Lindström in 1978. When ratings for their 5 pm broadcast failed to move the needle, she was relocated to early mornings for cut-ins during the *Today* show.

"I thought we were pretty good," Lindström recalls. "People said we were pretty good. I thought it was an interesting combination."

Tolliver and Lindström held the distinction as New York's first female anchor team, but were they trailblazing? "No, I don't think in those terms. I wasn't trying to blaze a trail," Lindström laughs. "I was trying to keep a job."

Tolliver admits, "I felt my contract did not allow for him to just remove me from anchoring."

Wanting Tolliver's talent so badly, WNBC paid for half of her salary while on the teaching break.

"Maybe I should have learned from John Johnson," Tolliver admits.

Once at 30 Rock, she was given headliner status for her own newscast, *Melba and Company*. Short-lived, they placed her with Lindström before the bottom dropped out when Kershaw took over.

"I wasn't fired; I just refused to go in," Tolliver says about her move to mornings. "That was the last thing I would want to do."

Ultimately, Tolliver lost in arbitration and was forced to finish out her contract, "which made me one of the highest paid general assignment reporters," because it was not renegotiated.

"The guy [Kershaw] was wacko, so I have no idea what was in his mind," Tolliver says about racial overtones. "I never knew him well and I certainly wasn't one of his favorites."

As for Lindström, she remained an anchor on *NewsCenter 4* into 1979, when she gave up her role as theater critic, thinking that she was "really doing well."

"And then it was gone," she says. "Then I didn't have the theater reviewing job anymore because I had given it up, and Katie Kelly took it."

But Lindström, who persevered at WNBC for the next 17 years, understands the fluidity of broadcasting.

"If you don't like that type of business, you shouldn't be in there," she says of the industry.

She took on various interview subjects and reporter opportunities at Channel 4 in New York City. But medical reporter eluded her, despite her lineage.

Her father, Petter, was a neurosurgeon, whose marriage with Ingrid Bergman ended when the famed actress forged a relationship with Italian director Roberto Rossellini. Her stepmother was a pediatrician.

However, she maintained the entertainment connection at WNBC, primarily with celebrity interviews in brief segments.

"It's almost embarrassing to run around saying, 'Can I talk to you for a minute and a half?'" Lindström jokes. 'Tell me about your life in two minutes.'"

She also covered the red carpet many times at the Oscars, a trophy her legendary mom won three times. But she says that didn't have a bearing on her career trajectory.

"The way it works is, people are curious and they might want to see you and say hello. But they don't keep you working for years and years," Lindström says.

***

"The broadcast landscape was so different," Carol Martin says. "Who knew that back then, but it feels as if it was."

Martin, a Detroit native, started her professional on-air career in 1975 in Washington, DC. She never aspired to become a TV anchor. Her dream was to produce children's shows when she attended college, leading to a journalism major at Wayne State University.

The female anchor, today a standard part of every newscast, was almost nonexistent. That's why Martin didn't even "go there" in her mind and had no role model in the business.

But Martin relied on her strong writing until she was positioned for a career-path change.

"A series of things happened that I think had all to do with Affirmative Action," she said.

Ed Joyce, the former news director at WCBS, praised her abilities in his autobiography. He cited Martin as one of the reporters he found "who could write and report their stories with flair and style without degenerating into the silliness that plagues some local television."

"What a lovely lady," Rolland Smith gushes. "She had the ability just to put you at ease with her smile and her soft way of communicating. I loved her. I still do."

Fresh out of college, Martin wrote for the Detroit News station, WWJ, doing public service announcements.

"It was a nothing job. I think I made $75 a week," Martin recalls.

It was the station of venerable Mort Crim, who Will Ferrell's *Anchorman* character is based on.

While working in DC, Martin got a call from WCBS news director Eric Ober. They were taking serious notice of the up-and-coming reporter/anchor and wanted to have a conversation about her future.

After thinking someone was pranking her, Ober convinced Martin that it was legit.

"I was blown away," Martin recalls. "But I didn't have aspirations to live here."

Humble to a fault, Martin was almost willing to sell herself short and forgo the major move north. "Because being a Black woman, maybe subconsciously this was in my mind, 'What are you going to do? There's nobody who's doing anything more than this. This is a decent job.'"

Although she wasn't quite ready to hit the top market, Martin did turn the interview into a $2,000 raise in Washington.

"I go back to the newsroom and I was like a queen."

It leaked that she came close to the WCBS gig, causing people to gush, "You might work with Jim Jensen?"

But Martin was not as enthralled.

"I don't know these guys," Martin would say. "I just didn't have that deep an ambition."

In October 1975, Ober made good on his promise to reconnect with Martin. She was hired, beginning a 19-year run at WCBS. She came in the door, joining established stars Smith, Jensen, and Marash.

"It was a team to be proud of being a part of," she said.

Still light on ladies, her best friends at the "Deuce" were reporter Chris Borgen and anchor/reporter Vic Miles. She says the first-time meeting with Rolland Smith and Dave Marash was as smooth as their on-air personas. Her introductory hello with Jim Jensen, however, caused some angst.

"It was cool, but I remember I was so nervous," Martin says. "I didn't know what I was up against just to meet Jim."

However, Jensen couldn't have been nicer, encouraging her to ask him for advice at any time.

Martin didn't take up the offer, but says she never had a problem with the veteran anchorman. Five years later, Martin and Jensen would begin a daily on-air partnership at 6 o'clock.

"I miss him even now," Martin reflects. "He was a complicated human being, but a lot of tough things happened to him."

As is the case when people work so closely for many years, "their problems became our problems," Martin says. It was an era of "every man (or woman) for themselves," but she thinks that camaraderie is gone. "Today, I don't know if that's how it feels."

Right around the time of her maternity leave for her only daughter in 1980, Martin assumed weekend anchoring with John Tesh, several years before he exploded on a national level at *Entertainment Tonight*.

When Martin returned, she was upgraded to weeknights, remaining entrenched for the next 14 years. Her first desk mate was Tony Guida on the 5 pm, before her tandem with Jensen at 6.

"It was probably the best times of life, and I didn't even know it," Martin says.

However, an earlier attempt to put her opposite Jensen hadn't worked out.

"It wasn't like it was job-threatening," Martin recalls. "I think they were just trying it out."

Eventually, Martin would co-anchor the newly created noon broadcast along with the 5 and/or the 6 pm.

"That was my terrain; it became my safe haven."

Safe or not, it wasn't always easy. In 1979, Jensen started a downward spiral, dealing with substance abuse and depression after his son Randall's death. The junior Jensen was killed in a hang-glider crash.

"It really spilled over to all of our jobs," Martin recalls. "CBS was exemplary in giving him as much support as he could have."

If Jensen wasn't battling demons, Martin thinks it could have been different for her as well.

"If Jim and I had been like Sue and Chuck, I might have still been there. You never know," Martin says. "It was a difficult work situation, and it rolled through the 80s and into the 90s."

At the height of Jensen's struggle with his demons, viewers watched an infamously awkward exchange with WCBS anchor Bree Walker in 1988. Walker just completed a report about her rare birth defect that leads to fused fingers. Jensen, dropping many jaws, asked her, "Have you ever discussed this with your parents, had there been the technology available then, and they had known about your condition before you were born, would they have aborted you?"

It was clearly a tension-filled studio, and likely for viewers as well.

"Everyone was dying," co-anchor Martin remembers. "You could have heard a pin drop."

But Jensen wasn't done. Knowing that Walker's condition could be spread genetically, Jensen asked if she would abort if her children showed signs of the defects.

"Well, I consider that a personal question," Walker responds. "I would not. I would not, and I'll answer your personal question, because I personally don't think this is a very big deal, and I have very strong feelings about that."

She eventually had two children who inherited the condition.

While Jensen is grilling Walker, Martin does not interfere. She seems momentarily thrown off, and they can't get to the commercials fast enough.

"I wouldn't have said a word beyond that to save my life. I just wanted it to stop," Martin says.

Once the two-minute session is over and Martin and Jensen are back on camera, she has a look reminiscent of WNYW's Dari Alexander years later: her mouth open in stunned disbelief when Ernie Anastos made his infamous "keep plucking those chickens" remark.

Martin is not as demonstrative, but equally shocked. For two seconds that feel like two weeks, there is silence, until Jensen finally tosses it to his colleague with a "Carol."

It's subtle, but her "OK" as she clasps her hands was akin to, "Why did you do that? And, "Did I have to go through that with you?"

"Nobody, when we went to break, said a word," Martin says.

She also doesn't think Jensen apologized for the personal questions.

"He was not a mean-spirited kind of guy that way, but I literally don't think he had a clue what it sounded like."

There were other, less controversial moments, showing a lack of focus from the once great anchor. There's a time when he blames the "new computerized system, which is supposed to modernize everything, and it's set us back about two centuries" as the reason for his embarrassing fumbling of the next script.

After Jensen's death in 1999, Howard Stern, who frequently mocked the anchorman's drug abuse, reflected on the Walker faux pas.

"What a nut," Stern said about the on-air abortion question.

When Stern was fired by WNBC in 1984, he made the rounds for local TV interviews. There was Jensen for the one-on-one. Stern recalls he wore the top half of a suit and jeans under the desk away out of camera view. After the short conversation, Jensen gave Stern a big hug and handshake.

Martin says aside from the odd exchange, Jensen didn't act any differently, so it was hard to know which version of the "franchise" would show up on set.

He was accused of acting like Ted Baxter at least once, when a producer gave the stage direction to Jensen in the teleprompter: "Ad-lib to sports here," which he promptly read on air.

Despite Jensen's illness, the veteran anchorman had the backing of his newsroom. Still, Martin maintains the unexpected nature was an unfortunate part of Jensen's addiction.

"You didn't know for sure what he was going to do any given day at that point in time," Martin says. "God, may he rest in peace, if he was sitting with us tonight he wouldn't even remember that. I guarantee you. He was so far out of there. He was really not well."

Martin didn't anchor the high-profile 11 pm news, and that was by design, because she wanted to be home at night to raise her young child. By the early 1990s, she was increasingly frustrated by changes at Channel 2.

"Here's how the universe goes, I used to pray that I wouldn't have to drive across the GW Bridge one more day . . . I wanted to try something else."

In 1994, that new venture was the Roger Ailes's now-defunct *America's Talking* cable network in Fort Lee.

Former Cleveland mayor Carl Stokes broke the color barrier when WNBC hired him as the city's first African American anchor in 1972.

His niece, Lori Stokes, a popular figure for 17 years of morning news on WABC before joining WNYW/Fox 5, says she's proud to have her uncle's Emmy from WNBC.

"He loved being with the people, relating to them," Stokes says. "He told me to have a thick skin, but to be compassionate and find the difference in telling a story."

"[It] was an interesting and curious experiment, but I don't think anybody thought it worked particularly well," Dave Marash says of Carl Stokes's on-air work.

The elder Stokes was given *The Sixth Hour* news, where ratings needed a serious injection opposite upstart *Eyewitness News* on WABC and perennial also-ran WCBS with Jim Jensen.

The Grimsby/Beutel broadcast averaged 1.5 million viewers, a big drop-off for "The Deuce," with 1 million tuned in. But WNBC, at the time of the Stokes decision, could only muster 650,000 viewers for the early evening news.

John Chancellor, the NBC News anchor, led the opposition to keep Stokes from getting the high-profile gig. He felt Stokes, just off his political role, was an impropriety. The *New Yorker* published an article the same day Stokes would debut on WNBC (May 15) that Chancellor was "dead-set" against the hiring.

The network news division, which still held the hiring power, required a stronger lead-in for Chancellor's *Nightly News*.

An NBC executive thought Stokes wouldn't be good at the start, but others believed the ratings were so poor that the newscast helmed by Stokes couldn't get worse. There's some positive reinforcement!

Stokes, a neophyte behind the camera, was teamed with Paul Udell, a TV news veteran from Los Angeles.

While *Eyewitness* hit the mother lode with the *Cool Hand Luke* theme, the news WNBC team was given a portion of *Shaft* for its opening. The set (which *The New York Times* described as miserable) was created by veteran Broadway designer Robin Wagner, famous for his work on *Jesus Christ Superstar, A Chorus Line,* and *Dreamgirls. Time* magazine was less critical, calling the NBC set "ultra-glossy," but there was nothing slick about the set. The *Eleventh Hour* in 1972 featured a vomit-yellow base with faux-wood paneling. The main anchors sit in the front, flanked by "desks" behind and to the sides.

The same *Times* article also highlighted a gimmicky technique where the anchors Stokes and Udell would pause to provide instant analysis of said story.

"The comments have been at best awkward and useless, at worst banal and pretentious," the newspaper declared.

Channel 4 broke another racial barrier a decade earlier, when Bob Teague became one of the city's first Black reporters. He stayed at NBC for nearly 30 years. By 1965, Teague was anchoring his own *Sunday Afternoon Report.* While delivering news from studio or street with an air of sophistication, there was no condescending. Viewers respected Teague.

"The news in New York City, like most of the rest of the country, has been losing weight since I got into it," Marash says. "[It] has become less ambitious, less journalistic, and real news has been replaced much more by body bags and bust lines."

***

By the time John Johnson made his debut at WABC, he was already a network correspondent with a "past life" as an art history professor. But as the civil rights movement gained steam, Johnson became more active with Black Power. He decided to use reporting to help the cause gain footing.

Early on, the network offered Johnson a job, but he politely said no. His work with Black Power led him to penning an essay, "Super Black Rant," for a book in 1968. ABC also tried to get him as a guest for his expertise at this pivotal moment in history. Instead, Harry Belafonte balked at the future news personality appearing at his side because he was too revolutionary.

The network wanted him for writing documentaries. Johnson wanted to focus on his education work and Black Power, but Charles Hamilton said it was important to get into a media outlet and have a voice. Hamilton and Stokely Carmichael co-authored *Black Power: The Politics of Liberation*.

At the time, Johnson was teaching at Indiana University and finishing his doctorate.

"ABC made me an offer, which was astounding because I couldn't believe how much money I could make compared to being a professor," Johnson recalls. "So, I did it because of the movement and the money."

But Johnson admits, "The day that some of my paintings were shown as part of an exhibition at the Metropolitan Museum of Art was the far greater day for me than ever being an anchorman anywhere."

As documentaries fell out of favor with viewers, Johnson got to work in front of the camera, an anomaly for people of color at the network. He was given a raise as a correspondent. Ultimately, Al Primo brought him to the fledgling *Eyewitness News* in 1972 with another salary boost.

An early highlight for the burgeoning journalist was covering the Attica riots. He estimates delivering more than 90 TV and radio reports in just one day as the upstate New York inmates led the infamous uprising.

Johnson says he was gassed while standing near a prison wall. He was trapped as the attack between inmates and officers escalated beyond the metal bars.

"They were screaming, 'nigger, nigger, nigger, kill the nigger!'"

"And I was saying, 'No, don't, don't, don't.'"

While Johnson was diligently broadcasting from the tense scene, he refused to report one crucial detail—that the inmates murdered the hostages.

"In the long run I proved to be right," Johnson says. "The attacking police killed the hostages."

That moment caused strife for the blossoming correspondent at ABC, as Johnson was considered an agitator, or at least a troublesome worker worth keeping an eye on.

"I was not [an 'Uncle Tom'] nor will I ever be, nor was I at ABC," Johnson says. "I had to cope with... these racist, white motherfuckers."

The family man who grew up in Bedford Stuyvesant and Harlem says he had to maintain his dignity as a Black man, despite actually being biracial.

"My ethnicity is traced through my DNA and my ancestry of half-German and half-Black. The only reason why you can call me Black is because my skin tone is a nice brown hue."

Johnson was the only African American man at ABC, but not the case when he went local. Channel 7 had the likes of Tolliver and Gil Noble, both of whom became entrenched in weekend anchoring.

"It was specific to color," Johnson, who also had a Saturday and Sunday presence at the station. "The weekends meant you would have a Black anchor doing one of the shows, or both."

He and Anna Bond (also Black) spent time leading viewers through the weekend headlines. Noble, famous for *Like It Is*, a public affairs show geared to a Black audience, anchored a late Saturday newscast.

Seeing a person of color in the 1970s meant so much as a role model for Blacks, but in an anchor role, the visibility was limited. So, when Gil Noble hosted *Like It Is* each Sunday, not only was it important for the Black community at large, it was telling the stories of the most influential Blacks of the day. Noble had famous interviews with Malcolm X and Paul Robeson. The show was created in 1968 in response to the assassination of Martin Luther King. Noble was interviewer from the start, but took over as host after Robert Hooks went back to acting.

Hooks would win an Emmy Award for producing *Voices of Our People: In Celebration of Black Poetry*. He'd appear in several films over 30 years, and in guest-starring roles on television from 1966 to 2000. *Seinfeld* fans will recall

Hooks as Joe Turner, the man who lets George watch *Breakfast at Tiffany's* on his couch (before spilling grape juice).

In addition to the celebrity conversations, Noble used journalism to shed light on the plight that average African Americans faced. Noble got his start at WABC thanks to the Kerner Commission, a report ordered by President Lyndon Johnson in 1967, examining why "Negroes" rebelled that summer. Among problems uncovered: The white news media did nothing to help ease tensions. It claimed that the virtual all-white industry saw the world from their perspective.[2] The commission recommended they start hiring Negroes urgently. It got Melba Tolliver, already in the door at Channel 7, fast-tracked to talent. And it got Noble on the air as well.

"The mass media had been caught with their zippers down," wrote Noble in his 1981 memoir, *Black Is the Color of My TV Tube*. "Red-faced executives scurried about, seeking Blacks for on-air and other job activities. What more logical place to find Black media persons than the so-called soul stations and newspapers? Within a year, many of us found ourselves downtown at major radio and TV stations.... None of the stations said we were being hired because of the prescriptions of the Kerner Commission's report. They all maintained, and they still do, that they are committed to being equal-opportunity companies. If asked about pressure, they would say, 'What pressure?'"

Aside from the mounting government intervention, Noble and other Black journalists were needed to cover stories in the Black communities effectively that whites could not in 1967 and 1968.

And so, one of Noble's first assignments was literally a trial by fire—at the Newark riots in 1967.

"I wearily returned home to tell my wife the good news, and was acutely aware of the countless brothers and sisters who were still encircled within the

---

2. Burroughs, Todd Steven. "Black Was the Color of His TV Tube: Asante Sana, Gil Noble and WABC-TV's 'Like It Is.'" Black Agenda Report, October 25, 2011.

National Guard barricades," Noble wrote. "Their uprising had been at least partially responsible for my new employment."

It was another watershed moment for African Americans, and Americans as a whole, that led WABC to create *Like It Is*. The assassination of Martin Luther King in April 1968 spurred the station to allot an hour on Sunday to showcase the Black experience.

Gil Noble continued the show for decades—a beacon for African Americans each Sunday—until he suffered a massive stroke and ultimately died in 2012.

By 1970, WNEW (Channel 5) added its own version for viewers when *Black News* debuted, first on Saturday afternoons and more known for years on Sunday nights with anchor Bill McCreary. By 1987, he was promoted to VP at the Fox New York station and was given his show, the *McCreary Report*, where he also served as executive producer.

As *The New York Times* said prior to the May 1970 launch, it would be "staffed and produced entirely by Blacks."

McCreary, a Baruch College graduate, died in 2021 at age 87. He was a mainstay at Channel 5 for more than 30 years.

Like It Is was the most visible way *Eyewitness* handled racism, but not the only way. Johnson recalls a subtler bout with racism that permeated the newsroom, involving staffers having to work directly with him.

"I had one editor walk out of the room and was problematic," Johnson remembers. "But my attitude was, if you wanted to take it outside in the street, that was fine. If you didn't want to work with me, that was fine."

Unlike at WCBS, Johnson says WABC had the appearance of being more "overtly racist," because Channel 2 made him the main anchor. "ABC refused to do that."

In short order, the personality and prowess led to respect from John Johnson's colleagues.

"Nobody would really fuck with me. I would have no fear of people," Johnson admits.

That seed was planted at an early age. As part of the first token integration, Johnson was taken from his Bedford Stuyvesant school to an all-white junior high school, a move that didn't sit well with the community.

"The entire neighborhood turned out at the school to beat me up," Johnson says.

Tolliver, one of the earliest visible Black women doing news in New York, says this is a racialized country.

"The newsroom was no exception," Tolliver admits. "People didn't write 'nigger' on their desk, but I'm sure there was a calculation in everything that [Al] Primo did. Not that he did it based on race, but he certainly took race and sex of the reporters into consideration."

Vic Miles may have been the first Black man in a "starring role" as an anchor. He sat next to Rolland Smith for a year when Dave Marash exited and acted as the stopgap until Michele Marsh took the seat. Miles would remain a reliable weekend anchor and a weeknight reporter at WCBS for many years. He died in 2011.

"He was a delight as a co-anchor because I knew he did his homework," Smith says.[3] "So you weren't left out there if you needed help."

A few years before his untimely death, John Slattery called his friend the consummate professional. "Vic won the hearts of those who knew him by offering friendship and sound advice. God bless my old buddy, Vic."

Miles's *Our Block* popular features were award winners bringing a special perspective to neighborhoods in New York.

Before the quarter-century of Miles at Channel 2 starting in 1971, he was part of another legendary shop at Pittsburgh's KDKA. During those five years, Miles was also splitting time between anchor and reporter, a skill that he appeared most comfortable displaying.

"I think he liked reporting a lot, because he was naturally suited to it," Carol Martin recalls.

---

3. Diamond, Edwin. "Anchorpersons Aweigh!" *New York Magazine*, August 18, 1975.

Not only was he building his street cred, but Miles was also expanding his TV presence to children. There were a couple of appearances on *Mister Rogers' Neighborhood*, also taped in Pittsburgh. Miles would play himself as a reporter of *Neighborhood News*. One time, Miles was on hand to provide authenticity for the courtship of Neighborhood of Make Believe puppets King Friday XIII and Sara Saturday for the royal birth of Prince Tuesday.

Unlike John Johnson and Melba Tolliver, who appeared prouder to display their Blackness on television, Miles was a newsman who just happened to be a different color. As *New York* magazine stated about the WCBS personality in a special 1979 edition called "Black Power in Crisis": "Miles rarely moves in the established Black circles and is often criticized for his aloofness and non-involvement."

When John Johnson joined WCBS as anchor, Dana Tyler was given a seat alongside the *Eyewitness News* castoff. Thereafter the outspoken journalist had the choice between Tyler or Michele Marsh. He says the chemistry with Marsh was top notch and carried over to WNBC, where they co-anchored a noon broadcast.

"Even though [Dana] is mixed, she really had a problem with Black guys, as I remember," Johnson intimates. "She was very uncomfortable with me and very uncomfortable with Reggie Harris. Michele and I were far more compatible." Tyler and Harris had the distinction as the first African American anchor team in the city.

Harris had a two-decade career in New York, first at WNBC, before joining Tyler for the historic partnership at WCBS. He was part of the station's infamous "Black Friday" purge in 1996. WWOR gave him a lifeline, where he worked until his untimely death in 2000 at age 46.

Tyler, by contrast, never moved from CBS or the anchor desk. After 34 years, she announced her departure in March 2024.

"Somebody just the other day said to me, 'I've grown up watching you.' It's the biggest compliment ever," Tyler said on her final broadcast. "I say thank you Channel 2 viewers. You're loyal. You're kind. You keep us on our toes."

Chris Wragge and Dana Tyler gathered at the New York Emmy Awards in 2013. [Jerry Barmash]

***

When Johnson found his way to CBS in 1995, he failed to get the support from Jim Jensen, who was in the closing chapter of his stellar career.

"I think Jim was upset that I became anchor," Johnson says. Staying diplomatic, he thinks Jensen's reaction "was more to do with his working there than with me."

Overall, Johnson says his arrival at WCBS didn't come with fanfare. It didn't help that on his first day an *Esquire* magazine cover story hit the newsstands, and hit like a punch to the gut, with Johnson's ex-wife E. Jean Carroll portraying him as a "jerk."

Carroll writes, "Actually, as I never asked for any alimony, I don't even count John as a husband."

In the piece where she examines the four loves of her life, Carroll says she sweated big time for Johnson. "I can't say precisely when I fell for John; it happened so gradually. But I believe I can date it from the night I first heard the gigantic salary he made."

(Carroll made bigger headlines in June 2019, when she accused President Trump of sexually assaulting her in the 1990s and would win a $83 million civil lawsuit in 2024.)

Johnson did have the backing of news director Jerry Nachman, but admits, "I don't think pretty much anybody else did at WCBS."

With two decades in New York television news, Johnson was no stranger to newsroom politics. However, he felt like an outsider at Channel 2.

"I was not from the CBS club . . . why didn't they promote from inside? So, there was that hostility also," Johnson says.

John Roberts, who would go on to White House duty for CBS and Fox, was bumped at Channel 2 in New York in favor of the "outsider."

Money was likely another cause of consternation: Johnson was bringing in a hefty salary, more than most of the established talent.

"I made a nice sum of money. I know that was one of their big things."

After a slow start, Johnson showed off his charm and talent with his new colleagues at WCBS as their relationship grew. But he wasn't greeted with open arms. It was only a 18-month tenure before the "Black Friday" mass firings.

Johnson and co-anchor Michele Marsh were abruptly dismissed at WCBS. He ended the October 2, 1996, 6 pm newscast by saying: "I'm John Johnson. Michele and I will be back at 11." Moments later, they were out, along with five other anchors or reporters.

Ultimately, Johnson gave up a big payday when he resigned at WNBC after 30 years in the business. He took the money earned from his TV news career and resumed his painting, with occasional art shows. Johnson has an art studio, and his wife has her photography studio in their home.

While proud of the journalistic accomplishments, Johnson remains bitter.

"We don't have to work for any fucking media outlet. Thank you very much."

22

The Future Is Now

As the anchor was evolving in the 1970s, the news industry began to make its mark on pop culture.

The Academy Award-winning *Network* (1976) is as timely as ever, where hard news is transformed into sensationalism to grab ratings and ad revenue. Peter Finch's extreme characterization of Howard Beele won him a posthumous Oscar. His portrayal of a "mad as hell and not gonna take it anymore" anchorman was a commentary on where broadcasting was heading.

In some ways, the Paddy Chayefsky script was a stark warning of a divided country and its equally divided media.

A topical version came to Broadway in 2018 starring Bryan Cranston, which landed him a second Tony Award.

Network was prophetic as just a few years after its premiere, the 24-hour news cycle came to TV sets.

Crowds lined the Belasco Theater to see Bryan Cranston's commanding performance. [Jerry Barmash]

CNN was born and the bastardization of the news industry would gradually follow. From Newsmax on the right to MSNBC on the left, a home for all political views means the fractured television audience can always find its information or disinformation.

Whether on cable or local newscasts, tabloid TV was the new way for viewers to receive their news. However, the media world isn't always trusted these days, in part because broadcasting has become narrowcasting.

Less controversial but equally as popular was *Broadcast News* (1987). The Oscar-winning film centers on a love triangle in the newsroom. Here we see a knowledgeable but less camera-ready anchor (Albert Brooks) versus the anchor who could have been brought in from central casting (William Hurt).

But if you want a movie set in the 1970s with a focus on the world of TV news, albeit as a satire, then look to the Will Ferrell vehicle: *Anchorman* (2004). Although it received mixed reviews from critics, the film gained a cult status with fans as a comedy franchise.

Despite the wild storylines, *Anchorman* went full-on vintage with its sets and costumes. Ferrell's Ron Burgundy was modeled after veteran anchor Mort Crim, who would work with Jessica Savitch at KYW in Philadelphia before she became a star at NBC News.

The 1996 movie *Up Close and Personal* was loosely based on Savitch's life. The screenplay was initially based on the book *Golden Girl: The Story of Jessica*

Savitch. Producers ultimately found it lacking commercial appeal and made changes to the script.

***

Movies aside, TV news has made strides where it means the most—with loyal viewers.

As you watch each night's newscast in New York, and anywhere else in the country, diversity on the anchor desk is now the norm. As you learned in these pages, the newsmen were, well, just that. But slowly, after years, talent of all genders and minorities finally got the chance to show their abilities.

Each woman and minority on camera is building a future for the next generation. Undoubtedly, countless young viewers who've watched Sue Simmons, Melba Tolliver, Carol Martin, Reggie Harris, Maurice DuBois, and Dana Tyler, have followed their career path in TV news.

DuBois, who grew up on Long Island in the 1970s, logged seven years at WNBC, primarily on the early morning newscasts. He marked 20 years at WCBS in 2024. DuBois got the station's plum assignment in 2011 — when he joined Kristine Johnson as co-anchor on the 5 and 11 pm broadcasts.

Local news has faced challenges from the dozens, if not hundreds, of channels on your set. And where to find that news is only half the story. Younger folks are fluent in social media and streaming apps to get connected with headlines on X (formerly Twitter), Facebook, or even TikTok.

So on-air talent, in the field or in the newsroom, are logging in and heading online to promote what's coming up at 11 pm. It's a world that Jim Jensen and company probably couldn't have envisioned, when the big technology jump was switching from film to videotape, long before the advent of high definition.

Viewership for traditional newscasts is down, on average, by more than 1.2 million from 2016-2022 across the affiliates of ABC, CBS, FOX, and NBC. [1]

While that trend could seem daunting to the bean counters, another report offers a more promising prospective.

Each market's local broadcast news gained an audience 8-12 times larger than all the streaming counterparts combined. [2]

Analysis from TVB, the trade association of America's local broadcast television industry, compared one-day viewing of local broadcast news to streaming services, which included Netflix, Amazon Prime Video, Hulu, Apple TV+, Disney+, and HBO Max.

A sampling of the numbers shows that TV remains the "gold standard" for delivering local news with reporters and anchors.

In New York, the 59 local broadcast news programs totaled 6.6 million in the Adults 18+ demographic, while 4,942 news programs on the streaming services reached 718,000 subscribers. [3]

It's clear: New Yorkers, and viewers across the country, rely on their anchors and trust them to report on the most difficult moments and share the best times as if they were part of the family.

Perhaps Dana Tyler said it best in her March 2024 farewell to WCBS.

---

1. Pew Research Center, Local TV News Fact Sheet, Sept. 14, 2023.

2. BusinessWire, Local Broadcast TV News Delivers a 10x Larger Audience Than Subscription Streaming Viewing According to New Study, June 6, 2023.

3. BusinessWire, Local Broadcast TV News Delivers a 10x Larger Audience Than Subscription Streaming Audience According to New Study, June 6, 2023.

"I've always felt privileged for these 34 years that you've invited me into your homes, your firehouses, your bodegas, and on your laptops and on your cell phones. I always tried to be respectful, compassionate, and bear witness because every story is an individual, a family, [and] a community."

About the Author

J erry Barmash is a veteran New York-based journalist and broadcaster, who has written about the media for such outlets as the *New York Daily News*, *Broadcasting & Cable,* and *Barrett News Media*.

He's a news editor at Patch.com on Long Island.

Jerry is a versatile on-air talent, with decades of radio experience. His voice has been heard on WABC, where he handled news anchoring and reporting duties. During Jerry's time as an evening anchor on Bloomberg Radio, he was on the air as Barack Obama was elected president in 2008. He worked for WINS as a sports and traffic anchor and at Wall Street Journal Radio, where he was a network business anchor.

He also had a national presence at Westwood One News, Blaze Radio, and USA Radio.

Jerry amassed an array of interviews, including John Bolton, Bob Costas, Bob Eubanks, and Dr. Anthony Fauci.

This is Jerry's first book.

Jerry lives in New York with his wife, Shuli, and their cat, Sophie.

For more information visit jerrybarmash.com

Made in United States
North Haven, CT
12 June 2024